ABOUT THE AUTHORS

Bobby is a veteran of the punk rock and football fanzine scenes from the past fifteen years – being a mainstay of the Wolverhampton Wanderers magazine *A Load of Bull*. He has also contributed chapters in books about football and wrote the History of German Streetpunk. Bobby is still a man who thinks the world can be changed for the better by three-chords, a pint of cider and a flash of Robbie Dennison magic. Oi! Oi! Oi!

Margaret is a local earth woman famous for her impersonations of the rich and famous. An infectious character she has a passion for justice and righting the wrongs around the world.

Bobby Smith & Margaret Oshindele-Smith

One Love
Two Colours

The unlikely marriage of a Punk Rocker
and his African Queen

Matador
9 De Montfort Mews
Leicester LE1 7FW, UK
Tel: (+44) 116 255 9311 / 9312
Email: books@troubador.co.uk
Web: www.troubador.co.uk/matador

ISBN 978 1906221 393

Typeset in 11pt Stempel Garamond by Troubador Publishing Ltd, Leicester, UK
Printed in the UK by Cromwell Press Limited, Trowbridge, Wiltshire

Matador is an imprint of Troubador Publishing Ltd

One Love Two Colours

No spin, no political propaganda, just the truth

The African Queen

Those shining eyes, they sought me out.
Burning like beacons, drawing me close to the flame.
I can touch them now, they're so fierce to behold.
A thousand stories all waiting to burst forth.
Of loves lost and reborn once again.
Betrayal, deceit, sorrow, all this and more.
These feelings show as lines, etched on your soul.
They gouge deep inside, scarring your beauty.
But a life lived in the past is one sorely wasted.
Taste the future and let it overcome you.
So open your arms to embrace the warmth,
for our love can fan the fires of a million hearts.
Doubts spring to mind, is this right, this affair of ours?
No-one to ask but your intimate inside.
Our love is not an illusion, painted by an artist.
The canvas that supports it is strong, formed from leather.
And so my love is beating on your heart with a handful of feathers.
A Duracell battery of love with a black & white top.
So be sure my love that we are a force together,
and purse those pretty lips that bring a smile to my face.
Why worry what the future may bring?
We will leap the barrier that fate lays before us.
Trust me!

A poem I wrote for Margaret when we were courting in 1996.
God I was naïve!

Contents

Acknowledgements

Bobby

My heartfelt thanks go out to the following, without whom this book would never have happened:

David Nunn – art work.
Lidia Ponti & Sue Howard – proof reading and belief.
Tony Hewer – fellow punk and print master supreme.
Scott Allin and Andy Price – ideas, inspiration and criticism.
My parents – for bringing me up in a loving home environment.

Thanks to all those whose actions, stories and experiences helped me to create *One Love*; My sister Dawn, Big Chris, Auntie Doreen & Uncle John, Lisa, Bev, Charlene, Amy and the rest of the Stratford crew, Daphne, Nikki Upperton, Janet Croker, Glyn Jones, Ade, Sheena (Miss Ghana), Natasha, Norma & Colin, Carol, Nik & Alex, Rodney, Vanessa, Nathalie, Big Dave, Steve & Gina Prout, Adebo, David Anthony, Robbie Dennison, Sade, Andy & Jon Gwinnett, Neil & Simon Kirk, Tars Sandhu, Asif Dar, Jim Heath, Charlie Ross & *A Load of Bull*, Slime, Cherlyne in the States, Anne & Lawrence Dennison, Julian & Tracey Smith, Glen 'sausage roll' Baldwin, Tricia and Gareth Ondrak. Jeremy Thompson and all at Matador.
To all the punks and skins around the world: keep on keeping the faith.
RIP: John Trice & Marie Baldwin.

Lastly a big thanks to the guy who attacked me on the train on the way back from football. This book is dedicated to you – for providing the last spurt of inspiration I needed.

Margaret

Many thanks to God the Almighty, who has given me life, hope and redemption. To my dearest parents. My beloved sister Anne. Auntie Mrs Biola Humphrey. My special friend Anita Asubo. All the people that Bobby mentioned and a special thanks to Phabs and her fantastic hair salon – for making me look beautiful.

Introduction

Hate. We all do it, often without realising. Black against white, Muslim against Christian, Mod against Rocker, Sikh against Hindu, Israeli against Palestinian. Hate. It gets you nowhere and screws you up. So why bother?

Time for a new approach.

This is our true story, a tale of two people who just happened to fall in love. There is no logic to our union for one is black, Christian and Nigerian. The other is white, a punk rocker and English. We can't stand each other's music, clothes, food and humour yet we have been happily married for ten years. How we have managed to achieve this is the basis of the book.

Our book is about discovery, conflict and human nature. It is a tale with no absolute ending but a story that takes the reader through the entire gamut of emotions hidden within any relationship. Via our experiences the book delves into the areas where both tortured pain and delicious pleasure are to be found, as it addresses head on the pitfalls that need to be negated for mixed, or indeed any, marriages to work.

On paper a successful marriage (for us) should be harder than most – given our cultural differences, yet for some strange reason our marriage has been a success. It is a mystery to others how we make it work.

Over the years so many people have told us they cannot fathom how we are together. Surely, I am normally informed, my wife should be adorned with tattoos and body piercings topped off with a mane of pink hair – all on account of my being a punk? She, in turn, is expected to be married to someone who shares her religious conviction and love of Nigerian food. People are therefore surprised when confronted with the reality of my bondage pants or Margaret's African attire. For both of us this is no big deal and our mutual love proves that cultural appearance is much overplayed where finding a life partner is concerned.

So why have we decided to write about our experiences on the rocky road to marital happiness? Well, our inspiration stems from the fact that mixed marriages are so often cast in a negative light, by talk shows, magazine articles etc. Truly, I have lost count of how many times you can pick up a tabloid newspaper and read a story about some middle-aged white woman, who gives up her cushy English life to go and live in the bush with a Masai warrior. Inevitably these stories go on to question the woman's sanity; how could she fit in culturally with an African man? She must be mad. But supposing the woman is genuinely happy with her lifestyle choice? Who are we to suggest otherwise?

And this is the crux of the matter with mixed marriages – it is a choice that only the two people involved can make. Following on from that it should be stressed that what works for us may not work for everyone, we have just written about our marriage to show that racial segregation is an unnecessary evil. Within these pages we will try to show the benefits of mixed marriages, and demonstrate that those who do take the plunge into more 'exotic' fields, do so for reasons no different to any other.

So how 'exotic' am I?

Well, I'm a thirty-nine-year-old punk rocker with a sad but true cider belly. My hair is greying and the first beachhead has been established at the top of my head by the receding hair army. Exotic? I don't think so.

My wife, on the other hand, could certainly be described as 'exotic'. Not for her colour but because she comes from regal stock. She is forty, comes from the Oshindele family and has a Chief for a Dad.

My father, as a contrast, was a Postman.

Somewhat strangely we have found that our two lives have followed much the same pattern – even from our childhood. Despite our superficially different backgrounds many of our 'cultural' experiences were running parallel to each other. This is certainly one of the points we want to get over in this book; that cultural similarities are often overlooked when society tends to look only at the problems of mixed marriages. It would be foolish to argue that there are no differences in a marriage, with ours being no exception, but generally the shouting fits are outnumbered by the cuddles.

Some readers may find this publication uncomfortable to digest in parts as it is very much a warts and all account of our relationship together. Because of that we were forced to look more closely at certain aspects of our union. As a result we now have a clearer understanding of the underlying tensions within our marriage.

Our experiences also illuminate what is actually happening on our streets under the banner of race and ethnicity, it being a theme that runs concurrent with our story throughout the book. Race comes to prominence every now and again in England – at election times and whenever there is a 'race' riot. It is always there though, bubbling away beneath our feet. How someone's race can influence a couple's relationship is very much a factor in our story.

For many reasons fair-minded white people generally steer clear of talking about race or ethnicity in this country. They recoil in horror at 'uncomfortable' words such as race, black or Asian. The reasons for this range from ignorance, prejudice or the fear of being stigmatised as a racist. To both of us this is stupid. Race is a subject like any other.

By heaping mystique and taboo onto race we are just putting it on a higher plain – unable to be debated like other issues. This then leads to myths, stereotypes and ultimately, hatred. This is wrong. If ordinary men and women are not allowed to mention race it becomes the preserve of radical politics. It is time the silent majority had a voice, a voice we have tried to express within the pages of this book.

Throughout *One Love* we highlight all those who espouse racism. It matters not a jot to us if the person giving out the abuse is black or white. As we will show; racism is a bile that affects everyone and is a disease that strikes in many different ways.

But surely we are misguided? Surely England is a nation that ignores race and appreciates 'diversity'. Yeah right.

Hardly any of its disparate groups mix with one another. All are becoming more insular, as outside factors apply racial straight jackets to those who want to live their lives free from the constraints of race. *One Love* acts as a reflection of our times, being both a personal celebration and damning political critique of multiculturalism. It is the truth behind the propaganda.

The chapters in this book concern subject areas of particular interest and importance to us. Each highlights our views and concludes with a short summary (normally by me – Bobby) outlining how either of us compromised to make it a success.

How a white man can love a black woman and reciprocate her unconditional love is an underlying theme of this book. It is a question we hope the reader remembers throughout. It is a simple question and yet one that puzzles many – given the conversations we have had.

So many books of this nature come from a political viewpoint – seeking to convert the silent or preaching to the converted. This is not one of those. Neither of us belongs to any political party and we are not devotees of either the left or right-wing. Oh no, we despise any who are politically extreme; George Galloway, Nick Griffin, Ken Livingstone, to name but three. Legendary German punk rock band Slime perfectly summed up politics for us with their 1980 song: 'Ich Hasse Sie Alle' (I hate them all.) Spot on.

Equally we are not part of the literary jet set, whose opinions on race are acquired via text books, and are written up from within the safety of pretty country cottages, away from the friction of our cities. Nope, we are the real thing!

Enclosed is just an honest practical story of how an ordinary couple can make a mixed marriage work. An ordinary Mr and Mrs Smith you might say.

Of course, two other people will have a totally different story to tell, we can only write from the perspective of a white punk rocker married to a black African Princess. We are Bobby and Margaret Smith.

Welcome to our world.

CHAPTER 1

First Impressions

Bobby

When I first met Margaret we were both working for the government as civil servants. At that time I had been in the service for a number of years, plodding along as only a civil servant can. I had slipped into the civil service in 1986 – attracted by its lack of dress code and flexible working hours. It is fair to say I drifted into it not fully understanding the life of purgatory I was letting myself in for. In truth I know no one who deliberately chose the civil service as a profession. When I was growing up I went through all the usual dreams when it came to my future job prospects: train driver, fireman, astronaut... err... civil servant.

Doesn't quite have the same ring to it does it?

But the Civil Service it was to be and I bumbled along happily enough, surrounded by the usual odd characters that decide to make public service their goal in life. For some reason the service tends to attract more than its fair share of oddballs, eccentrics and absolute psycho nut jobs. Really, I used to look at many of my colleagues and wonder what other employer would have granted them employment – they were that strange. It was no surprise to me that one of England's most notorious serial killers, Dennis Nilsen, was also a civil servant. Still, I learned to cope with my colleagues peculiarities and even adopted some of them as loyal friends. It was hard work but the camaraderie kept me going long after the novelty of working for a living diminished. So why did I stay? I was only eighteen at the time and just starting out in the world of work. I did not know that better jobs existed so I was happy enough with a few pounds in my pocket and a pint of cider for lunchtime. I remember an old hand in the service, Ray Newlands, who asked me in my first week: 'Mr Smith, do you really want a career in the Civil Service or are you just here for some work experience?'

Truthfully I answered that I was just going to see how it panned out. I had no idea that I was damned to spend the next nineteen years of my life helping those less fortunate than myself. I had signed my life away to the Devil! My colleague told me: 'If I stay for a month I will be in it for life.' I guess he was wiser than I thought at the time.

Then, out of the blue, my life was transformed. I was informed by my boss that a new member of staff (Margaret) was being transferred into our office. I was also told that she was a 'troublemaker.'

Believe me when I say this sort of office gossip was endemic where I worked. For some reason colleagues felt compelled to cast comment about other members of staff without checking up on their facts, with Margaret being the latest in a long line. Having been warned of her potential disruption we awaited her entrance eagerly. The result? A plump black lady of limited height who smiled a row of sparkling white teeth. Being a normal hot blooded bloke I also couldn't fail to notice she had a pair of extremely impressive breasts; a deep revealing cleavage that blossomed into two large melon like balls of fat that cried out; 'mind the gap'!

Other than that, though, there was nothing that jumped out of her and demanded attention. She was a typical TAT kind of woman: tits, arse and teeth. I should also mention her hair, a tight curly perm, as it quite simply looked appalling. It was so bad she could have gone on *Stars in Their Eyes* as a female version of '70s singer Leo Sayer. So I can't say it was love at first sight as her hair and mouth (she was very loud) frightened me off.

Still, we worked together for a few months and I began to realise she was actually quite a nice person and not a troublemaker at all. Not having had a girlfriend before I didn't recognise the feelings that were beginning to stir in my loins whenever she entered the room, putting the tingle in my genitals down to my wearing the wrong size pants. Eventually, though, I realised that certain parts of my body were not for urinating alone and decided to confront the matter head on. Conquering my nerves I asked her if she would like to spend some time with me. Luckily she agreed and we decided, (as friends), that I would attend a Pentecostal Church gathering, in return she would watch Wolverhampton Wanderers FC with me.

On the morning of the church visit she met me in my studio flat for breakfast. After giving my abode a brief frisk Margaret declared herself satisfied and we departed towards Tottenham. I must say that the Church service was an education for a non-believer such as me. The sight of grown adults rolling around the floor together, whilst being exorcised by a preacher, was certainly one that has stayed in my head. The last time I witnessed so many bodies entwined was at a Doctor and the Medics gig back in the 1980s, when we 'rode the beetle' on the dance floor. Being a gentleman, my first instinct was to help the young ladies up from the floor, foolishly thinking they were in pain. Suffice to say my assistance was not required. I actually did attempt to lift one of the women but she was kicking and shaking so much I had to let go. And boy did she have a lot to shake!

After a couple of hours of this we went back to my flat for lunch. Not knowing what to cook someone of Nigerian origin, I went for the tried and tested Marks & Spencer's chicken pie, accompanied by my infamous mashed potatoes. Margaret sat down on the sofa next to me and wolfed the lot down. After talking for a bit she grew sleepy. Before she knew it she had fallen fast asleep, her head resting on my skinny shoulder. Trust me dear readers when I write this was the nearest thing I had had that even vaguely equated to a sexual experience. I sat there not daring to move, smelling Margaret's sweet perfume.

After an hour or so she awoke and pulled herself up from me, dazed and confused at lying next to such a hunk. I was told a few years later this was the moment she first considered me as a potential life partner. She was apparently impressed that I didn't try anything on with her whilst she was sleeping, which doesn't say much about the quality of men she knew before I turned up on the scene.

To keep her part of the bargain Margaret did as required and attended a Southend v Wolverhampton match at dilapidated United's Roots Hall football ground. Wolves lost the match 2-1 but I was more than happy. Yes, for once in my life I was walking around with a pretty woman in tow, despite her awful hair. For her part Margaret enjoyed the trip, but she was perplexed by the sight of grown men swearing at the referee and the mindless fury they showed in public. Of course, at this stage in our fledgling relationship, Margaret didn't appreciate the heavy drinking culture that exists in the West Midlands. A culture that I demonstrate to her whenever I return, pissed as a fart, from a match at Wolverhampton's Molineux stadium.

Back in the humdrum world of work, we grew more accustomed to one another and the fateful day came when I plucked up the courage to properly ask her 'out'. Now 'out' means many things, such as trips to the cinema or theatre, or even a candlelit dinner for two. But, it also means that sex is potentially on the horizon in the near or distant future. Was I ready for this at the ripe old age of twenty-six?

Yes, was my obvious answer, so I took the plunge and confessed my admiration for the petite figure of fun whose company I had grown to enjoy. Margaret, flattered by my shy charms, accepted the invitation and I now had to think of where to go. Not being much of an expert at these matters, I

3

plumped for the cinema and suggested we see *Rob Roy*. Thankfully Margaret accepted and we agreed a date. Next problem; what to wear?

Being a hardcore punk rocker presented me with a few challenging issues – as my wardrobe consisted of bondage pants and obscure German punk t-shirts – hardly appropriate if one is trying to impress a young lady. In the end I decided upon a Julian Cope sweatshirt and an old pair of jeans. Not exactly a style-*meister* I'll grant you but I was presentable if nothing else. Just before departing I sprayed half a can of deodorant under my arms, a squirt between my legs (in case I got lucky), and brushed my teeth into a Colgate ring of confidence. Wow – what a cool dude!

The movie was quite good in a sweaty, earthy type of way and we watched in silence until the credits rolled at the end. I felt nervous as the cinema emptied and she remained in her seat; did she expect me to kiss her? Seeing as how I was in un-chartered territory, I lost my bottle and just suggested we went home via a taxi. This we did, each of us seemingly content with the others' behaviour during our 'date'. Indeed, we were so content at the others' performance that the next few nights were filled with long telephone conversations between the two of us. At the time I thought I must have impressed her – due to the hours she spent lapping up my sweet words of romance. However, I have since come to realise being on the phone everyday for three hours is normal for Margaret. To be fair though, she does share this affliction with every Nigerian woman I have met.

So that was how we started – way back in June 1995. Given my less than flattering comments about her hair, the obvious question is what was it that attracted me to her to start with? I must confess it really was not her looks – apart from her sexy flat nose. No, I was more taken by her easygoing approach to life. Not for Margaret the sneers I had taken for granted from other men and women concerning my choice of clothes/music. Margaret took me at face value and looked at the person inside the wrapper.

I should point out that the idea of Margaret being a black woman was completely irrelevant to my decision to ask her out. I saw, and have always seen her, as just a woman. For me this is a crucial point, as some people in mixed relationships are attracted to someone's skin colour first and their personality second. I would always be highly dubious if someone liked me, even initially, for the fact that I am white. If I had thought that Margaret was 'Caucasian curious', I would never have asked her out. Margaret, I am glad to say, agreed with my attitude.

So we were off and running – a relationship that seemed unlikely to many – but natural to us. A relationship that would soon be tested, purely because of our different cultures.

But just how did Princess Margaret end up with some dead end job, hardcore punk rocker? What was it that sent a shiver down her spine and screamed; 'This is the man for you.'

Margaret

When I first saw Bobby I cannot say I was impressed. He wasn't, how you say in England, masculine! Indeed, even his friends re-christened him Charles Hawtrey (from the *Carry On* films) for his lack of masculine qualities. Prior to returning to Britain, I came across the expression a 'man's man', and was excited by the prospect of meeting some of these proud yeomen of England. My lustful mind fooled me into thinking I would be rubbing shoulders with macho James Bond types, boasting bulging biceps and a hint of danger to match. Alas, I was to be disappointed, as Bobby's character and demeanour was more akin to Frankie Howerd than Sean Connery or Roger Moore. Certainly he has a type of exaggerated femininity about him that is all too apparent, especially whenever someone meets him for the first time. Our dear friend David Nunn perfectly sums Bobby up when he describes him as being; 'camper than a row of pink fluffy tents.'

Tall, skinny to the point of anorexia, and with a strange, eccentric type of humour – that was my Bobby. To be fair, I have since come to realise that a lot of English men share this type of humour. The cultural difference here is that in Nigeria Bobby's 'jokes' would get him killed – as sarcasm and irony are just not recognised as a form of amusement.

And, as for the rest of Bobby's appearance, well, if I tell you he was a dead cert for a TV makeover programme, you may get the point. He hadn't had a girlfriend before I arrived on the scene and it showed. His clothes were shabby and obviously hadn't been introduced to an iron, whilst his beetle crusher shoes had, apparently, once been in fashion. I haven't even begun to describe his hair, suffice to say that he cut it himself and it kind of resembled a badly mown lawn. He said it was punk to do it like that, I just thought he didn't own a mirror.

Still, he seemed a pleasant man when he introduced himself to me. In fact, he told me he was a 'punk rock star', presumably so I would buy a copy of his *Death to Pansy Pop* EP – a record that he proudly shoved in my less than enthusiastic face. Feeling sorry for him, I bought a copy so he would go away.

As I began to work in more close proximity to him, I couldn't help but be impressed by his sincerity and respect towards complete strangers. The more I got to know him the more I found he was not at all like his public image. Bobby was just a straightforward, down-to-earth guy who didn't have a pretentious bone in his body. He really didn't care what people thought of him and just got on with his life. This was just as well, though, as I'd heard numerous comments about him being a bit strange. The funny thing is, even I described him as being 'weird' to my then boyfriend at the time. Never in my wildest dreams could I have imagined him as my future husband.

I should explain that, prior to Bobby, I had only ever dated Nigerian Yoruba (my ethnic group) men, and so couldn't understand his strange English eccentricities. He was very much a step into the unknown for a woman used to the Yoruba way of doing things.

After my long-term relationship with my previous boyfriend failed, I became totally disillusioned with all men. I seriously looked into becoming a nun. Yep, it was that bad. I had signed up to the 'all men are bastards' school and did not want to know them anymore. But then Bobby had the nerve to ask me out. I answered 'yes' to his question at the time, it was early morning at work, but spent the whole day regretting it. What have I done? I kept asking myself over and over. Yes, he is a nice man, yes, I get on with him, but...

He was *white!*

On this point I should explain that I had been asked out twice before by white men but had refused their invitation. In my head I kept on imagining they only wanted me as an 'exotic experiment' or a sexual plaything. So the two men in question were given short shrift. In all honesty, I actually felt insulted by their suggestion.

Looking back now with hindsight, I realise my hostile reaction was prompted by the myth that African women, who go out with white men, are prostitutes. I used to work with a Congolese woman, and she told me African women, who date white men in the Congo, *all* wear fake hair, have long nails, short skirts and high heels — classic prostitute garb. Taken by itself, this could be dismissed as an innocent, albeit ignorant, comment. Only this was not an isolated case. I heard similar words from Africans whose country of origin was not the Democratic Republic of Congo.

However, I do empathise with them because I once shared similar beliefs. For I myself was brought up to be a proud Yoruba woman destined to marry a Yoruba man and have his children. So no, I could not do it; I could not cross the colour line. At the time, I tried to pass it off as a cultural thing and not the prejudice it quite clearly was. But then, along came Bobby.

The irony is; I had purposely moved to Enfield, North London, from Brighton so that I would meet more Nigerian men. And here I was arranging to go 'out' with a white man – and a camp punk rocker at that! What would my parents say? Come to think of it – what would anyone's parents say?

Telling my parents, though, was still someway off. At this point in our relationship we had merely been out on a couple of informal trips; the church and the football, simply as friends, nothing more or salacious, for the gossip-hungry hounds at work.

Prior to our first church 'date', the thing that stuck in my memory was the spotless appearance of Bobby's flat. This was such a surprise to me – given his less than tidy personal fashion sense. Fair play to Bobby though, for his flat had the pleasant smell of wild lavender and not a speck of dust was to be found on his book shelves. I have truly never met a man like Bobby when it comes to tidiness.

As I later discovered, my husband extended his neatness into other areas. By this, I refer to his habit of changing his underwear on a daily basis. I am sure many women reading this are nodding their head in agreement with me when I state this is a much undervalued aspect of a male's suitability for shagging. My previous boyfriends were sometimes remiss in this area and instead wore aftershave by the bucket-load to disguise their hygienic imperfections whilst attempting to woo the opposite sex. Yeuch! By way of contrast, Bobby was clean and hygienic even though he looked a mess!

One thing that will always stay in my memory was the stickers Bobby had decorated his flat with. It was covered with German words such as *Nazis Raus* (Nazis Out), 'Slime' and *Schlachtrufe BRD* (Songs from Germany.) I remember thinking, oh my God; I have walked into the house of a Nazi! Even his bathroom had German punk slogans daubed all over the walls. How peculiar, I thought at the time.

Luckily Bobby saw my startled expression and put me at ease by explaining his love of German punk/skinhead music. He then pointed out I should not jump to false assumptions, as German does not automatically mean neo-Nazi. Slime, for example, was a staunchly anti-Nazi punk band on the hate lists of far right organisations. This was all news to me and it came as a relief when Bobby clarified the German slogans. One thing was for sure – Bobby was turning into an enigma – nothing was how it should be.

At this point I made a pact with myself to find out more about this man, despite my racial misgivings towards his colour. To do this I would have to go on a proper 'date' with him. The reason for my decision? The Bible. Being a practising Methodist, I could see no reason for God to say that my relationship with a white man was wrong. In fact, the act of rejecting someone for purely his or her skin colour was un-Christian.

The odd thing about my decision was that my boss at work had, on the very day Bobby asked me out, called me into a room and advised me to be careful of Bobby as he was known to 'swing both ways.' The truth, as I later found out, was Bobby hadn't swung any way at that point in time!

So, not only was I a potential experiment for a white guy, I was also an experiment for a 'hetero' curious man as well. Oh dear I thought, what was I, a proud Christian woman and not a prostitute, getting myself into? I really did think about changing my mind and pulling out before I got in too deep. I felt scared of Bobby on two levels; his masculinity and his ethnicity.

But I read my bible, swallowed my prejudice, and went with Bobby on the bus to the cinema. All I remember about the ride was that I prayed no-one would see me out with a white man. I was petrified of what strangers would think of me – dating the 'enemy.'

Sadly, despite progress in society generally, the very act of a black woman (in England) dating a white man was still frowned upon by some communities. As a result of this, I was going to have to confront some demons if I continued my relationship with Bobby. Demons that, in many cases, lurked in my own head.

For now, though, I was content merely to enjoy our time together and to be treated like a lady by a man who respected me. Not for Bobby the demand for coffee in my flat and a fondle of my voluptuous breasts. No, the best I got was a polite nod of his head before he departed on his long walk home. Bobby was certainly not treating me any different because of my colour. In actual fact, he never mentioned my being black or 'exotic' at all.

Slowly, even though I fought it, I couldn't help myself; I was beginning to warm towards my English punk rock friend with the strange sense of humour and even stranger clothes.

Bobby also wrote a succession of lovely poems that touched my heart. One of these had the rather stereotypical title, *The African Queen*, but was so good it won first prize in a poetry competition and was later published in a book. Romantic with a capital R; that was Bobby. Sadly, the poems have largely dried up now that he has had his wicked way with me. Indeed, his feelings towards me now are best summed up by the song he recorded to commemorate ten years of our marriage, 'Ghana Braid Girl' – the lyrics of which are reproduced at the back of the book.

So, our voyage of discovery was beginning – with two stowaways on board; the 'troublemaker' and the 'gay swinger.'

Where would our journey take us?

Summary

Not much to add in this chapter. We both concentrated on the individual and not the colour of his or her skin. Our minds were beginning to open.

CHAPTER 2

Our Childhood and Adolescence

Bobby

A slight intermission in our story here as we take a step back to our respective upbringings. Given our different backgrounds, would we have anything in common?

I lived a fairly typical life, being brought up in a loving family environment by two parents who always put their children first. Without a shadow of doubt, my mother and father imbued in me a true sense of what is right and wrong, and I will always remain grateful to them for this. It is only as time has gone on that I realise I was lucky to have the benefit of a stable childhood. In England this is a luxury denied to so many.

My dad was a hard-working man who worked his way up the corporate Barclays Bank ladder until one day they decided he had outlived his usefulness – around the age of fifty – and sent him off into early retirement. He then found other work as a postal worker.

Thinking back now, I didn't realise how much this affected my dad's self esteem. He certainly deserved more from an employer that he had dedicated most of his working life to. In all his years I never once remember him phoning in sick and crying off work. And what did he get back in return? A reduced pension and a kick out the door.

In contrast to dad, mother stayed at home for the duration of my childhood, so my environment was the stereotypically normal; bloke working, woman looking after the kids type of family. Seeing as how I was such a pleasant child my parents had another and my sister Dawn was born. Initially we grew up in Edmonton, North London, which was quite a nice place to live in during the Seventies. Even today, I can still fondly remember playing war games with the local 'street urchins,' as my mother used to call the likes of David Avery and her *enfant terrible*, David Wignall. Life was good; I had friends, stock car racing at Haringey stadium, *Battle and Action* comic and *Doctor Who*. In short, I was popular.

I write that I was popular but even at this early age I had problems. I always recall our street party for the Silver Jubilee celebrations in 1977 – an occasion marked by 'socially cohesive' get togethers and declarations of Royal allegiance. What a glorious sight it was; a nation united behind the Queen with all the pageantry of old. United, that is, unless you were part of the Sex Pistols entourage, who partied on a Thames river boat in the name of anarchy. Oh, how I would love to write that I too was on the boat, rucking with the law whilst sticking safety pins through my school uniform, but I can't. Instead of rebel rocking, I was toasting her Majesty with a plastic cup of orange pop, not quite in the same league as *agent provocateurs*; Rotten, Jones, Cook and Vicious.

I remember the street party vividly as I managed to win the prize for making our roads best hat, ably assisted by my *Blue Peter* inspired father. Good old dad had spent hours on a variety of cardboard boxes to concoct a passable imitation of HMS *Belfast* – the venerable old Royal Navy ship currently moored in the Thames as a floating museum.

Proudly I collected my prize – a bottle of Black Tower wine – and passed it over to my equally proud parents. This was all too much for one boy who, in a fit of pique, smeared a cream cake in my face for my having the nerve to relegate his papier-mâché Tardis into second place. What did I care though, as I licked the Victoria sponge from my cheeks, I was a winner and had the acclaim of my peers. Little did I realise that having jam all over my face was to be the height of my pre-pubescent popularity. Life was about to change.

As my parents grew more affluent, we joined the lower middle classes and jumped ship. Yes, for us the white flight started early (Edmonton had a growing Greek Cypriot population at the time) and so, in 1981, we moved further out to Broxbourne, Herts. Our new house was pleasant, with a large garden, an even longer drive but, sadly, no butler.

For those of you not familiar with Broxbourne's population breakdown, it is even today a 99 per cent white area. I went to a school that had only one black child in it. The nearest I came to experiencing 'diversity' in my youth was via the likes of Kunte Kinte, Chicken George and the rest of the cast of TV smash hit *Roots*.

What made it worse is that school never taught me anything about black people, not even the slave trade. The history syllabus I followed had plenty of stuff about Nazis, Commies, Tudors, Romans, but nothing at all about a person I might bump into on a bus at the end of my road. So if anyone was growing up in a one dimensional racial world it was I. Despite, or maybe because of this, I never thought of someone's colour as meaning a great deal. The first time I was aware of colour was when I heard racist remarks by my sister's boyfriend. In everyday conversation he used to make reference to 'Paki' shops and 'Coons.' 'How strange,' I remember thinking, why use such words?

Our next-door neighbour also made much of the fact that she would never sell her property to anyone who was 'coloured', presumably to reassure my mother she would never be living next to a mysterious 'ethnic'. My parents, though, were unimpressed by her comments and welcomed any who crossed their path.

So, Broxbourne became the white canvas for my adolescence.

Although I had two loving parents around me at all times, I was something of a disappointment to my father. He so much wanted a boy he could play football with and to whom he could act as mentor. Instead he got me. Me, a boy who was more interested in his Matchbox and Airfix toy soldiers than the merits of the latest Tottenham Hotspurs footballer. Dad persevered, though, and took me to watch Tottenham a few times. Sadly, for my father, I was not impressed by his efforts and refused to be drawn to White Hart Lane. It is fair to say I was more in rapture with the pleasures of plastic figurines than the skills of Ossie Ardiles. I could reel off by heart the statistics of Michael Wittmann's Tiger tank but not the goal scoring record of Steve Archibald. Poor dad, he tried his best but I just didn't connect with his interests or his idea of a father and son relationship.

Living just round the corner from Broxbourne School, it was inevitable I would be palmed off to my local comprehensive. And so, satchel and cheese sandwiches in hand, I daily walked the hundred metres to school. Initially, I had no complaints as it was a good school, where discipline was believed in and its educational standard was high. However, whilst my education thrived I was to have problems in other areas.

For me, writing about the experiences I had at school is hard, as I have tried for years to blot them out. I was that most invisible thing – a victim of bullying. Oh how I used to dread waking up each day to go to secondary school (1981-1984) and the insults that would follow. It is fair to say that school and I did not agree. Not from an academic point of view but from a purely survival one. *The Krypton Factor* TV programme was a big hit at the time and it felt like I was running its assault course just to get through to home time. I can still recollect the impact of a knife being hurled against my leg before a lesson started, and the helpless feeling of being trapped under fifty chairs piled up upon my skinny body. I shall never forget the insults that were ten a penny and the social exclusion I suffered from. So why was I bullied? Why is anyone bullied?

Because they are different in some way from the social 'norm'. It could be because the person is fat, spotty, poor or possessing of a stammer. Whatever, there will always be some spiteful child who will use their difference to isolate someone. For me, I fitted quite neatly under the spotty category. My hard-working parents also never had the spare cash to go on vacation, so I used to be abused about my non-existent holidays on the 'Costa Del Broxbourne.'

I was manna from heaven for the bullies – I fitted two categories; I was a buy-one-get-one-free type of victim. It, therefore, only took a couple of weeks for me to become the point of main effort, the *Schwerpunkt*, of their aggression. Seeing as how I was a bullying victim, I was also ostracised from the other pupils – after all, who wants to be linked to the class punch bag?

Being a somewhat shy individual, I did not seek solace from my parents. They suspected something was wrong by the constant state of disarray of my school uniform but knew nothing concrete. The only concrete I was familiar with were the lumps thrown at me in the school playground.

Looking back, I realise I should have confided in my parents about the problems I was having. Now that I myself am a parent, I can feel only guilt that I did not seek out mum and dad at the time, as I would always want my children to be able to talk to me about anything troubling them. I do not want them to replicate my mistake if they are unfortunate enough to go through what I did.

So I suffered, alone, endless days of torment at the hands of people who knew the value of power and ruled with a rod of iron. Did these children know no mercy? Did they have no compassion? I guess not.

I have often wondered what happened to those children for whom violence came easy. Are they happy in their lives? Do they regret their actions from earlier? I know the website 'Friends Reunited' exists and I've often been tempted to set up an alternative version: 'Victims of Bullying Reunited.' I suspect it could get a bit depressing, though, with all the endless stories of childhood misery.

Just about the only good thing about school was that I discovered the fantastic world of *PUNK ROCK* – my first true love. Come evening time I would lock myself in my bedroom and play those tiptop three-chord sounds that soothed my furrowed brow. Without being too melodramatic, it was punk rock that saved my life, as I often used to think about suicide. Luckily for me, I developed a passion for music. It was this that got me through a few bad years. At last I had found my identity, my sense of belonging, in a world of hate.

However, even punk rock got me into trouble on a couple of occasions. I vividly recall getting beaten up – in Broxbourne of all places – the week after the infamous 1990 Poll Tax riots. The reason? I looked like one of the scruffy anarchists whose picture was shown on the telly during coverage of the disturbance. Because of my appearance, I was accosted by a couple of spotty herberts on the way to the local train station. I recall one of my assailants shouting: 'Take that you dirty poll tax protestor,' as he whacked me from behind. To be fair, I did milk this attack for my punk rock credibility but it was still a shock to my eight-stone weighing system. Life as an anarchist was not for me, I decided – even though I sympathised with the anarchic ideals of bands like Conflict and Crass.

Another abuse story concerns the humble bus stop. I remember waiting for a bus in Broxbourne (in 1985), decked out in a t-shirt that had Lenin's slaphead image plastered all over it. In addition, I was modelling a rather fetching pair of multi-coloured patchwork shorts and a variety of punk badges. Whilst twiddling my thumbs at the stop, I noticed a parka wearing Mod riding astride a Lambretta scooter. Upon spotting me on the pavement, he pulled over and shouted at me for my choice of t-shirt. In his words, I was a 'traitor' to my country for sporting such an obvious symbol of Russian Communism. Before I could explain that I was in no way shape or form a Russian sympathiser, he kick-started his souped-up kiddie scooter and zoomed off. I must say, I am probably the only *Daily Telegraph* reader who has ever been called a Communist! Bloody hell, Ronald Reagan could go to Bitburg unscathed but I was having problems catching a number 310 bus from the bottom of my road! Had the Cold War moved its epicentre to humble old Broxbourne?

Cor blimey, I was discovering that being a punk was hard work. I should have joined the burgeoning ranks of the New Romantics and had an easier life. Then again, all that Spandau Ballet nonsense would have done my head in. I liked proper music; music that was hard to get and even harder to attract the girls with.

I mentioned earlier that I couldn't connect with my dad's idea of what a father/son relationship should be. It is only fair to point out that father played a blinder when it came to indulging my punk rock taste in music. Most weeks, he would go down to the Our Price record shop, near to where he worked in London, and order records by bands, such as Blitz, Mau Maus, Yeah Yeah Noh and a whole host of other groups. I daresay, he must have suffered a few curious looks from the counter staff before explaining they were for his son. Whatever the looks, though, dad put me first and came home with the precious vinyl. I remain indebted to him to this day for assisting my musical development. I may never have discovered the joys of German Oi! punk but for dad. Only a true father would do this for his son.

Eventually, my ordeal at school ended and an average child was thrown out into the big bad world. Not knowing what to do, with only a trio of O-levels to show for years of bullying, I opted for a Business Studies college course at East Herts College, and here, at least, I met some interesting people. My good friend, Nikki Upperton, (destined to be my 'Best Man' when I married Margaret), Joanne McCaffrey and fellow punk enthusiast Martin Pearce. Martin was a cool guy despite his uncanny resemblance to David Sylvain, from the pop band Japan. I discovered shortly after meeting him that, rather than liking the art-school poncy music of Japan, he was in fact a mad keen Sex Pistols devotee. We, therefore, immediately hit it off and started borrowing each other's records.

Even though we were both punks, I should remind readers here that this is 1984 and not 1977. It is fair to say I was always a bit behind the times. Martin and I soon became good friends and accompanied each other to see numerous punk bands. I can still raise a smile at the memory of pogoing down the front of the stage to bands like: The Fits, The Damned, The Nomads, Crazyhead, Southern Death Cult, New Model Army, The Violent Femmes, Julian Cope, The Prisoners and the legendary Doctor and the Medics (before their 'Spirit in the Sky' monster hit.)

To digress a little, Medics gigs were simply brilliant; organised chaos set to a laughter soundtrack mixed in with paisley waistcoats. Sounds strange, I accept, but they really were a top night out. So, whilst most of the population was getting to grips with bands such as Duran Duran, Bucks Fizz and Imagination, I was heading in the opposite direction. I was on a rock'n'roll trip to hell. My poor parents, only just getting over the bullying stage in their son's development, worried about my weird taste in clothes and the peculiar sounds coming from my bedroom. But they were at least content that I stayed away from alcohol/drugs and had found both an interest and a couple of friends.

Following on from my passion, I bought a guitar at this time and formed a band with Martin (bass) and his Morrissey type brother Russell (guitar/vocals.) Martin was not a very punk name, though, so he changed it to Olaf! To this day, I am puzzled by his decision. Olaf? Gene Vincent, Sid Vicious, Kurt Cobain, Elvis and...err...Olaf. I am sure you will agree that Olaf does not sit easy in the pantheon of rock and roll names, sounding like something from the days of the Vikings and certainly not 'punk rock.'

Maybe he should have called himself Martin Matlock – to reflect his Pistols obsession? Whatever, he had started a trend. A trend I just had to follow. So I, in a flash of madness, changed my real name of Paul to Bobby. Cool or what?

At the time, if not today, I thought Bobby had charisma and a hint of masculine charm. Most people I know just think the name is stupid. Still, no matter what, I was living the punk lifestyle to its max.

If memory serves me correctly the band was called The Consumptives and played at the Bull & Gate pub in Kentish Town – a venue renowned for hosting the inept, the limited and the unloved. However, I did have two major problems with being in a band; I didn't have a clue what to do with groupies and couldn't keep time with other 'musicians'. So, after a short career as a guitar hero, I was ejected, due to musical differences, and instead formed a one-man band. I still play the guitar to this day but have never mastered my two handicaps – even though the spots have gone.

How bad was I with the groupies? Well, it is true to say I was never a big hit with the girls. In my entire adolescence I can remember only one incident of sweet romance. The lady in question went by the name of Sarah and plied her trade where I worked. She was kind of cute in a manly sort of way and I could visualise myself wrapped up within her muscular arms. So, after much wringing of hands, I eventually asked her out. To my surprise she agreed. 'Great,' I thought. Maybe I should get her some flowers. Big mistake. Not having any experience as to what you buy to impress your intended, I pottered off to my local florists. What an array of flowers greeted my virgin eyes! How on earth do I make up my mind? Eventually, my eyes spotted salvation in the form of a rather large and sumptuous-looking bunch of strawberry coloured carnations. They looked like they would do the trick, so they were duly purchased for £20 and sent off to her. I breathed a sigh of relief and sat back, content that nothing could go awry. How wrong I was.

I had cunningly arranged it so the flowers would turn up on the day of the date (bizarrely, we were going to see funk band Five Star) and was confident I had covered all angles of attack for the un-suspecting young lady. I spruced myself up, bade goodbye to my parents, and got ready to make an important step on the journey into manhood. I ran down to my local train station and waited, dry mouthed and perspiring, for my potential beloved to accompany me. I waited for thirty minutes. I waited for one hour. I checked my watch and waited a further thirty minutes. Finally at around 7.30pm I went home, alone.

Puzzled as to why the young lady had not turned up, I asked a mutual friend. The answer? The sumptuous-looking 'flowers' were a wreath! Needless to say, the young lady was not impressed and so left me to sit alone on a cold platform. Mona Lisa, I thought to myself, what have I done?

So that was that, my one and only attempt to enter the murky world of teenage love affairs had failed. It was back to the tissues for me!

I say that was my only proper foray into the teenage kicks lifestyle, but I did have another, even less successful, attempt to engage with the opposite sex. This was again at my workplace, when I was eighteen. The lady who caught my eye was a punk rocker, placed in my care for the day, so I could show her the ropes of the job. A punk rock girl – with me. Talk about landing on my testosterone feet for once.

Sadly, my enthusiasm for punk was to torpedo any hope I may have had for the two of us. In the three hours I was showing her around, I managed to inform her of just about every punk band in the world that I liked. Thinking she would be impressed, I suggested we go and see the Fits (Blackpool based punk band.) She told me she would think about it and went off to lunch, whilst I contemplated having a punk rock girlfriend. She never returned from her sandwiches. After the event I discovered that she resigned on the spot, due to my being a punk rock bore.

So no, it is fair to say, that romance and I never got acquainted on first name terms.

Meanwhile, back in the academic world, my college course finished and I left for the adventure that is work. An adventure that would eventually bring me into contact with my dear wife of today. Little did I know that, in Nigeria, a small girl was experiencing equally traumatic times in a boarding school in Ogun state. Unfortunately, for her, she did not have punk rock to come to her rescue.

Margaret

England was blessed twice in the year 1966: they won the football World Cup and I, Margaret Oshindele, was born in London of Nigerian parentage. The year was not just successful for the England football team it was also good for the Nigerian pound v English pound exchange rate. My dad therefore decided the family would be better off by moving to England. So in 1962 the Oshindele family made a new home for itself in the run down paradise that was Clapham Common.

Despite the usual stories of racism/prejudice that was directed at black people during the Sixties my parents put down the roots that led to my birth. So how bad was the prejudice? Quite bad and more than a touch bizarre. My mother told me the strangest comment she received was from a white woman of around thirty years of age. Apparently, this lady genuinely thought that black people had tails attached to their backs. As a consequence, the woman used to linger outside any toilet my mother was using – no doubt hoping to get a quick flash of tail when the cubicle door opened. Nowadays this lady would be called a stalker but at the time my poor mum had to tolerate her ignorance.

Despite hindrances like these, life was relatively good and by 1966 my parents could afford to have me, their second child. The first born in our family was my dear sister; Anne Oshindele.

Blessed by the financial power of the Nigerian pound, my parents were able to afford to send me off to foster carers, the lovely Mr & Mrs Anderson in sunny Brighton. Cashing in on the oil wealth that Nigeria was now swimming in, my parents set up an oil franchise business back home and lived off the proceeds in London.

Father did not neglect me though and came to see me on most weekends. A different type of upbringing compared to Bobby, but my experience was not unusual for young Nigerians who had parents in the swinging '60s London Nigerian scene. Sadly, the Biafra Nigerian civil war erupted for the period 1967-1970, and ruined the hopes and aspirations for Nigerians both at home and abroad.

Without wishing to bore the reader, who may know little about the Biafran War, it is important to have knowledge of it in order to understand the current day situation in Nigeria. The war basically centred on who controlled the oil in Nigeria and the monetary gain to be had by exploiting it. In May 1967 the Ibo (tribe) dominated Eastern Region broke away from the Yoruba Government, led by General Yakuba Gowon, and set up the independent state of 'Biafra'. This was the spark that caused armed conflict to break out. Eventually government forces emerged victorious but not before the free state of 'Biafra' had received assistance from the international community due to sympathetic reporting of their plight. This was mainly because they were starved into submission via a blockade. The famous author, Frederick Forsyth, was one of many who highlighted the abuse of ordinary men, women and children in the Biafran 'state'. The inter-ethnic conflict that occasionally breaks out in present day Nigeria has many of its origins from the Biafran War.

A little diversion from our story but the war is an important part of Nigeria's development. It is also a history that many in the West do not know.

Today, the continent of Africa is still scarred by similar disputes. Only when peace comes will the continent fulfil its undoubted potential.

After the war though, life improved for the winners and the oil prompted financial gain for a large number of Nigerians. It should be admitted, however, that this wealth windfall has been largely wasted by fraudulent leaders and oil companies who have grown fat on the sweat of others.

With the war over, my parents returned to Nigeria and so I left England to return to their hometown state of Ibadan. Ibadan is a state of around five million people, around one hundred kilometres north of Lagos. It is a town where the houses are big and the dreams are bigger. And, boy, do we Nigerians like to dream.

I, though, had no time for dreaming. After being reunited with my parents, I was promptly despatched to a boarding school in Ogun state. At the time I thought nothing of this; I had been away from my natural parents for so long it just seemed normal.

After my birth my parents had three other children, my younger sister Kemi and two brothers, who were not born in England. Kemi now lives in America but my brothers still live in Nigeria, away from their two sisters who miss them dearly. Money was still plentiful for us at this time, although my parents had to put in the hours to earn their money. As a consequence, I learnt to cherish the limited time I had with them. Again, this is a fairly common experience for young children growing up in Nigeria. We were always aware that business comes first and appreciated the sacrifices our parents made for us to attend private school. I, therefore, determined to prove their investment a correct one.

Any doubts I had to make an effort at school were cast aside the moment I entered the disciplined world of the boarding school. For those of you educated in England the following may be hard to understand, as schools in England certainly have a different approach to the enforcement of a teacher's wishes. For example, when a teacher entered the class all pupils had to stand to attention. What a contrast to England, where kids qualify for the Duke of Edinburgh's Gold Award if they attend school for more than five days in succession.

This old style discipline was backed up by a fear factor, and anyone transgressing a person in authority was soon made to realise the error of their ways. Corporal punishment in England is frowned upon, but in Nigeria it is seen as the normal way to admonish a misbehaving child. Retribution was painful and always swift. I remember some of the children at the school were bullying other pupils. The head teacher was told and their penalty was to stand outside in the hot sun all day. I should remind the reader here that we are talking about a Nigerian sun of thirty-five degrees centigrade and not an overcast day in grey Manchester. It was like a scene from the film *Bridge on the River Kwai* as the bullies passed out one by one. Nowadays such 'discipline' would be frowned upon as an infringement of their 'human rights' but it certainly stopped them from bullying.

Unfortunately, they were not the only bullies at the school and I got to know the majority of them on an intimate level. Like my future husband, I too had the misfortune to endure their cruelty on a daily basis. My crime? I was a short girl of around eleven years old. I should explain to those not familiar with Yoruba Nigerian culture that being short is synonymous with Satan. I was, therefore, subsequently taunted for being the 'Devil'. Unlike present day England, Nigeria is a country where issues regarding religion are taken very seriously. To be called the Devil is both upsetting, and potentially lethal. Even to this day, children are being abused and killed purely because they are suspected of being possessed by evil spirits.

I should add that this is not unique to Nigeria and is actually more prevalent in other African countries. For me, this abuse was extremely distressing. Because I was the 'Devil', I was refused food by the prefects in my class and not permitted to use the showers. As a result, I started to smell rather bad and loose weight. I was so hungry; one day I had no alternative but to eat sand. And all because my genes decided I was to be vertically challenged.

Luckily my dad, on one of his weekend visits, noticed my poor health and demanded to know what was wrong. Being of a somewhat fragile disposition, I unburdened my heart to him and told him about the bullying. Feeling the need to replicate the robust approach of the school towards discipline, dad drove up to one of the boys that was bullying me and tooted his horn. The boy obediently walked over to my father's car, for in our culture it is the custom to respect our elders and never to question their role. Once he reached the window, my father whacked him several times with a leather belt and told him to leave me alone in future. I guess these days my dad would be imprisoned for such an act but, yes you've guessed it, the boy stopped abusing me.

However, there were others who readily took my tormentors' place and my persecution continued. Apart from one dear girl, who passed away whilst at school, I was without a friend. Life was hard and I used to cry myself to sleep. If only I had someone to confide in.

Suddenly it happened; the event that would transform my life. I had a spiritual awakening by an image that hit me in the middle of the day. I was lying down resting in the hot afternoon sun when I saw Jesus calling out to me. He was talking in a soothing voice and giving me his assistance and strength to beat the bullies. He wanted to comfort me and take me to his chest. With much joy in my heart, I mentally accepted his invitation and took his hand. From this moment on I really felt I was no longer alone and that he would be there to guide me. I had found my friend. This friend would not let me down, he would not call me the Devil, he was kind, compassionate and forgiving. From now onwards, I felt safe and strangely at ease with my situation. Sure, the bullying did not stop but the abuse couldn't touch me any longer. I was being looked after by the Almighty.

Unfortunately, my newfound spirituality could not help me academically and I still ended up failing my WAEC (West African Education Certificate.) This was not only a disappointment to me but also to my parents. They had put their faith and money in me, their daughter, and I had betrayed them by not being a good student. I felt so ashamed and vowed to re-sit my exams in the hope of achieving my true potential. Fortuitously, at the re-sit I was more mature and managed to attain a creditable four General Certificate of Education passes. The way to higher education was now open. It was 1986 and time for me to return to England.

Arriving back home in dear old Blighty, I attended Middlesex University and studied for a degree in Social Policy and Economics. At this time I was living with my fellow student and sister Anne, and my long-standing friend Anita. The three of us were inseparable and shared everything we had between us. England, though, was a bit of a shock. Not, as you may expect, for its weather. No, I was perplexed by the bank automatic cash dispenser machines. What a nice job I thought; to sit there all day dishing out free money to customers. I could only marvel at how disciplined the English were as the queue to use these machines did not stretch round the block.

It is fair to say that English money was turning into a bit of a mystery for me. I remember going to a supermarket with my sister to buy some food. The bill came to £160. Food was cheap in Nigeria and this was somewhat of a shock to us. We only had £40 in our pockets and had to look on shamefaced as items were removed from our trolley.

To make ends meet, and to avoid any further embarrassment at the check out till, I took on a variety of poorly paid part-time jobs. How poorly paid? I was paid £1 an hour by an Iranian man to work in his fish and chip shop. That sounds innocent enough but this man expected me to work ten hour shifts for this pittance. To all intents and purposes the slave trade was alive and kicking in England. Not only that, but because I lived in the small flat above his shop, the man felt it was his right to walk into my bedroom at any time of the day – whatever my state of undress. I should have resigned my job at this point but felt compelled to put up with these awful conditions as I needed the money, however low it was. Luckily the minimum wage has since been introduced, a policy that has gone someway to easing the financial burden and exploitation of legal migrant workers in England.

Unfortunately, many employers still treat their fellow human beings with similar distain. It is also a matter of shame that many abuses committed against vulnerable illegal migrant workers are instigated by those who have only recently arrived on our shores. I know of a Nigerian man whose company pays £2.50 an hour for its illegal immigrant African workforce. He knows full well they cannot complain for risk of being deported so he laughs all the way to the bank. In many ways the system has not changed since I struggled to make ends meet. It is also ironic that the owners of these companies are usually at the front of the queue, when it comes to slagging off African leaders who flaunt their wealth. Pathetic.

When surviving in my slave existence, I also did those unpleasant jobs that many in England would not dare contemplate to do. Yes, I was that cleaner at 6.30 in the morning, scrubbing away the grime of the previous day. Yes, I was that invisible person who worked as a cloakroom attendant in the dead of night, whilst the disillusioned socialites got off their heads on drink and drugs. If you look around today, you will see thousands like me then, working for a few crumbs, invisible until the British National Party (BNP) make a claim that jobs are being taken from whites. Then, we are the spongers, the asylum seekers, the poor, and the needy, with their caps out begging for money. Just how many more newspaper headlines will seek to blame migrant workers for the state of modern day England?

As for me, I did the jobs that no one wanted to do, so I could save up and buy the books I needed for my studies. When I wasn't working hard to earn a living wage, I studied conscientiously and long into the night. I knew I had one chance to succeed and had to grasp it with both hands. Through sheer hard work and determination, I completed my degree and graduated with 2:2 with honours. What a relief! Despite what the bullies had put me through I had managed to prove myself a good student.

After I graduated I had such high hopes and expectations. I had repaid my parents trust in me and looked forward to being able to send money home to them. It was 1992 and the world was my oyster. Surely I only had to sit back and take my pick of the elite jobs about to fall into my lap?

My financial dreams were shattered as I joined the Civil Service.

Summary

As you can see, we both had difficult childhoods. A bully in Nigeria is the same as one in England. Both are odious creatures that do so much long-term damage to individuals. Bullying is a pain that never goes away, remaining a scar on the memory even as one progresses through adult life.

As a consequence of our background, we are both quick to react today when we see someone who bullies others. The memory of the pain they cause is always there at the back of our minds. Time has certainly healed some of the wound but the scar of being a teenage bullying *victim* – how we both hate that word – remains. But eventually we were both saved.

Margaret by Jesus. Me by Johnny Rotten!

CHAPTER 3

Reaction of Parents/Friends to our Relationship

Bobby

When I first told my parents about Margaret I think their initial reaction was one of relief, as girls had been a subject pretty much on the back burner, to put it mildly.

According to a June 2006 MORI poll, the average age for losing one's virginity in the UK is seventeen. Well, all I can say is, an awful lot of under seventeen year olds must have been enjoying sex, given my late start in matters of a physical nature. I was that rare thing, a virgin at the age of twenty-six and not really bothered about having a girlfriend at all. Of course this had to mean I was gay, didn't it?

Not being one for gossip, I grew tired of constant questioning of my sexuality at work and just got on with my life. Not for me the endless discussions of my male colleagues. Discussions that tended to revolve around breasts, orgasms and cars. No, I was content to withdraw into my world of music and Wolverhampton Wanderers and let the gossipers do their worse. I guess this partly explains the comment made to Margaret when she was getting to know me, about my 'swinging'.

I will never understand why so many people in an office like to wonder about someone's sexual choice. It is a matter for the individual to make. Increasingly though, we live in a world where being stupid is seen as a desirable state of mind. A world where what happens in celebrity relationships is more important than what happens in Iraq. Still, at least my parents always accepted me for who I was, rather than who they imagined I could be. It was because of this I was confident they would extend this courtesy to Margaret. I was correct. To this day, I am eternally grateful they accepted her with open arms. In the press/chat shows you hear so many stories about parents disowning their offspring because of their choice of partner, so I will always respect my parents for ensuring this was a problem I didn't have to face.

Margaret was worried though, the first time she met my parents. Why? I had convinced her (I make no apologies for my strange sense of humour) that I came from a family of nudists and that, as a family, we liked nothing better than to prance around in the nude. Margaret was naturally horrified that her first view of her mother-in-law might be a bit more revealing than is the norm! Indeed, she was so worried that she actually hid behind the front door as they entered my flat in Enfield. I will never forget the look of relief on her face when she realised they were fully clothed. My poor mum, unaware of my 'joke,' must have wondered what was going on. Once Margaret emerged into full view, they settled down and she immediately impressed them, by showing them the respect they deserved as elders. They responded with unconditional love.

The only cultural thing that they found strange, initially, was Margaret addressing them as Mum and Dad – as Yoruba custom dictates. Since then though, they like the fact they have acquired another daughter, so to speak.

With Margaret being a devout Methodist, they also grew to understand the spiritual aspect of a person and have since asked many questions about the bible. Like a lot of English people my parents are not religious, in the Yoruba sense at least, although they do believe in a higher being. Centuries ago the missionaries went to Africa to preach religion. I now had Margaret doing the same to my parents. The world had turned full circle.

In many ways, Margaret was more a mirror reflection of how the English used to be in the nostalgic days of the Fifties – when my parents were growing up. Therefore, rather than finding Margaret's Yoruba culture a stumbling block, they actually found it reassuring as its ideas and core values were so similar to their own.

I once asked my mother why she went out with my dad. She replied; 'because of his manners; he knew how to approach a woman in the correct way.' This is so true of my father as he still believes that respect for a woman is the foundation of any male/female relationship. I have tried, and sometimes failed, to carry on his good work. These days, a short walk down a high street shows that men have lost this simple art of conversation. In our lovely, modern world, a woman is lucky to get a wolf whistle and a 'nice arse' type of comment. This is not the way I was brought up. For me it is normal to open doors for ladies and to give up my seat for them when the bus is full. Small gestures for sure but I feel better for acting this way.

The only real problem they had, and occasionally still have, is Margaret's accent. It is fair to say it is quite unique in the way it blends a hint of Brighton/London with a big dash of Yoruba. I know many people of Nigerian origin and still have never heard anyone sound quite like Margaret. Even her sister, with an identical background, has a more defined vocal style. It is kind of sexy in a way, but as it's a sensitive subject with my missus, I will move swiftly on.

I should add here that Margaret's grasp of English words, whilst good in the technical sense, sometimes lets her down when it comes to slang or swear words. As an example, she really did not know what a wanker was until she went out with me! Really, she didn't.

She does now.

One of the beneficial aspects of my parents' acceptance of Margaret is that they feel totally at ease in her presence. Even my dad, normally a reticent talker, opens up when she appears. Good old dad, he really seems to have an empathy with Margaret and other Africans in general. He did National Service in Kenya so Margaret often jokes with him that perhaps he has a Kenyan daughter that will appear when his will is read out! Knowing my dad, the nearest he got to any nubile young Kenyan woman was being served by the tea lady.

For her part, Margaret finds talking to my parents so relaxing and it is certainly not a chore visiting the 'in-laws.' Indeed, Margaret has grown to love my parents in a way that goes beyond the call of duty.

Relations between the two sets of parents are a little harder, mainly because Margaret's normally reside in Nigeria. When they do meet up it can also be a bit of a struggle to communicate due to language difficulties. Even I find this a bit of a handicap at times although I do persevere.

I certainly admire my other 'Dad' though for his constant, never ending thirst for knowledge. How many other seventy-five year olds do you find buying a laptop and enrolling for computer courses? Well, my father-in-law does. I take my hat off to his desire to improve his brain and his reluctance to vegetate in front of the telly all day. My mother-in-law also keeps her brain active. When not sewing my bondage pants, she still runs her oil franchise business. Seeing as how Nigeria doesn't have a welfare state, my in-laws have no option other than to keep in business. Not for them the easy option that we sometimes take for granted in the West.

Following on from this, I fully understand my financial help is needed to support my extended family in Nigeria. This will not be news to anyone of African origin, but people in Africa, with relatives in Europe, expect their sisters and brothers to work long hours to send money 'home'. Sometimes, I do wonder if people 'home' actually realise how expensive and hard it is to live in the West but is it fair to blame them if they have never lived here? Margaret's cousin, Joyce, has the best slant on this, referring to the early years of living in England as 'the struggle'. Spot on. I can only admire those cleaners/carers that work so hard to support others. My wife knows people who are employed for one hundred plus hours per week just so they can send a few pounds to relatives. It is more than £1 per hour but the fish and chip owner syndrome of Margaret's youth is continuing. No wonder black African children are sometimes neglected in England, their parents are too busy working to give them the care and support they need.

And yet, all of this is invisible to the naked eye. Without the majority population knowing it, a whole world of people are slaving away for a few dollars more, their stories untold and their lives unknown.

So, if my parents were happy with Margaret, what about the rest of my family?

My sister was okay with my choice of partner once she had gotten over the shock of a woman finding her brother attractive. In reality, with only one exception, all of my family accepted Margaret into the 'clan'. The one exception? An uncle who didn't attend the wedding as he 'doesn't approve of that type of thing.' I tried to explain that Margaret was a woman and not a 'thing' but he had made up his mind. Ah well, his loss I figured. After years of bullying, a mild comment such as his is easily dismissed as an irrelevance.

And my friends? Well Margaret's colour was never an issue for any of them. Sorry to disappoint any who presume that white men always ask 'What was it like to have sex with a black woman?' It just never happened. My friends had a similar attitude to my sister, in that they couldn't help but find it funny that Bobby had a girlfriend and had suddenly started talking about 'adult' subjects.

So, I was in the clear, my big secret was out, I had finally reached maturity – I was a man!

Margaret, though, had her own hurdle to jump over and she would encounter prejudice of a more ingrained nature.

Margaret

When I first told my parents about Bobby, they were initially disappointed and more than a little concerned they might lose their daughter. I guess, like myself, they had always assumed I would settle down with a Yoruba man and provide them with the grand-children they had always desired. My going out with Bobby shattered that assumption and forced them to contemplate Plan B. For my part, I was worried how to approach mum and dad with news of my new boyfriend – knowing them to be typically conservative in their views on such matters. Bobby, with his pale skin and 'alien' culture, was going to be a step into the unknown for two elderly Yoruba parents.

In fairness, I should add that my mother would have had at least the same, and probably more objections, if I had married a man of Caribbean origin – as many Africans have a downer on people from that part of the world – for reasons we will elaborate on later.

Still, I did have one trump card to play, with regards to smoothing affairs with my parents – my sister Anne. She had already met Bobby and given her seal of approval to our relationship. In actual fact, she had dealings with Bobby before I did, whilst attending the DSS where Bobby worked. I remember when I told her I was going out with a white guy from work, she just asked; 'Is it that nice man who is polite to everybody, *even us Africans?*' She was overjoyed when I confirmed it was. I learnt afterwards that my sister had not been the only one impressed by Bobby's manners. It turned out that other Nigerians had also commented to her about Bobby's kindness towards them and his lack of prejudice – especially given Africans' generally low status in English society. Sister Anne was, therefore, confident I had made the right choice to go out with him.

Where would I be without my dear sister, I sometimes wonder? She has certainly always been there for me when the need has arisen: my rock when times are hard. Mind, it would have been better if she had married Bobby as she is definitely his number one fan. Whenever I have a problem with him she always takes his side, normally with the prefix 'Ah, poor Bobby, don't be too harsh on him.' That's easy for her to say – she doesn't have to listen to his music, laugh at his jokes or eat his food!

Despite her blessing, I was still nervous at the thought of approaching my parents with news of my English gentleman. At this time they were still living in Nigeria so any contact with them was via letters and the odd snatched phone call. They often used to ask, when I was seeing Bobby, if I had a boyfriend. My answer was always the same: *NO*. Although I wanted to tell the truth, I just couldn't bring myself to tell mum and dad I was dating a white man. To make matters worse, my new lover didn't even have the consolation prize of a degree – as education is something that impresses every Nigerian parent. So I had no choice but to keep Bobby locked away as my little secret.

Despite Bobby being hidden from my family, our relationship deepened.

Indeed, it got so deep that Bobby packed his bags and moved into my flat. He then proposed to me on Christmas Day 1996. I accepted immediately, my mind ecstatic at the prospect of spending the rest of my life with a football obsessed punk rocker who didn't know the meaning of fashion. My joy, however, was short lived. I would have to tell my parents.

I decided the best medium – yes, I know I was a coward – was through a letter. I duly sent it via an acquaintance of the family (the Nigerian postal service is not what it should be) that was visiting Nigeria at the time. I sat back and waited, each day secretly dreading the arrival of the post or the ringing of the phone. It took a while but eventually a letter was delivered by the slightly more reliable Royal Mail. It was not good news. My mother especially asked me to reconsider and confessed to praying everyday so I would realise I had made a mistake. In later years, I also found out she had fasted in an effort to make me see 'sense.'

How could I do this, she wondered, did I have no respect for our Yoruba culture and customs? What would the rest of the family say? Why would I throw away centuries of tradition and beliefs all for the pleasure of a white man? Sadly, that was all Bobby was, a white man. It did not matter about his character, manners, or even his naff clothes. He was being defined simply by his skin colour.

My parents viewed the situation so seriously that an old friend of the family was despatched to see me to try to get me to change my mind. I listened to her worries and sympathised with the reasoning behind her words. I though, like my namesake, was not for turning. I stayed strong and made the decision to go ahead with our marriage, despite the misgivings of my parents. In my mind, I was not rejecting Yoruba culture I was merely mixing it with another. To this day I still find it annoying that by marrying someone from a different culture it is automatically assumed that the person has lost something. I certainly had not lost anything; I had merely gained an insight into an English culture that, hitherto, had been hidden from me.

So, if that was the immediate reaction of my parents, would telling my friends be any easier? Unfortunately, it got worse before it got better. I had been part of a group calling itself the 'Committee of Friends'; a loose gathering of Nigerians from the local area. We got together every month or so to discuss Nigerian issues back 'home'. It was an informal meeting where one of the main benefits was hearing Yoruba spoken by all. Plucking up courage, I eventually informed them of my decision to marry Bobby. They were surprised at my news and out of the 'friends' I invited to the wedding only two came. The others, I guess, also did not approve of that sort of 'thing.' In disgust, I left the committee.

29

A relative of one of my friends also rejected Bobby. I recall her saying she did not want to visit me anymore because our home 'smells like a white person's house.' I am not sure what she was referring to by this, maybe the smell of potatoes? If so, how sad that a humble potato can affect the way one is viewed. This was not the last problem I was to have with potatoes.

I recall another black male friend who warned me about white men in general. I was told, 'Be on your guard. I work with them and I know how they operate – you cannot trust them'.

Eventually, most of my friends did accept Bobby – albeit with a shake of the head at my choice. I recall my good friend Sylvia merely commenting, 'Fine if you have to go out with a white guy but why Bobby? He is so eccentric.' I guess he is but his eccentricity is attractive in a funny kind of way. However, despite acceptance of our union I was told many years later that, behind our backs, the usual comment was 'It'll never last, they are just too different.' This happened especially at work when news first broke of our relationship. Ah, it is so sad that office life revolves around gossip and back stabbing with truth a poor substitute to innuendo and rumour. Have these people nothing more substantial in their lives?

I also remember visiting my old friend Anita and her husband Chucks after they had found out about our dating. Chucks wanted to delve into Bobby's interests and started at what he thought would be an uncontroversial subject – music. He asked Bobby what music he wanted to be played at their house. He suggested jazz, soul, funk, rap or gospel. Bobby waited for the list to continue. It didn't. 'Have you got any punk rock?' came his knee jerk response. 'Err, no,' came the inevitable reply. The conversation fizzled out. Even today, I know no-one in my circle of friends who accepts Bobby's musical taste as they find it bizarre in the extreme.

To be truthful, I was more concerned with obtaining my friends' blessing than worrying about Bobby's musical choice. Despite a few raised eyebrows most people eventually gave their blessing for our wedding. Mum and dad though were taking longer to come round to Bobby.

Now that we were destined to be as one, Bobby did try to integrate by learning Yoruba and he can manage a few words such as *ba wo ni* (hello), *ki lo se le* (what's happening) and *o da bo* (goodbye). His trademark, though, is the slang word; *jabajantes* (rubbish.) If we are ever at a Nigerian get together, I can guarantee he will use this word within five minutes as it always gets a laugh.

He can also say 'ah ah' when the time arises, although this is becoming a boring private joke that he insists on carrying on. I should explain here that the 'ah ah' sound accompanies the sharp intake of breath that Africans give out when they are shocked by something. If you spend five minutes on a London bus you will hear 'ah ah' many times.

At the actual wedding, Bobby also did a speech in Yoruba that was well appreciated, if not exactly understood. However, the wedding was still a few months off and my parents had time to send yet more emissaries to dissuade me from my decision. The next occasion was when an aunt and uncle came to visit the two of us. This time they noted Bobby's kind and respectful manners and just asked us both to consider what we were doing for the sake of my parents. I explained that Bobby came from a good family and that he had promised to look after me. They departed not entirely happy but at least beginning to understand what I saw in Bobby.

My father also received a letter from my intended and was much impressed by its contents. In it Bobby described how he would care for me and not cut me off from my culture. He also asked for his blessing of our union. If you watch old 1950s movies you will see this scene played out time and time again; the man asking his prospective father-in-law for permission to marry his daughter. Bobby may not have won any Oscars for his perform-ance, and he was a bit late with his letter, but it was well received by my dear father.

Luckily the letter did its trick and my dad even planned to come over to England for the wedding. My parents may not have fully accepted Bobby but they knew I was not going to change my mind. Therefore, they swallowed their pride and made the best of the situation.

I realised by marrying Bobby I was not going to have the usual Yoruba wedding with all the razzmatazz and a flexible guest list but I was now confi-dent I had made the right choice. Even though my parents initially objected to Bobby, they were brave enough to eventually accept him for who he is as a person and have only occasionally let his colour/culture become an issue. This is important, as it would have broken my heart to have had to make a choice if they had threatened to disown me. I was fortunate but others who travel this route may not be quite so lucky.

But just what did my mother, especially, find so objectionable about me marrying a white man? One of her concerns is that she felt she would have to make an appointment to see her daughter. I should explain here for non-Yoruba people that you do not invite your relatives or friends over to your house – they just turn up when the whim takes them. In contrast I know most English people like to phone before attending someone's house as a matter of politeness. In Yoruba culture this is not a social necessity. Equally it would be wrong for the person to say, 'Sorry I am too busy to see you.' Bobby finds it strange that Yoruba people do this and, as he always observes, 'Supposing you go out and no ones at home, the person would have had a wasted journey.' That is Bobby all over; always looking at the practical nature of a cultural 'clash'. But he now accepts the Yoruba way and merely shrugs his shoulders.

His two concessions to this? The first is, I have often found him laying an extra place at the dinner table, just in case a visitor turns up. The second concerns his habit of locking the door at all times of the day. Why does he do this? To avoid any further embarrassment with my family. By this, I refer to an incident he had with my mother a few years back. As is the way with Yoruba people, my dear mum once let herself into our house early one morning. Poor Bobby, unaware of my mother's entrance, had just come out of the shower and was drying himself. He had the shock of his life when my mother appeared out of nowhere and viewed him stark naked. To be fair to my mother, who was probably also suffering from shock, she quickly regained her composure and remarked approvingly; 'I can see why my daughter married you!' At the time, all three parties found this awkward but, nowadays, I laugh to myself at the image of my red faced husband covering his genitals with his small hands.

Mother was also worried that I would cut off my siblings back in Nigeria, both financially and emotionally. Of this she needn't have worried, as I have always been aware of my responsibilities in this field. I give when I can.

So finally, our union was to go ahead and we could start planning our wedding. Nothing could stop us now.

Summary

This was the first (real) time that Margaret and I had to face the reality of attempting to merge two cultures into one. Two different families, two different continents; it would have been naive in the extreme to think the path would be smooth. But we persevered and think that both families have gained by knowing a bit more about the others' culture. This is certainly a positive for us and, as an old Yoruba proverb goes, "No knowledge is wasted."

The odd thing, though, is that every time Margaret meets someone new and they find out she is in a mixed marriage, they always ask the same question: 'Did Bobby's family accept you?' Not once does anyone ever ask: 'Did your family accept him?' For us, this is an important point as it presumes any prejudice to come from the 'white' rather than 'black' side. I know people mean no offence by it but it is interesting that others think this way, probably without even knowing it. The truth, as we have demonstrated, is not as simple as black and white.

CHAPTER 4

Religion

Bobby

I must confess I was tempted to leave this chapter blank. The nearest I got to God was standing in a urinal next to Robbie Dennison (Wolverhampton Wanderers winger) in the Charlton Athletic toilets!

As you may have gathered by my less than serious start to this chapter, religion has never been something close to my heart. I can't state that God does not exist, only that I can neither disprove nor prove such a belief. So, yes, I am Mr Sit-on-the-fence, an agnostic. Or, as Margaret often refers to me in her strange version of English, an acoustic.

I have tried to understand my wife's religious core but I truthfully cannot feel her passion for the good Lord, so I accept her religion will remain something I cannot relate to. In many ways I wish I could as I can see the religious zeal that hides behind Margaret's oval eyes. It must also be comforting knowing that wherever you go in life, you are not alone. But I just can't do it. I cannot fake an interest in God.

Funnily enough, when I was a child, I did pray every night – praying that the bullies would leave me alone and pick on someone else. Unfortunately, seeing as how 'someone else' never turned up, the abuse continued. I guess from that moment on I stopped putting any trust in God.

I did try though, and even attended the Boys' Brigade religiously (pun intended) for a few years, but came out when I got bullied there as well. Apart from the 'in-house' bullying, I was also threatened by a knife wielding country boy during a Boys' Brigade camping trip. As these experiences were running concurrently with my troubled school years, it appears to me now that I should have had an entry in the record book as: 'The Most Unpopular Boy Ever.'

So, God and I were off to a bad start. A start that went rapidly downhill given my choice of music. Two of my favourite songs when growing up were The Damned's 'Anti-Pope' and The Upright Citizens German punk classic 'I Hate Church'. I soon came to realise going out with a spiritual woman like Margaret would lead to problems.

Certainly Margaret finds it hard to accept she is married to a person who does not share her Christian beliefs. She feels we cannot connect on that level and she is probably correct. It really is frustrating for Margaret that I do not share something so central to her. Without wishing to trivialise her faith, I find it equally annoying that she cannot recognise the genius quality of a band like Die Lokalmatadore.

Faith differences can be overcome in relationships though, it just needs a bit of compromise. In our case, I have made all the strategic withdrawals over this issue. To be fair, it would have been unjust of me to object to Margaret's Christian way of life, especially as I have nothing spiritual to replace it with. I can imagine it would be far harder if both individuals belonged to a different religion. As it is, with us our children are being brought up as Christians and regularly go to church. Even though their Dad stays at home on Sunday to make the roast dinner. I have no complaints about the children being brought up this way as it will hopefully help to keep them on the straight and narrow road into adulthood.

The only problem to date was with the circumcision of my son. Writing as a man who is un-touched by a knife 'down below', I could see no reason to mutilate my son's genitalia purely because of religion. In contrast, Yoruba Christians have their foreskin removed at an early age. Something had to give. In this case it was my son's foreskin. Even to this day I still get upset by this and will never accept that it is more 'hygienic' for it to be cut off. I really do not see any difference between female/male genital mutilation, especially when a child has no input over the matter. But, as usual in religious areas, my objections were dismissed and the wicked act was carried out in Brighton. Joshua had to endure the pain of the knife just to be 'pure' in a religious sense.

Looking back now, perhaps I should have raised more of an objection and put my foot down but I lacked the moral strength to do so. It is a subject that will always disturb me, even though Joshua doesn't notice the lack of his 'winter warmer' or 'jacket potato.'

My son is curious though as to why I do not attend church with the family on Sunday. Frequently he asks me, 'Daddy why have you lost God?' I am never quite sure what to answer so I invariably just reply: 'Wait until you are older.' A cop out I know but I honestly haven't got a clue what else to say. Maybe I should turn the question around and ask, 'Son, why have you lost your foreskin?' Mind you, I shouldn't go on about this part of his body as he seems to have an obsession with it – like most eight-year-olds. He, also, once asked me, 'Daddy, when I grow up will my willy be as big as yours?' I replied, 'Only if you are very unlucky son.'

I guess, one day, I will have to explain to him that not all people are God worshippers. I dare say this will cause a religious clash in our household, as faith needs its blind devotees in order for it to survive. I just hope I can be honest enough with my children to explain there is always an alternative. Doubtless and needless to say Margaret will have other ideas.

Margaret

Religion for me is a very deep subject. After I received my 'vision', I made a conscious decision to dedicate my life to God, and The Holy Scriptures now guide my actions/morals. Without them I cannot see how a human being can live a spiritual life. It is the core that my actions spring from. Whenever I need guidance it is God I turn to. He never lets me down, as he is a forgiving God. No person is without sin so I cannot understand why more people, especially in England, do not believe in his words.

As it is, we seem to have substituted religion with physical forms of satisfaction, be they drugs, alcohol or rampant sex. The moral aspect of life has been completely overlooked. This is saddening to me, as I genuinely feel sorry for people who do not know God. These other forms of 'entertainment' do nothing for the soul. They do nothing to help people understand others. They merely blot out the reality of life. Is life really that bad that we need to live in a fantasy world with only our 'Make Poverty History' bands to remind us of the real world?

Rather than wear fashionable slogans, people should learn about God and realise there is so much more we can do on a practical level to aid others. By this I do not mean giving money blindly to those evangelical Pastors that abuse their positions of spiritual power. No, I mean being welcoming and friendly to each other, irrespective of background. All people deserve respect. They could be white or black, Christian or Muslim. It does not matter. We are all God's people.

One of Bobby's relatives, his kind hearted Uncle John, often talks to me about God and laments the way the English have lost their belief regarding religion. He truly finds it refreshing listening to me discussing religious matters and only wishes that the rest of the population shared my passion for the righteous way of life. So do I. However, the question must be asked; why did you lose this passion?

So, how can I balance my beliefs with that of my 'acoustic' husband? Simple. Christianity does not force itself on anybody. It is a benign religion, spread by those who know God's word to be true. If Bobby decides not to believe in Jesus Christ I cannot coerce him into being a Christian.

I do find this frustrating because Bobby does exhibit many Christian like character traits. He is a potential Christian, as I like to call him. I really do hope that one day Bobby will share my faith but I am also a realist and accept this may not happen. Still, at least our children are both being brought up as Methodists and I respect Bobby for not causing problems over this issue. The problem will be if he continues to inflict his awful punk rock on them as they enter their teenage years. How confusing it could be for my children to hear 'Anti-Pope' or 'I Hate Church' when their mother returns from Sunday service.

Bobby often asks me why God has not come to the rescue of people throughout history, such as the Christians in the Roman arena or the Jews in the Concentration Camps. Bobby's argument is; if God existed he would surely have helped such innocent victims? My answer is; God has a way for everything, we just do not know his plans. I know I sound a bit like a Nigerian information minister here, as, whenever a plane crash happens or an oil pipe is ruptured, you always hear this explanation given, but it really is true – no mortal knows his intentions. We can only give him our loyalty and trust in his wisdom.

I will conclude this part by quoting one of my favourite passages from the Bible. Proverbs, chapter 9, verse 10; "the fear of the Lord is the beginning of wisdom and the knowledge of the Holy One is insight."

Summary

We live in a Christian house, even though I do not believe that God definitely exists. To my mind, religion acts as a divisive tool used to segregate people from different communities. So many conflicts around the globe are centred on religious issues that I find it hard to see religion as a force for good. I hope I am wrong but the hardening of attitudes we are seeing around the world, mainly between Muslims and Christians, does not bode well for the future.

On a personal level though, I have compromised over religion as my wife has such a strong belief in God. As a result of this, there was only going to be one place where we were going to exchange our marriage vows.

CHAPTER 5

The Wedding – July 1997

Bobby

It is fair to say people have never attended a wedding quite like ours. Where else could you hear a selection of music that was as diverse as: Whitney Houston, The 4-Skins, Luther Vandross, The Buttocks, Fela Kuti, The Exploited, The Neurotic Arseholes, Anita Baker and Slime? They all got an airing at our reception.

I must say, I found it interesting as the dance floor filled up whilst Margaret's Nigerian sounds were being played. How could so many people find that music entertaining? It was also quite comical watching a variety of rotund bottoms swaying to the sounds from the Dark Continent. Suddenly though, the dance floor emptied as three chords started up, a noise that could only herald the start of another classic Oi! anthem! The dance floor was now barren, apart from four punks pogoing like mad. I am sure many guests at the wedding were perplexed at the sight of the bondage pants on display and the bovver boots pounding away on the tacky linoleum flooring. Suffice to say, when the next jazz funk garbage came on, the non-pogoers resumed their bottom shaking. Yep, it was certainly different from other weddings in our family.

The union itself was very much a religious affair in my wife's local Methodist Church. She turned up about an hour late for the service but apart from that everything went smoothly. Mind you, it nearly never happened as Margaret didn't recognise the strange man standing in front of the altar. This was my fault as she had never seen me in a suit before. Once over her shock, she remembered her lines to perfection and claimed her 'man'. In contrast, the biggest shock for me was the smell of her awful hairspray. I guess it was designed to make me feel all weak at the knees in her presence but I just thought she had a bowel problem!

Was I such a bad prospect, I mused, that the idea of marrying me turned her stomach? Yes, the odour really was that bad. It was like sniffing the toilet the day after a hot curry mixed with egg sandwiches. It was so revolting I was tempted to put my fingers over my nostrils but figured she may be offended by this. Being a man, I just grimaced silently. Somehow, I managed to put the stench behind me and duly whispered the lines that condemned/blessed me to a life-time with Margaret.

So that was that – we were now married and committed to growing old together. Now the regrets started. Had I done the right thing? Like a lot of married couples I agonised all the way back to the reception hall. I was happy with Margaret but would the future be kind to us? Ah, what the heck, I thought ruefully, it's done now. Best to concentrate on the reception and have a few drinks. So I opened my first cider tinny, left my regrets behind and entered the hall.

The reception was a mad affair with too much food and loads of beer. You can go to some weddings in England and find yourself paying for drinks, this, though, would never happen at a Yoruba wedding. A few trips were therefore necessary to the local supermarket, where I exhibited my usual shopping skills. I certainly had the right idea when it came to the cider and got enough in to keep apple growers in business for a decade. I listened, can in hand, as the speeches started.

I should explain here that Yoruba weddings always have a head table where the main guests sit. Much like an English wedding you may be thinking. You would be wrong. The first major change was the DJ who introduced each member of the two families to the table. Doesn't sound too bad at face value but I have neglected to mention that each person was called out as if they were about to enter a boxing ring in Las Vegas! My dad especially was rather taken aback by all the hulla-baloo but joined in in good spirits. It was certainly culturally different from other weddings in our family.

To continue the 'alternative' theme, the Best 'Man' – old college friend, Nikki Upperton, did her speech. Unfortunately, poor Nikki was so befuddled after drinking some Budweiser, that her speech managed to include the fact she is a lesbian! I must confess I found this part quite hysterical, although my new wife was a tad embarrassed by her revelation. I am not sure if the word lesbian has a direct translation in Yoruba but I suspect not, given the hand movements her dad was using to explain the concept to an Auntie. The Auntie, it is fair to say, looked horrified. Then again, I saw her afterwards explaining it to another relative, only this time the hand had been replaced by a tongue and the movement was more animated.

About an hour later, after all the speeches and prayers had concluded, the feasting began. Ah, the food. What was served up was a variety of Nigerian and English dishes, as befitting our symbolic union. Old friend, Glen Baldwin, was happy merely to consume vast quantities of sausage rolls whilst the Yoruba contingent (and Julian Smith) polished off the jollof rice.

I, by this stage, was not hungry, the excitement playing havoc with my semi-legendary stomach. If memory serves me correctly, I think I managed a single sausage roll to accompany the cider that was flowing quite nicely. So yes, I can't deny it, I was on the way to becoming pissed!

Somehow, I managed to stay reasonably lucid and participated in the usual wedding day rituals. One of these involved my wife cutting a piece of wedding cake and slipping it into my mouth. The whole purpose of this was for my parents' benefit – so they could see how Margaret would be caring for their son in future. I would have preferred a fishfinger sandwich but I swallowed the cake anyway. I then returned the compliment to Margaret.

The dancing and drinking continued well into the night as sweat mingled with beer and clothes bore the brunt of food stains. A lot later in the evening, I ditched my cider sprayed suit and changed into my own Yoruba attire. I was hoping that most of my friends would have departed by now but unfortunately quite a few were still there. Suffice to say, the appearance of me in my Nigerian outfit (complete with Tommy Cooper style fez hat) topped the evening off for many.

Eventually, the whole enjoyable day came to an end and Margaret and I started to tidy up the hall. You would have thought that with all the Africans at the reception we would have managed to invite a few cleaners to help us but no, no such luck, we had to do the clearing up ourselves. Hours later, we retired to our home, mentally and physically drained by the whole affair. As a result my wedding night will certainly stay in my head for all eternity. For the non-stop rampant sex? No. I was up until 3.30 doing the washing up and actually ended up sleeping by myself on the couch. Not quite the usual marital night of bliss! Never mind, I made up on that score during our honeymoon in Rome. Over to you dear wife.

Margaret

Thinking back to my wedding is strange, as it seems like two decades have since passed. Was it really that long ago? Where has my youth gone? Sadly it has gone for good. In its place is the lined face that now greets my mirror reflection. I have to face facts, for there is no point denying it; I am past forty and beginning to feel my age. My genital defences have been breached, my body ravaged by time and my brain aged by stress. God, what a life! What has Bobby done to me?

Casting my mind back, I felt so different as the day of our wedding dawned. I was so excited by the coming activities and the prospect of betrothing my life to Mr Smith. Strangely, what I recall most is the rushing around in the morning, making sure the food and my dress were okay. To the uninitiated I should emphasise that food to Nigerians is very important, especially at celebratory occasions like weddings. So many different types of rice, so many meats to be cooked. It was a huge task and one I am indebted to my sister for helping out with. After many tribulations all was eventually well. So I, the blushing bride, boarded my limousine and arrived at the church, albeit a little later than expected. A lady should always keep her man waiting and I certainly lived up to the saying.

I must say that Bobby looked smart in his bus driver's suit although slightly nervous. I wasn't sure if this was because he was marrying me, wearing a suit, or his presence in a house of God. My beloved dad gave me away for free and the rings were exchanged. We were husband and wife. Now the eating could commence!

The reception passed by in a whirlwind of rice, peanuts, yam and potatoes as bellies swiftly became full to bursting. The mixing of Bobby and I into one was unfortunately not replicated at the reception as most Nigerians (and Julian Smith) positioned themselves near the food. The majority of Bobby's family were on the other side of the room. Luckily, the both of us have friends from a variety of ethnic backgrounds and these people happily mingled. Well, until the music started at least.

I couldn't bring myself to insist that Bobby didn't play his music so we compromised with the choice. This did mean that we couldn't have a traditional 'our song' moment as we do not share any of the same musical interests. Indeed, of his entire collection I can only tolerate one song; 'Westworld' by German streetpunk stars Oxymoron. This song though was not appropriate for the wedding. Instead, Bobby played 'Baby Baby' by the Vibrators and even by doing this he thought he was conceding ground. He also kept on disappearing throughout the evening when he should have been doing some of the official duties. The reason? He was convincing the DJ to play some more of his punk 'tunes'.

It was a very pleasant wedding though. Bobby and I were determined to enjoy it to its full and this we did. I especially liked it when he changed into his Nigerian attire as this was showing respect towards the culture his wife was from. His Yoruba speech was also funny and went down well, although some of my relatives thought he was speaking English, his accent was that bad.

By the end of the day, I felt contented that we were now married. Not only were Bobby and I as one, the two families were also joined. Our union was their union.

So, I was now to be known as Mrs Smith to the world. No more would I have to spell my maiden name to people (Oshindele). I was now demonstrating my assimilation into English culture by adopting my husband's surname. I had sold out. Or had I?

Summary

What a day our wedding was. A glorious mixture of two cultures. I have often argued that we must have had the most politically correct (PC) wedding in history. I married a black African woman and my Best 'Man' was a lesbian! I should have had London Mayor Ken Livingstone there to give it a seal of approval. On second thoughts, though, he may have asked for the congestion charge to be applied to the car park.

In all seriousness, our wedding did not entirely pass off without problems. Margaret, I know, missed the fact that she was not married in Nigeria and therefore suffered the absence of a large chunk of her family. Despite this, we got on with things and managed to pull it off successfully. Even today, friends of mine still talk about our wedding and how mad it was.

A pleasant spin-off of its success was; it showed to everyone who attended that two cultures could intermingle and be tolerant/respectful towards one another. Our wedding was not about one culture coming out on top – it was about a Christian occasion celebrated by all.

So, with the marriage over, we were now expected to produce children. But, perhaps more importantly, sex was lawful under the eyes of the Lord.

CHAPTER 6

Sex and Sexual Attraction

Bobby

The first time I had sex it was with Margaret – sometime into our relationship. How long into it? Some things should remain private! What I remember the first time is that, whilst Margaret waited, legs apart, for her 'English gentleman' to get physical, I was preoccupied with putting a video into the recorder to tape *Coronation Street*! Not the most romantic idea for any young men or women wanting sex tips. Well, I remember thinking, I had waited this long to enjoy the sins of the flesh, I can wait another couple of minutes. I can see now that this may (!) have seemed to Margaret a tad insulting. I am only surprised that her legs remained open. A lot of women would have had them shut quicker than the Thames Water Barrier when I mentioned the video.

Luckily though, Margaret was patient and she waited until I had fumbled with the remote control. Taking a deep breath, she ushered me into her with the tried and tested line: 'Go ahead punk, make my day.'

Dirty Margaret, I don't think so!

To be honest I didn't have to worry about taping *Coronation Street* as the dirty deed was over so fast I would have only missed the introductory credits. What I also didn't realise were the thoughts going through Margaret's head as we consummated our relationship. She really did think all white English men were into kinky sex.

After our squelching was over, I laid back and considered my virgin performance. For a first attempt I thought I did well, confirmed by Margaret's constant sighs of passion well past the end of our 'session'. Hindsight has instead taught me that the sighing was nothing to do with my bedroom prowess. No, she was just relieved I had put the kinky theory to bed.

There are so many myths concerning sex between different races. Certainly enough to fill a book just on that subject. Most though are just that; myths. As an example Margaret, and other Nigerian women, have told me the reason white people kiss so much is because white men take a long time to obtain an erection. Other comments heard include the idea that a woman needs both hands to peel back a white man's foreskin, like say a banana. White men are also heavily into bestiality; hence our love of dogs. Then there is the use of props such as whips and chains. We all like this, apparently.

I know they sound funny, but these attitudes towards white men really do exist, tarring us all with this sexual pervert image. So why is this? I am told it stems from the English tabloid newspapers that are on sale in Nigeria and England (although I don't recall any that covered the 'elastic' foreskin story!) When Nigerians read salacious news stories about rampant sex orgies or 'dogging' activities, as in the notorious case of disgraced former footballer Stan Collymore, they genuinely believe that these acts are commonplace in England – that we are all constantly on the lookout for ways to 'spice up' our sex lives. The key cultural difference here is that if these stories were published in a Nigerian newspaper, the editorial column would condemn these acts as un-Christian. In this country they pass without comment from the newspaper editor. Is it, therefore, fair to blame Nigerians if this is an image we are happy to export to others? Newspaper editors really need to be aware of how they portray the English, as our public image is not what it should be. What may be titillating to one person is insulting to another.

But what is perversity and what is 'normal' in a relationship? Many Nigerians I have spoken to regard oral sex as a perversity and not something to enhance a couple's sex life, an attitude shared by Margaret's past Nigerian boyfriends. A Caribbean origin friend of mine also told me a story about a Jamaican man she knew, who would not do the 'blood clot ting', as he was not white. Why was his colour important I wondered – presumably he has a tongue.

Sex between couples should be a demonstration of mutual trust and love. There should be no coercion into what a couple do in the bedroom; it is a matter of give, take and compromise. Just like every other aspect in a relationship. That is why I find it strange that some people cling onto culture when sex comes up, as it has no place in bedroom politics.

Having mentioned black myths about white sexual behaviour, it is only fair that I point out some I have heard about black women. An old white colleague of mine once told me that I must get a lot of sex at home as my wife is African. Hmm, not sure about that one. Since when did someone's colour influence the amount of times they felt in the mood?

The image of the highly charged sexual black woman is one that has permeated throughout the western world. This invariably shows itself when Acquired Immunedeficiency Syndrome (AIDS) is mentioned in the press. You would think that Africans spend all day long having sex given the self-righteousness on display every time Africa's AID's deaths are mentioned. Margaret informs me this partly stems from Seventies TV documentaries that used to show black women running around topless in Africa. It seems that breasts are viewed primarily as a means to sexual titillation in the West; whilst in Africa they are seen mainly as a woman's tools for the trade. As a consequence, what to Africans is mere nature conflicts with Western sexual imagery, best shown by page three of *The Sun*. I am not sure I totally agree with my wife but it may be a contributory factor. Ironically, where sex is concerned, I have found that African women are deeply conservative over it and are reluctant even to talk about the subject.

Anyway, in England we are too open to the charge of arrogance over this issue and need to confront our own inner demons before demonising whole continents. Weak sexual control is seen on many of our city streets late at night, as the drunken hordes stumble out of pubs. Just how many children are conceived out of wedlock in this country as a result of one too many Bacardi Breezers?

So, why then am I attracted to Margaret? What is it about her that puts a spring into my genitalia? I should confess here that I never found her attractive in a sexual sense when we first stepped out as a couple. In fact, my confession needs to be extended, as I never found black women remotely attractive. It sounds funny to write this, I know, but that was the truth for me growing up. I have tried to rationalise this now, and can only imagine it was because I was never around black people in general. Stuck in my own private white environment, I never saw black people as being part of my life. I had no negative feelings towards them, they just never entered my world. Instead my teenage years were spent lusting after white icons such as Glynis Barber (Soolin in *Blake's 7*) or Elizabeth Sladen (Sarah in *Doctor Who*) rather than Naomi Campbell. But then Margaret entered my life and a brave new world opened up.

Although not a 'hot babe', Margaret was pretty enough in a plain Jane type of way, but nothing that really stirred the loins, although her breasts were impressive and her mouth blossomed into a chubby entrance to joy. It was only when I got to know her character and saw her compassion for others that I noticed a feeling of desire towards her. Recognising a winning lottery ticket when it came up, she responded to me in a physical sense and our relationship deepened. It was her soul, though, rather than her body, that provoked this reaction.

Nowadays, I seem to have gone full circle, as I do not find white or Asian women attractive. I cannot explain it in adequate words, but for me only big bottomed black women (not that they all possess large *gluteus maximus*) hit the spot.

So, how come my opinion changed regarding the beauty of black women? My 'crossing over to the dark side,' as my mate David Nunn terms it, happened a few years into our marriage. It was a cold February and Margaret had departed for Nigeria to top up her sun tan. During the month she was away, my sex starved eyes had a tendency to flit over any woman my mind deemed attractive. Somewhat to my surprise, I noticed they were all black and mainly West African. How strange, I thought to myself and tried to rationalise it out. So why am I only drawn to these women? For me it is not primarily a sexual motivation. No, it is the general character that I have found in West African women that I find attractive. Not for them inane conversations about celebrities or what clothes to put in the washing machine. In my experience they are more spiritual, serious and more understanding of the suffering that goes on in different continents. It is the basic resilience and humanity that attracts me to these women.

That is not to say they do not talk about washing machines and mundane trivialities, just that they put them into the correct perspective. After all, if you have an extended family to support back 'home', what is going to be more important to you, a net curtain or a plate full of food on the table? In contrast, I find that too many white women are only interested in tabloid tittle-tattle and soap operas, seemingly ignorant of the world around them. A generalisation I accept, but one I see every day of the week.

Then again, perhaps I am drawn to black women as Margaret has been the only woman who has shown me any affection? Maybe, because of this, my brain has eliminated white and Asian women from my heart, penis and eyes, as I have never enjoyed satisfactory relations with such women?

It may even be down to the fact that I have been surrounded by black women for these past few years with only a sprinkling of white and Asian females to aid my diversity.

It is quite obvious to me that I am now so immersed with the beauty of black women that I fail to recognise beauty in others; I have succumbed to the idea that 'black don't crack' and can never envisage a situation where I would shack up with a white lady. I guess, at the heart of it, I just love the smell of cocoa butter on a woman's skin!

I suppose my one dimensional outlook on beauty is not healthy in the long-term but all the above are contributory factors for my unconscious decision.

Of course, what I am writing goes against the stereotype that white men go out with black women merely for a taste of the 'exotic'. I truly cannot believe that this myth is still so strongly believed in the 21st Century. Undoubtedly there are white men like this but the vast majority are attracted to black women purely because they like that particular individual. Many of my white friends are married to black women and all agree with me. Basically, they got spliced to females they loved who just happened to be black. There was no desire in them to seek out women deemed historically 'exotic', such as Saartjie Baartman, The Hottentot Venus, a Khoisan South African woman, whose buttocks were economically exploited in 19th century London, by white men genuinely seeking 'exotica'. Thankfully life has changed since then. Indeed, not once has Margaret demanded payment when my clammy hands reach for her wobbly behind! Long may this continue.

In all honesty, if it was 'exotic juice' I was after I would go down the supermarket for a litre of mango. It is cheaper and also lasts longer than the human version.

But, even if you are attracted to someone initially for his or her skin colour, is that such a crime? Surely, it is just the same as liking blonde or brunette colour hair? Yes, I would argue. So what that I only like black women, I cannot help the body my brain is trapped inside. I am way past the stage of lying awake at night wondering if my penis is racist because it only springs to life at the sight of black women – it is just the way I am.

Strangely, I am not attracted to mixed race ladies either – the person has to be a dark shade of black to get my brain and lower regions interested. An old, white, female colleague of mine has a similar 'problem'; only with her she is attracted purely to black men. We are like peas from the same pod. Does she worry about this? No, she just accepts it and gets on with her life – whatever black women may say to her about her choice of partner.

Sexual attraction should be a matter purely for the individual. If it works for you then go for it. If not try another shop. Luckily for me, I found my shop at the first strike.

I am not sure, though, if England's relatively liberal attitude to sex and black/white relationships is shared in other countries. As an example, during our honeymoon in Rome, Margaret was called over to a passing car and propositioned by the driver. The white occupants thought she was a prostitute merely because she is black. I know that a lot of Nigerian prostitutes are 'working' in Italy but to presume that every black woman is one, is both demeaning and morally wrong. The amount they offered (around £5) was also insulting. Still radiant from her wedding and energetic honeymoon, Margaret looked a million lire or, at the very least, a fistful of dollars.

Unfortunately, I compounded Margaret's annoyance when she came to me for help over this approach. Feeling a bit pissed off by the car load of sexually aroused Italians, she demanded that I protect her honour as a lady. Thinking quickly, I considered an appropriate response. 'Tell them to double the amount before we enter into negotiations.' Bloody hell did my wife go mad! I was cussed every name under the sun for this innocuous one-liner. It's fair to say that pimping one's wife out is not without its complications.

Examples, such as the one above, merely reinforce the often-expressed view that white men see black/Asian women purely as sex objects – a view held by many black women I have met. I would agree that the sex tourism scene is populated with such people, but, on a day-to-day level, in this country, the numbers are small. Then again, Italians, as I am told by Margaret, view black women as extremely desirable commodities when it comes to choosing one's sexual partner. I have also been informed by numerous Nigerians that groups of Italian filmmakers go around luring young Nigerian women into the adult film industry. Really, I have lost count of the amount of times this mythical group of Italian men crop up. Does this really happen? Are these films part of Nollywood?

Sadly, those who perpetuate this black woman as sex 'object' stereotype, are replicating the sick mentality of slave masters, who raped the black women toiling on the plantations. It is truly tragic that this slave master mentality has left a legacy that affects black women to this day.

During my research for this book, many black women told me they blame slavery for their reluctance to enter into relationships with white men. To a degree, I can understand this feeling, as even Margaret feels guilty at times. The thought of giving yourself freely to someone, whose ancestors may have enslaved yours, is a difficult one to overcome. Difficult yes, impossible no. Even the black female friends we know who married white men, confessed to viewing whites as 'no-go areas' in their youth. I honestly find this attitude disheartening, as it is hard enough to find a partner these days without restricting one's choice. Surely the best way to show up the inhumanity of the slave trade is for a black/white couple to physically/spiri-tually commit themselves to one another, only on equal terms?

If only one could transport these slave masters into the present time. What joy it would be to show them that black and white couples can make successful marriages with the absence of racial superiority theories. Even though *Doctor Who* has recently made a successful comeback, there is, regretfully, no way to make this dream come true.

To conclude this chapter, I have to confess, when I re-read these words, that I seem to come over like a complete hypocrite; as I mentioned how patronising it is to be attracted to someone for the colour of his or her skin – and then admit to only liking black women. My point, though, is it is not only the skin colour I am attracted to but the personality. Splitting hairs? Maybe, but I cannot explain it any other way.

Finally, I should advise the reader that I do think Margaret is sexy these days, but I still do not find Naomi Campbell attractive (tennis player Serena Williams, singer Jamelia or TV presenter June Sarpong are my idea of dream babes!). Then again I have gone off Glynis Barber as well – although this may have more to do with her advanced years than my taste in women.

Margaret

What went through my mind the first time Bobby and I decided to have sex? Well, I was really scared as he undressed as I still believed the stereotype I had been told about white men in the bedroom – that they were prone to sexual perversion. What on earth was he about to do to me? What would my mother say? Putting my anxieties to one side, I closed my eyes, bit my lip, opened my legs and thought of Nigeria! And when it was over? In my best cool-as-cucumber voice, I huskily asked Bobby: 'Do you feel lucky punk?' Of course, he answered yes and went on to profess his undying love for the woman who had made him into a man.

The question remains though, just why did I relent to his physical 'charms' given the sexual concerns I confessed to having about white men in general? I guess I had got this far with our relationship with no major shocks so I just went with the flow to see what would happen.

Once it was over, I began to realise that sex with a white man (albeit with my limited experience of this subject) was pretty much the same as sex with a black man, despite the myths that persist about penis size. The image of the predatory black man with an enormous member, who demonstrates his sexual athleticism in the bedroom, is a racial stereotype that does black men no good at all. The problem is; some black men feel the need to live up to this image, an image that dates from slavery times when white women were imbued with a fear of black men. Surely, in this day and age, we can end this legacy?

So, I was relieved, and maybe a little disappointed, when Bobby didn't attempt any 'perversity' with me (only joking mum!) No, truly, it was a normal run of the mill experience; there was nothing to be scared of Bobby in a sexual sense. Of course, other black women may have less pleasurable experiences with white men; I can only base my opinion on the union between my husband and I.

The strangest thing about our first bonking session was the film Bobby took me to see – to get me in the mood for sex. Was it a romantic movie full of sweet words and sentimental scenes? Oh no. To get my juices flowing, my naive husband chose *Amistad* – the uncompromising Stephen Spielberg slave drama. White men, a warning. If you are trying to impress a black lady to the stage where you want to get inside her panties, do not take her to see a film that features wanton scenes of cruelty and oppression of black people. Orgasm inducing it is not.

After we had sex some of my friends asked me, 'What was it like with Bobby and his foreskin?' I always answered, 'That is only for me to know.' Until this book, that is how it has been. So why write about it now? Because of all the ridiculous myths that exist over matters of a bedroom nature. Bobby has already mentioned the stereotypes in his piece so I will not repeat them again. I do find it depressing, though, that we live in a society where sex is seen as the number one priority in a relationship. Why should Bobby have been sneered at and looked down upon just because he lost his virginity so late in his adult life? To me, he was a man comfortable with himself and at ease over his lack of sex. He did have a lot of tissues at his flat but I put this down to his all too frequent colds!

I have since realised that too many young women are pressurised into having sex in their teenage years. This is tragic, as careless decisions made at such a tender age can have a dramatic effect on someone's whole life. As an example, the recent upsurge in British chlamydia cases shows that Western society still has a lot of improvement to make. To my mind, Bobby should have been congratulated and not commiserated on his lack of sexual experi-ence. Sure, he had to wait until he was quite old before he experienced the sins of my flesh but so what? At least I was worth waiting for!

Believe me, writing as someone who has had her heart broken, a man who can exert sexual control is much to be desired. There is nothing exciting about a man who has numerous sexual partners. It just means he will soon get bored with you and seek pastures new.

In Nigeria we have our own problems with sex, where it is seen as the man's right in a relationship. As a result, it is normally the male who decides how often and with whom sex takes place. The poor woman just has to accept her lot and give in to her man's needs.

I have also found that Nigerian men are very reluctant to use condoms, giving a variety of excuses for their lack of family planning. Number one excuse has to be that they are not large enough (oh please). Another popular reason is that they are 'uncomfortable.' This means Nigerian women are often having unprotected sex – leading to the increased risk of HIV/AIDS. We really need men to wake up to this and stop pressuring partners into such activities. Women, though, are often to blame for this attitude. A Sierra Leone woman once told Bobby she liked sex 'flesh to flesh' without a hint of rubber in sight. This is okay in a stable relationship but extremely risky if your partner changes on a regular basis.

Unfortunately, it is the women who are bearing the brunt of this lax approach to contraception. The latest figures by The World Health Organisation (WHO), released in May 2006, show that 59 per cent of all AIDS infections in sub-Saharan Africa are women. This is a catastrophe that can and should be halted. To do so, we have to confront the African man's relaxed attitude towards sex, and point out that a man should not be ruled by his penis alone. At the very least we, as African women, need to insist that men use condoms before touching our flesh.

In some ways, I think I was always destined to end up with someone like Bobby. I remember growing up in Brighton with my carers, Mr and Mrs Anderson. Mrs Anderson frowned at the TV one day when the black children's presenter Floella Benjamin came on the telly. Mrs Anderson (who was white) told me that Mrs Benjamin is married to a white man and that she doesn't believe in sex between different races. Despite this, she went on to say she would not object if I ended up marrying a white man. What a confusing discussion for me to be burdened with at the young age of twenty! Of course, at that time, I myself would have thought the idea of going out with a white man was abhorrent.

Thinking back now, I just cannot rationalise Mrs Anderson's comments. If she were against that 'type of thing,' why then would she have no objection if I, her foster child, were to go against her beliefs?

Anyway, it was immaterial, as I was still going through my Denzel Washington and Johnny Gill stage – my bedroom being adorned with their photogenic images. The other posters decorating my walls, though, are harder to explain. I had pictures of white movie stars such as Michael J Fox, Sean Connery and, a bit more bizarre this one, Dolph Lundgrun. Apart from his colour, Bobby certainly doesn't resemble any of the above – especially in the muscle department.

So, just why did I find these images of Caucasian men attractive, if I was so much against going out with a white man? I honestly cannot explain why. I can only think it was because their faces were continually on the TV. A puny reason, I grant you, but I have no other theory to produce.

It is funny to think that years spent looking at Dolph Lundgrun affected my sub-consciousness to such a degree that I would end up having sex with a white stick insect like Bobby. Marrying him has made me realise we should all have more open minds when it comes to dating people who look different, as the difference is often just skin deep.

Even Bobby though, finds this reasoning hard to adhere to, as for him beauty only comes via a dark shade of black. Over the last few years, despite my pleas for him to stop, I have noticed his lecherous look at any sexy black woman who happens to walk past him. This is most annoying but, what I find harder to understand, are his lustful looks towards...wait for it.....black showroom dummies! Yes, that's right, black showroom dummies! How on earth can he find a plastic model attractive purely because they have been dipped in black dye? And yet, more than once, I have seen him purse his lips in appreciation at these black inanimate objects. He really should see a shrink about this.

Although my personal sex 'hurdle' has been cleared, I do feel saddened by the number of black women put off relationships with white men for the reasons we debated in this chapter. Most of these reasons are just excuses and should be dumped in the bin. We, as black women generally, need to liberate ourselves more. We may have burned our bras in the Sixties but our sexual prejudices largely remain.

So, after having sex with Bobby, the next obvious step was to produce children. It was here where 'cultural' clashes would begin to appear with alarming regularity.

Summary

No real problems in this area. We quickly came to terms with the other's body and enjoyed it to the full! As a consequence it will remain a mystery to us why so many people refuse to enter into a relationship with someone, due to sex. As we have just described, in reality sexual differences are relatively minute in the pursuit of physical happiness, so long as the two individuals have no stereotypes about the other's potential performance. As I always say 'the mind should be able to control the body. It cannot, though, tell the body who to like.' Time to free one's mind I feel.

CHAPTER 7

The Birth of Our Children

Bobby

Our first child, Joshua Boluwatife (the brave leader) Smith, was born in 1998. Like most Nigerians, he has got a lot of other names but it would take up too much space to include them all. I was either good or bad at sex as he was conceived in two months flat.

If that bit was easy, Margaret's pregnancy was hard going, for both of us. Men, believe with all your heart that women have hormonal problems during pregnancy. It was like living with Stalin, Hitler and Margaret Thatcher all at the same time. I would much rather have been the one vomiting in the morning than having to cope with Margaret's bizarre eating habits (grass) and her ridiculous mood swings. To be fair though, eating grass was at least consistent with her personality as she was a right cow to live with at the time.

So, was I an unsympathetic male chauvinistic pig? Maybe, but I was provoked. My biggest mistake was in forgetting how hard she was to live with the first time and putting her up the 'duff' again. I blame the cider, or, more especially, the eight pints of the stuff I drank on the day my daughter was conceived. How come *Mastermind* never asks the question all men want the answer to, 'Why do eight pints transform women into page three models?' I should have stopped at seven that day and saved myself from her hormones!

Margaret, of course, denies she suffered from hormonal problems. However, I have since heard her sympathising with female friends during their own pregnancy and blaming it on their hormones. Pah! I was conned. I advise any men reading this to buy a flat somewhere and live in it for the nine months of their partner's pregnancy. Trust me, this is a decision you won't regret.

For women reading this who had less stressful pregnancies, your partners do not know how lucky they were. Have I made my point clear yet?

If the pregnancy was hard, the actual birth was a less dramatic affair (for me anyway.) I attended the hospital with Margaret for a number of hours. Being informed that the birth was still sometime away, I decided to nip off home to get some food and have a shower. This was a mistake. During the hour I was away our son was born.

To this day, whenever we have an argument, the same familiar line comes up; 'you weren't even there for the birth of our son.' To be honest, after seeing the blood stained walls of the labour room, I had a lucky escape. It was reminiscent of the John Hurt scene in the *Alien* film; the one where his stomach explodes. Blood, slimy entrails, and blobs of congealed body tissue made the delivery room a scene of absolute misery. I slipped the hospital cleaner a £1 tip that day and apologised for the mess my wife had made. Seeing as how I didn't get a response from the cleaner, I cracked a joke to make light of the guilt I was feeling, 'Cor, it looks like a Jackson Pollock on speed painting in here.' The cleaner, a Nigerian woman, kissed her teeth, brandished her mop towards me in a slightly aggressive fashion and replied, '£1, you give me one pound! Your wife ruins my nice clean ward with her bodily extractions and you expect me to be happy with £1?' With a look of genuine disgust, she continued 'and after that you expect me to laugh at your stupid English jokes?' She sucked her teeth into the Guinness book of records and finished with 'and anyway, what is so funny about a fish?'

Bloody Nigerians, what is it with them and English humour? At the time though, I shrugged off her cultural ignorance, my head full of remorse at missing Joshua's arrival in this world. I would have really liked to have seen my son's birth, even though I may have fainted, and I'll always remember the first time I saw him, so small and innocent, hair plastered over his scalp, little piggy eyes blinking in the light. So small, so fragile. It really is a life defining moment when you see your child for the first time.

Unfortunately, not being experienced with babies, I had no idea of how to hold him and nearly dropped him on the floor. If Margaret had had any energy left, she would have castigated me for mishandling him and being late, but her body was limp with the exhaustion of it all.

So I was now a Dad! If you had asked me a few years before that I would be a husband and a father I would have laughed in your face. But that is what I now was. It felt scary as it was very much a step into the unknown for me, even though I did attend all my pre-natal classes. Could I be that dependable man that Joshua needed to guide him into adulthood? Could I be to him like my dad was to me?

Nine days after his birth, we had his traditional Yoruba naming ceremony, where his names are announced to the world. A small party of guests attended the event held in our house: Margaret's father, my parents, Margaret's sister Anne and her beloved Auntie from Brighton. Prayers were said and the birth of our son blessed in the name of God. It concluded with a short speech by Margaret's father wishing him future prosperity. This being the first naming ceremony I had attended, I wasn't entirely sure about what would be happening. I just nodded my head at the prayers and helped with the drinks.

One thing I do like is that his Yoruba names have meaning. I find it disappointing that so many children are born in England with names like Shanice, Latoya, Porsche etc, names that either do not reflect their parents' heritage or are simply made up. To balance this up, I should mention that many Africans in England automatically assume English names have no meaning, without even checking up on their facts. I did not know this was a common belief until I met Margaret, but she's explained to me she often hears such disrespectful comments from colleagues at work.

Margaret, being a Christian, also insisted that Joshua's first name was chosen from the Bible. So, after a long absence of picking up the Holy Book, I gingerly opened it and found a name after much deliberation. Margaret, however, declined my choice; her holiness deeming it inappropriate. Personally, even today, I still can't see what is wrong with Beelzebub but, instead of digging in my heels, I gave in to my wife's deeper knowledge of biblical matters.

Laughing aside, I actually wanted to call my son Bodie (from the *Professionals* TV show) as I always had a soft spot for Lewis Collins in my youth. In fact, even now, I like to imitate Bodie's 'macho but stylish' walk. Margaret preferred Doyle (Martin Shaw) and it would have suited our son more – on account of his curly hair – but Joshua it was going to be.

Despite struggling with one child, we decided to try for another, and our daughter, Olivia Temitope (I am God's glory) Smith was born in 2002. Her pregnancy was also hard work but with at least one happy ending. Yes, you've guessed it; I was there at the hospital when she was born! This time I was taking no chances. I had ready-made sandwiches and sausage rolls made up from the time Margaret was six months into her pregnancy. True, I had to throw a lot of these in the bin, or give them to my friend Glen, but it paid off when she went into labour. Whilst Margaret was frantically throwing her toothbrush into her overnight bag, I was raiding the fridge for sausage rolls.

I called a taxi and held on tightly to Margaret's hand as it swerved round bends at sixty miles per hour. Luckily, it was 8.15pm so the roads and speed cameras were empty. The poor cabby, though, was having kittens as we motored towards the hospital. I guess he was desperate for his cab not to be covered in the blood and gore that I described earlier – a reasonable fear I think.

Once we arrived at the hospital, Olivia soon popped out, with a few lungfuls of gas and air for the pregnant mother and a cracked plastic seat for dad. Thinking back now, I can categorically state that I needed more than the seat. Oh how I wished with all my heart for a set of NHS earplugs as Margaret moaned at me non-stop throughout her labour. To this day, I don't understand why she made such a fuss about giving birth. After all, all she had to do was open her legs, pant a bit and wait for something slippery to slide out from her groin! How can that be a bad experience for a woman?

I was actually in the labour room, when Olivia was born, peering up inside Margaret's genitals (men a warning: you will be put off giving cunnilingus when you see this sight) when I first spied my daughter. 'I....ca ca can...see....a...head,' I informed Margaret. 'Put down that sausage roll and speak clearly,' came her somewhat impatient reply.

So I did, and managed to see Olivia enter the world. She looked just like Joshua, with one important difference. The same feelings of protective father-hood swamped me as I caressed her tender body. So that was that, my daughter was also born, with all her bits in the right place. I could relax at last.

Feeling a bit tired, I managed to convince the Ward Matron to let me stay with Margaret as she rested that night. I watched her silently sleeping, her large nostrils flaring up and down. Despite a comfy hard-backed seat, I could not sleep, and so sat there in silence, listening to the cries of anguish from other mothers. Margaret stirred at around 3.00am and I played my trump card. 'Have you got any food?' she whispered painfully. Quick as a flash I produced a couple of cheese sandwiches and a strawberry yoghurt. Margaret snaffled the lot down and gave out a satisfying belch. I had redeemed myself!

We also had a naming ceremony for Olivia that was pretty much the same as our son's, although by that stage I was an old hand at it.

So I now had two children and a stretch marked wife. We had the full set so to speak and a future life of worrying about schools, university, house deposits and drugs. Fantastic – I will be mentally burnt out by the age of forty.

People often ask us now if we will have any more children?

My answer?

I am going on the wagon!

Margaret

I had always imagined that I would have children. To a Yoruba person, children are God's creation and are there to be treasured. It would be almost out of the question for a Yoruba couple to be married and for them not to want to have children. Questions would be raised and the woman might be suspected of being barren if no children were forthcoming. In complete contrast, Bobby had never desired children, either before or after our union. But by dint of my marriage to him Bobby knew I was after his sperm, and I was not going to take no for an answer!

It could be argued here that this was a clash of cultures, as quite a few of Bobby's white friends have been married for a long time – but missing that obvious ingredient – children. Indeed, even Bobby's own parents were divided on this issue. In his case, his mother was against it whilst his father had always wanted kids.

I really cannot understand how a couple can live a happily married life without the blessing of children. In our culture a child is the perfect demonstration of a couple's love for one another. Without them, what do you have? Only a lifetime of material possessions and fading memories. Children, though, are a permanent memorial to the love that two individuals can bring to each other.

I also consider it to be selfish not to have children, as the pain and sacrifice that one's parents went through should be replicated by the next generation. That is not to say that parenthood is full of only pain and sacrifice, although at times it feels like it. For me, as a Yoruba woman, I did not view myself as complete until I had given birth. Without children, I was merely a burden on the world's resources. I needed to give birth to justify my existence on the planet.

Despite what Bobby has written, I enjoyed my pregnancy. Not for the vomiting, tiredness, or even the grass. No, I was pleased to be fulfilling the role God had reserved for me.

The first birth was a painful experience, made worse by my husband's insistence on going home to feed his face. I felt so alone as Joshua was born. If I had given birth in Nigeria, I would have had a cluster of Aunties or housemaids fussing over me, holding the baby and massaging my aching body. Here, on the NHS, you are lucky to be given a cup of tea and an overnight stay. It was this time, more than any other, that I felt like a foreigner in a strange land. Both my parents were in Nigeria, so only my sister, Anne, was in England. She, and Bobby (once he had finished eating), were a great help in the weeks and months after our son was born. Bobby's parents were also a source of comfort as they fussed over the first grandchild into the family. Luckily my father managed to come over for the naming ceremony and he also did his bit with the child – although this was a step into the unknown for him. In addition my Auntie in Brighton offered sterling service at this time, staying with Bobby and I for a week.

But for me, it was not enough. I desperately wanted to return to Nigeria to enjoy the special atmosphere that surrounds a new mother. In England, relatives like to give 'space' to the new parents, so that they can 'bond' with the child. In Nigeria, they are more likely to leave the baby with someone else, so the mother can quickly regain her strength. But as I was married to Bobby, I had to endure the reality of giving birth in England.

And, of course, once you have one child you have to have another! Despite Bobby's reservations, we 'spun the bottle' again and this time were blessed with a girl. I must say, it felt different having a baby girl, and I immediately felt sympathy for her predicament at being born a female. Why? Because I know that a procession of men (she has inherited her father's good looks) are going to break her heart. Is it unfair for me to feel this way towards my daughter? After all, surely my son (who has my good looks) will also break some other daughter's heart? That is true, and it is hard to reconcile my conflicting thoughts over this issue. It is just a physical/emotional response, I guess. Bobby, no doubt, would blame it on my hormones.

I did have a slight cultural problem when it came to Olivia's naming ceremony. One of my relatives thought she should have a Yoruba first name as Joshua had his Yoruba name (s) second. I did not wish to offend my relative but we had already decided on the name Olivia. So, that was how it stayed.

So, I was now a proud mother of two sparkling little children. Bobby and I had gone the whole way. In the eyes of the BNP and the black separatists, we had committed a crime and had made 'confused' or 'mud' children through our 'perverse' physical lust for each other. Both of us, though, just saw the children as a result of a man and woman's natural love for one another.

Having had the children, we now had to do the hard part; bringing them up in a country that gives too much freedom to children. It would be our biggest test to date.

Summary

I spent the first twenty-six years of my life doing my level best to avoid having children, seeing them as a curse on the purse. And yet, here I was, committing myself to the £500,000 cost it would take to successfully raise a couple of kids to the age of sixteen. What had I done? Was I mad? My love for Margaret must know no bounds if I was to go this far.

Despite my regrets Margaret was now in her element. She had gained the respect that a mother achieves in Yoruba culture.

Cultural differences were very much to the fore in this chapter. In England, a mother who stays at home to look after children is sneered upon for contributing little to society. Many even view her as a parasite on the state. In Nigeria, a woman who performs her natural human function, by giving birth, is doing God's work.

We, as a couple, had to make an informed decision regarding our suitability for the demanding role of parenthood. Margaret wanted them, I did not. Someone was going to be disappointed. As is now obvious, Margaret's feminine charms won the day and I duly accepted my role as a committed, albeit reluctant, father. I had conceded ground once again.

CHAPTER 8

Parenting and Education

Bobby

This, for me, is the hardest chapter to write. Even now, a few years down the line of being a parent, I still find it by far the most demanding and thankless task that God could ever have invented. For those nodding their heads in agreement, thank you. I know these words sound terrible but if you have never gone through it you cannot comprehend the truth. I really do feel guilty writing this but I do not always enjoy being a parent. Sure, it has some pleasures, watching *Doctor Who* with my son, making his Airfix models or giving my daughter a piggyback ride, but the relentless grinding nature of parenting wears you down. There is no rest. You are constantly at the beck and call of your offspring. Children always need either feeding, or cleaning, or amusing.

And even then, after devoting many hours to them, they complain that life is so 'boring'. Your own relationship with your partner also suffers as you spend less and less time in each other's sole company. I hold my hands up and admit that I am selfish by expressing this attitude, but it really is the way I feel. Of course, it is probably just that I am a bad parent that I am having these negative thoughts about parenting. A stricter parent would be able to discipline his children better and, thus, acquire more time to devote to his partner. Most other men, I'll wager, would not tolerate the way my children sometimes behave, with their non-stop chitter-chattering and stupid bickering. Honestly, they make so much noise that I am beginning to wonder if whining is a default option for their vocal chords.

Margaret would really like it if I were more 'Nigerian' over this matter. By that, I mean being more of a disciplinarian. For yes, it is true; I am soft with my children. Even though I try, I find it hard to get them to obey my instructions due to my less than manly authoritarian voice. As it is, I sound more like an angry pneumatic drill, and not a stern father, when telling them off.

I guess the influence here is that I was surrounded by love throughout my childhood by parents who were always there. Margaret had to fight for her right to attention from her parents – whenever she saw them. She is, therefore, less sympathetic to the needs of children, as she did not always receive the love I took for granted. This is definitely the area where we have most arguments. For any women reading this, Professor Bobby has some words of advice: *Do not marry a wimp if you want a real father.*

Poems and dainty words whispered into one's ear may help you during courtship but it will not benefit a young child growing up. The older I get, the more I feel the traditional role of the man, (in being the harder of the two parents), is the correct one. To give the reader the full picture, I am writing this from the perspective of a man on a career break from work, who has always been in touch with his 'feminine' side. Oh, how I wish I could be that strong Yoruba man who disciplines his child with a rod of iron. The truth is though, the memories of the 'rod of iron' from when I was bullied, are holding me back. The sad fact is, I doubt this lax attitude will benefit my children in the long term, as they are sometimes immune to the concept of discipline.

What, though, if I am mistaken? Maybe the Nigerian 'iron' approach to children is the one that is wrong? As an example, Margaret was brought up in a very harsh environment, her body being covered with marks administered by relatives, all, presumably, from the 'tough love' school of parenting. A whip was also used to further enforce the rule of parental discipline. Has it done her any harm?

In some ways I think it has, as her relationship with her mother is very much a complicated one. Margaret regrets mum not having much to do with her when she was first born. She also resents the fact that she had so little attention from her mother, due to her coming from a large family. Attention deficit disorder was not around in the Seventies but I do sometimes feel this lies at the heart of their relationship. As a result of this, Margaret has spent the last twenty or so years desperately seeking approval from her mother to make up for the time lost in her childhood. Sadly, her mum doesn't recognise this and just expects Margaret to follow the 'cultural' way of relating to her. By this, I mean total slavish obedience to her instructions. Both parties lose out over this; Margaret for not receiving the love most offspring take for granted, and her mum for not really understanding the delicate nature of her daughter.

Probably, the best attitude towards parenting would be a mixture of both our ways of doing things. Unfortunately though, we have too many flash points regarding the upbringing of our children for the dialogue to be constructive. If only Margaret could substitute me for a Yoruba man during the time we spend with our children. Would that solve the problem?

I really am trying my best, but discovering that 'best' is not good enough. Sorry Joshua and Olivia if you are reading this, but I really am struggling to act the role of the dutiful dad who dedicates his life to his children. I hope in later years I will feel differently towards them; it's just right now I cannot see the light at the end of the tunnel. Like my son's voice the strain of rearing children just goes on and on.

Does everybody have this feeling at some stage of the parenting ordeal? In some ways I hope so, as I really want to be part of the normal world over this issue. No one likes to think of themselves as a complete and utter bastard, but that is how I feel about myself regarding my children. It is so hard – always putting them before your own satisfaction. It is so hard – always having to think of them first. It is so hard that the relationship of the two parents changes, as time becomes a precious commodity. Our home has become a virtual battleground, all four combatants struggling to make their voices heard as conflict echoes within the four walls. To make matters worse, I am constantly told to enjoy this time with them and that these are the easy bits! I await their teenage years with trepidation.

But, at least, I am still in the home, coping with the responsibilities that being a parent brings. Other children are not so lucky when it comes to the parenthood roulette game. A report by the Institute for Public Policy Research, released in November 2006, stated that 50 per cent of UK black Caribbean children, born in the year 2000, do not live with their fathers. In comparison only 13 per cent of white British children live with one parent. The lone-parent figure amongst children from either an Indian or Bangladeshi background drops to 5 per cent.

Depressingly, it gets worse for people the lower down the economic chain they fall. The National Children's Bureau published a report in 2003 that stated 70 per cent of low/moderate income families, from Caribbean origin, were lone-parents. The figure for white lone-parents was 46 per cent. That these figures are so high is quite staggering and bodes ill for the future.

The key here is a lot of Afro-Caribbean origin women have no expectation that they will get married – statistically still the best environment to bring up children. With little hope of getting married, we should then not be surprised they have children at a young age and bring them up alone. After all, what is the benefit in hanging around if Mr Right has already bought his ticket and shipped on out of town?

British men and women of black African origin may be nodding their head at these words, but this single parenthood ideal is spreading into their culture too. Many Nigerian women I have spoken to, accept they will not get married in this country and are instead being forced to find husbands in Nigeria or to become single-parents. It should be explained that, in Nigeria, marriage is still looked upon as the first step you take if you want to be a mother. England, with its different culture, does not always view marriage as a necessity if you want to bear children.

The funny thing that always strikes me, is that advocates of marriage are generally portrayed in the media and life in general, as being conservative or right-wing. On the other hand, pro-single parent articles are normally to be found in left-wing papers such as the *Guardian* or *Independent*. I am puzzled by this suggestion. Marriage is a vehicle designed to protect the interests primarily of the children, as two parents can obviously give more time to a child. And, remember, it is time that a child cherishes more than guilt motivated presents. Left-wing concerns are also based on the noble belief in protecting minorities against social injustices. Surely then, they should be supporting, rather than denigrating, marriage? I shall explain.

Who benefits from a woman having to bring up children on her own? Not the child – largely deprived of a male role model. Not the woman – at an increased risk of financial poverty. No, the man emerges as the clear winner as he gets more free time and can normally escape the clutches of the Child Support Agency. Logically then, left-wing types should be more vocal in support of marriage than their right-wing counterparts, but somehow this message never crosses over into the mainstream.

Only when black women insist on a more stable foundation, will the black middle-class become properly established in this country. I know this is a risky subject for me to be drawn into, but truth sometimes hurts. Black men and women have to realise – although I am sure they already know – that their children are suffering because of the lack of parental examples being set before them. Is it really hard to wonder why a fifteen-year-old boy goes a bit wild, when all around him he sees family breakdown and absent fathers? It is easy to blame racism and inequality, both of which play a part, but black fathers should accept their responsibility over this issue, otherwise the black community in Britain will be left behind economically. As it stands at the moment, a lot of black boys are not introduced to male discipline until they meet a secondary school teacher, a discipline that then clashes with the hormonal need for a teenager to appear grown-up. The irony is most black parents I speak to, especially those in their thirties and forties, want proper physical discipline for their child at school, instead of the wringing of hands approach adopted by our authorities. Why? Because this is the way the majority were brought up, when fathers and uncles were around to beat 'picknies' (kids) if they misbehaved.

This then leads on to a myth that is cited as a gospel truth, that it is the cultural norm for black kids to live in single-parent households – due to the fallout from slavery when families were forcibly separated by whites. Whilst the fallout did undoubtedly influence black family structures, in the 19th and early 20th centuries, it should be noted that 78.4 per cent of black American babies, born in 1960, were born to black married couples. By 1994 the figure had dropped to 29.6 per cent, according to the 1998 *American Sexual Behaviour Report*. Single-parenthood is, therefore, a modern phenomenon. I know I probably come over like an English Bill Cosby with these comments (he made similar remarks a couple of years back), but so what – he was right.

I am also aware that my words, written as they are by a white man, could be deemed inflammatory or condemnatory. So, why do I have to pick out black children/parents? Don't white kids have the same types of problems? Shouldn't I stick to commenting on children generally?

To a degree this criticism is valid. White working-class children are also suffering from family breakdown and the educational under-achievement that follows as a result. A report by the Social Justice Policy Group, published in November 2006, found that only 17 per cent of white working-class boys managed to gain five or more A to C grades at GCSE. In addition, they also suffer from the idea that it is not 'cool to study'. So why have I concentrated just on black boys?

Firstly, because I do not feel constrained by my white skin to debate only those issues I am supposed to be comfortable with. I would argue it is sometimes better to spot mistakes when you look in from the outside rather than having a lifetime experience of being black. Because I am white I do not feel black peer pressure on my shoulders to act, or to express myself, in a 'black' way. I therefore feel free to give my honest opinion based on the evidence of my own eyes.

On this point though, I am under no illusion that many will read my words and come to the conclusion; 'just because this guy has married a black woman he thinks he knows all about black people'. Well no, I don't actually. But, if what I am saying is correct, why should it matter the colour of my skin? I actually feel part of the problem is the non-involvement in so called 'black' issues by white people. By this, I mean that white apathy towards black academic failure does far more damage than blatant white racism. The non-black person who shrugs their shoulders at the education statistics of black kids and dismisses them as 'not his concern' is the person we need to reach out to.

Why should white people not have a vested interest in the educational prospects of black boys and girls? We all live in the same country; we all have an equal part in shaping the future of this nation. A person's colour should really be irrelevant if that person genuinely cares about their fellow citizens. Anyway, seeing as how my kids are of mixed race I have a personal interest in the success of 'our' children in the education system. I have to get involved for their sake.

Secondly, and I hate to come over as patronising, (although I have probably failed) but black men and women are still often treated as second-class citizens in a world where white power and money rule. It is only by increasing the odds in their favour that black people will progress. That is not to say I am advocating positive discrimination as discrimination, positive or negative, is still spelt the same way. No, parenting is the key issue for the next decade. Men and women have to play an equal role in the upbringing of their offspring.

I truly want my children to grow up in a better world. A world where a child's potential is not stymied purely because of colour. This is my sole motivation for debating this issue.

But am I not a hypocrite for confessing that I am struggling with the role of dutiful parent? Possibly, but I do at least make sure I am there for them. As my children get older, I am really beginning to understand the importance of being a male role model to them. My son, especially, hangs onto every word I say. He shares my interests – even the punk rock – and just wants to be with me. Nearly every day he tells me he loves me and that he wants to grow up so that he looks just like his dad.

However, a boy who grows up without a dad has no-one to reciprocate his love and eventually that love can turn to rejection and hatred. This is so obvious to me that I find it hard to understand how some fathers can abandon their children to the influence of boyfriends/stepdads, etc. The mere thought of Margaret finding someone, who is not suitable to bring up our children if our marriage ended, petrifies me. It is a fear that helps to keep our marriage free from temptation.

Why then, do I find it so physically and mentally draining listening to my son's non-stop demands and complaints? Maybe, if he was a child who could amuse himself, I would appreciate that the years watching him grow are the years to enjoy? I know Margaret finds my attitude terribly disap-pointing. A Yoruba man would never admit to what I have just written. It would appear then, where parenting is concerned, that cultural differences show us to be miles apart.

I am not giving up though, and so I plod on, hoping and praying that I can mature into the father that my dad was. My children deserve nothing less.

I, also, have another warning here for men: do not fall for the old female trick; 'if we have two children they will play with each other and leave you alone.' Absolute rubbish. All that happens is they fight amongst themselves. Dear old dad is only needed when he's asked to play the role of the United Nations peacekeeping force. This role is invariably hard as one child or the other feels you are taking sides. My advice? Stick to one child and let them play card games like patience.

One issue that I should touch on is the fact that our children are 'mixed race' or, to use this year's description, 'dual heritage'. I guess this is better than the demeaning 'half-caste' but all are equally stupid. Our children are Joshua and Olivia, their ethnicity does not define them, their character does. And yet, every form I complete for them from the council/school demands that I enter their ethnic background. Am I alone in getting frustrated by this? Why is it always so important to people? Margaret says it is for the same reason that the Nazis recorded anyone of Jewish descent. When the time comes to 'chuck us out,' she says, 'they will have us on their lists.'

Melodramatic I'll grant you, but I do share her suspicion over this matter. As a result of this, I refuse to comply and merely add another box that I label as 'human being'. If everybody did this, maybe the thought police would move onto some other area of life and forget about the racial profiling of people. I, personally, think the more we emphasise a person's colour the more it promotes differences along racial lines. It may be with the best intention, but all this insistence just increases the racial disharmony that seems to be multiplying.

Another interesting area, where having mixed race children is concerned, is how others see them. By this, I mean on every occasion a black person meets our children for the first time they always say they look like me. In contrast, every white person we have introduced them to states they resemble Margaret. I think this shows the subliminal thought pattern of the brain. It just cannot recognise that a mixed race person is physically the same as them so it instead labels them as the 'other' colour – to reassure itself. I have nothing scientific to back this theory up, but it has been uncanny the amount of times this has happened.

One of the myths about mixed race children is; they grow up confused and not knowing who they are, forever to wander between two cultures. The people that think this should know the truth. It does not work like this in reality – for us, and our friends with dual heritage children, at least. Both Margaret and I never refer to an individual's colour in the house. As a consequence, our children have grown up not noticing colour as an issue. They know that people are different but it simply doesn't bother them that they themselves are half of one and half of another. The only time Joshua has asked questions about race was when he was reading a book about Zulus. Part of the book referred to white *Afrikaners* taking black Africans as slaves. This prompted my son to ask, 'Daddy, is mummy your slave?'

'No, son,' I replied in a bemused voice, 'we are equal husband and wife – we are both slaves – to the mortgage company'.

Not satisfied by my somewhat flippant response to his serious question he continued: 'But why are black people always poor?'

Touched by Joshua's inquisitiveness, I was tempted to launch into a lengthy tirade about the history of white oppression against blacks but decided against over burdening a young mind. I merely answered, 'They are not son, it's just your school books giving that impression'. Thinking about it later, I wondered if all these negative images of black people are having the desired effect on young black minds? By showing how they were enslaved by whites, we are in danger of inserting negativity into fragile brains – leading to difficult issues about race and identity in later life. Surely it is better to impart knowledge of the likes of Mansa Musa – the King who ruled the Mali Empire in the 14th century – than to continually brainwash kids into thinking they are in some way inferior due to past history. At the moment, my children are free from such burdens but will this continue as they progress into adulthood?

No, is the obvious answer. I have mentally prepared myself for my son to say to me at a later stage: 'but dad you don't know what it is to be 'black'. This is a question that I can only answer in the negative but hopefully he will get over this phase. I, naturally, will answer him: 'neither do you, you are half of me and half of your mother.' I dare say that, by then, society would have thought of another way of describing mixed race people – I wait with baited breath for the next exciting instalment.

In contrast to this, one of Margaret's friends has a child similar of age to my son, the child is always referring to black this or white that. She is 'pure' black and knows it. Is this the correct approach? Surely the children that are 'colour-open' are the ones that are blessed and not confused?

But the black separatists and BNP keep peddling this lie. If you watch documentaries from the Fifties and Sixties, you always see old white women, with their dandy purple rinses, commenting that they feel sorry for mixed race children and that it's just not right. This attitude is popular, even now, amongst black and white adults. One of the strangest comments one of Margaret's black friends said was, after my son had misbehaved; 'is it because he is half-caste?' How strange. It is comments such as these that are making us write this book. Over to you, dear wife, and please be gentle with me.

Margaret

For me having children is the whole point of marriage. To bear and raise children is a blessing from God for both parents to enjoy. That is why Bobby's comments disappoint me. I cannot accept his reasons for why he struggles with parenthood. It is selfish in the extreme not to love every minute spent in the company of one's children.

He complains he finds it hard to discipline them and this is certainly a key area that has led to problems between us. Why? Because both parents need to show a united front over child rearing issues. If one parent goes against the other, how will the child know which approach is best? However, in our marriage we both react differently to the children – with Bobby undoubtedly the big softy. This is definitely a cultural difference, as I have always believed the adult must show who is in control.

Poor Bobby, despite having a loving couple of parents, he is sometimes unable to grasp this and loses the initiative with Joshua and Olivia. This is the classic 'good cop' 'bad cop' syndrome that, whilst it may work well on the screen, or in the police station, is not appropriate in the home. He is too weak with them. Children should always have a 'fear factor' when in the same room as their parents. In Yoruba culture, the parents would not tolerate the sort of behaviour that our children sometimes get away with. If only Bobby would see this and come down harder on them, as the children do take advantage of his generous nature. Oh how I wish he would shout at them more and display the Yoruba parenting skills that most Nigerian friends of mine take for granted.

You may be thinking about giving social services a call here, but I am not referring to physically abusing a child. No, I am referring to stopping privileges and TV shows. My own background did include corporal punishment and, whilst I would agree that this does have a role to play, it is not the only way to discipline an unruly child. What I find strange in England is the idea that children have the same rights as adults. As an example, I am horrified when I see children of seven or eight years of age walking down the road brazenly smoking cigarettes. In Nigeria, any elder would shout at them and tell them to remove the offending item from their lips. The child would not run to the police or their parents to shout 'abuse of my human rights.' The child instead would be disciplined at home for displaying behaviour that shames the parents. Doubtless, they would incur a slap from the father and this may hurt for a few seconds. But, they would not grow up with yellow stained teeth and lungs to match. What is better for the child as they struggle into maturity?

And what about the swearing that goes on all the time? Every day I am forced to listen to youngsters cussing each other and giving insolent looks to any who frown at their behaviour. Why is this tolerated? Why do other adults not step in and tell these children off?

You see this attitude again, over here, when a child is in trouble at school. How many times do you hear or read about a teacher being attacked by the parents of a misbehaving child? Parents often seem to take the side of their offspring, whatever their crime. In Nigeria, the word of the teacher would always take precedent over the mere word of a child. Is this wrong? Of course not. Children tell lies all the time and are quite devious in the way they play teachers off against parents.

I should add here that Bobby agrees with me on these points. He always has the greatest respect for teachers and would be deeply embarrassed if our children ever did anything that warranted their attention.

In Yoruba culture, we have a proverb that sums up our attitude to education. It states: "It takes the whole village to raise a child." This is a very important point as a child needs guidance throughout its life – from many different sources. Parents play a key role it is true but Aunties, Uncles and even complete strangers have an input too. When I was growing up in Nigeria, I can often remember elders in the street telling me off for some minor infraction. At the time, I was annoyed by this but accepted it anyway – it was after all part of our culture. It was only after my own children were born that I now see the benefit of this approach. Unfortunately, too many parents are exhausted by work in England and have little energy left for any others but their own. We are seeing the results of this via the gangs of feral youths that roam our streets in the evening.

Adults have become disproportionately scared of children and show them too much respect. The England of the 1950s, where the mythical policeman clips a child over the ear for scrumping apples, has gone. In its place is the anarchy caused by bad parenting. We need to urgently adopt the Nigerian way and become more socially responsible as a nation to all our children.

In England though, we have a fear of paedophilia and many parents would not want strangers telling their children off. I can sympathise here but we also have paedophilia problems in Nigeria. It goes against the stereotype but not all paedophiles are white middle-aged men. In Nigeria, we have our fair share of men who abuse the 'Uncle' system of respect, even though, as a country, we try to pretend it doesn't happen. This is a difficult issue for many Nigerians to accept but the same child abuse that goes on in England is replicated throughout the world. Yes, even in Africa where we sometimes like to think of ourselves as superior regarding such crime. The worst thing about this abuse is that the victim often has nowhere to run for help, as our culture tends to apportion blame on the person being abused rather than the perpetrator of such acts. Because our culture is so 'strong', it keeps this type of affair 'in-house' and hidden away – in direct contrast to the way abused children are encouraged to tell the authorities here in England. To admit to being abused is to bring shame on your family and shame is a heinous crime in the eyes of Yoruba parents. As a result, boys and girls cry themselves to sleep at night, alone in their misery, whilst paedophiles, often from the same family, are free to commit their perversity.

This is such a taboo subject for most Nigerians, and I am under no illusion my words will cause much heartache in our community – as I will be seen as bringing attention to these practices – but times change and we should talk about the reality of male sexual behaviour for this abuse to end. As it stands at the moment, we are shielding these perverts from justice by refusing to admit their presence in our midst, mistakenly thinking the problem will go away if we ignore it. This is not acceptable anymore. Silence is no longer an option.

Physical abuse towards children, as committed by some African parents, also passes without the condemnation it deserves. The mistreatment meted out to innocents like Victoria Climbie, tortured and murdered by distant relatives who thought she was possessed by the devil, cannot be justified under any religious edict. It is abuse pure and simple. It is time those who perpetrate such acts are ostracised from our community as they cause immense sorrow and pain.

Ditto those parents who allow Female Genital Mutilation to be carried out on children – a disgraceful practice that refuses to go away amongst some African communities. Liberal social workers, who categorise and tolerate such behaviour under the odious 'respecting cultural needs' mantra, should also be disciplined and made to realise that 'culture' is not above the law of the land. If this child cruelty continues (eighty eight alleged ritualistic abuse cases since the year 2000 in London alone – according to Metropolitan Police figures), it just makes it easier for white Europeans to dismiss us as 'savages.'

So yes, I am strict with my children but only because I love them so much. I do not want them corrupted by the excesses of easy living that one sees on the street all the time. It is my great fortune that Bobby's parents share my concern and are equally as strict with our children. Joshua in particular is wary of his grandmother and obeys her every instruction. If only he would do the same for his father!

I also knew that, by having children with Bobby, I was condemning my children to being brought up within a western education system. If I had married a Yoruba man, we could have always sent the children 'home' to Nigeria if we were worried about the direction they were headed. Bobby, though, would not agree to this. He would hate to be parted from them for any length of time (despite his earlier comments.) How ironic it is that black parents living in England are now sending children 'back' to African or Caribbean countries so they learn to appreciate discipline in schools. It used to be that parents, living in Africa or the Caribbean, would dream of sending their children to be educated in England. How rapidly things have changed!

This is again a reason for us to adopt the lessons from Nigeria where education is concerned. Children in Africa generally know that education is the only true way for an individual to better themselves and so get on with it with an eager heart. I may sound a touch sanctimonious but I cannot imagine Nigerians wasting their lives drinking alco-pops when homework needs to be done. Of course, I am aware that by writing this I am at risk of coming over as a typical arrogant Nigerian where education is concerned. Many, especially in the Caribbean community, feel we act superior because of this. They are correct; many Nigerians do have this attitude. However, we do so because we wish for all children to share our thirst for knowledge. If it comes across as arrogance then so be it. The education of a child should be the most important exam for parents to pass – whatever their ethnic background.

How wasteful it seems to my eyes to see children in England playing truant and ripping up schoolbooks. What a contrast to the Nigerian student who truly appreciates the value of education. In England students who really want to learn are picked upon and sneered at, all for the crime of wanting to improve their chances in life. The terrible murder of Damilola Taylor – who was called gay because he was a motivated student – was a good example of the clash of Nigerian educational expectations against the peer group pressure of inner city London. Black boys, especially, have this problem to negate before they reach adulthood. It is truly tragic to see so many not realising they only get one shot at education. Instead, they find other reasons to get 'shot'.

So, do I want my son to be trapped within this system? No. Joshua must understand that education is central to his development. If this means he has to be sent to Nigeria then that is what must happen. It will lead to problems with my husband but I cannot bear the thought of him wasting his life.

Bobby has made some sweeping generalisations regarding black parenting issues and I would like to back him up over this. In actual fact, I think he pussyfooted around the issue too much. I also believe the number of black children being born out of wedlock has to decrease. We, as black people, complain about outside racist factors that hold back our children at school and in society generally. This does happen and is rightly highlighted.

However, we must also do what we can ourselves to limit any damage caused by such factors. We cannot just bleat about racism every time the statistics are announced concerning black children being excluded from school. This is not going to benefit 'our' children. No, we need to ask if the home environment of these children could be improved to increase the chances of the child developing in a way that is the cultural norm back in Nigeria. Having children means putting them first. That does not mean buying them the latest trainers. It means spending time with them and not having a procession of 'baby fathers' in the house. A proper man reads his child a bedtime story; he does not merely see them on the odd weekend.

It should also not be acceptable for some black men to boast about having so many children whilst doing little for them in the way of maintenance/time. It is getting to the point where we, as black women, should refuse to have children with men until they show us commitment – via the institution of marriage. I think we need to amend the popular Nigerian saying NEPA (Never Expect Power Again – a reference to our power cuts), to Never Expect Penetration Again! Trust me; they will soon come running when our legs remain shut!

Unfortunately at the moment, too many black kids know their fathers only as peripheral figures, or floating fathers as I like to call them – this is despite the best efforts of black self-help organisations such as 100 Black Men of London – whose aim is to assist 'our' youth fulfil their potential.

And yet, the funny thing is that I have lost count of the amount of times I have been told that black men 'love their children'. Really? If they loved them that much you would think they would want to stay in the same house as them. This myth needs to be ended right now. The barefaced reality is that black children are suffering due to the absence of black men in their life.

Largely because of this attitude, black children lag behind other groups when it comes to education. According to February 2005 figures provided by

The Literary Trust, only 37.5 per cent of black Caribbean children scored five C grades at GCSE level, compared to an average of 51.9 per cent for all state schools in England. By itself this is depressing enough. However, this is actually an improvement on year 2002 when only 30 per cent achieved this somewhat moderate pass mark. Black attitudes have to change for black people as a whole to progress. The question to ask is; are we ready and mature enough as a community to accept this? I think we are – although we have a long way to go to break down stereotypes.

Problems, however, do lie ahead, not least for me. For instance, I dare say some black women reading this would put my words down as being written via the pen of a 'coconut' – due to my marriage to Bobby. This is unfair. Why is it that I am scared to say/write what I think because of my marriage to him? Because of the hostile attitude I get back in return. So many times I have been told that I am no longer Nigerian due to my sleeping with a 'white man' or that I have 'betrayed my culture'. I have even had a man say to my face that I have no right discussing Nigerian issues anymore – due to my marriage to Bobby. How arrogant is that? My sister Anne shares my beliefs over male Yoruba attitudes, parenthood and many other issues. She, though, is free from the coconut slur. Why am I assumed to be the mouthpiece of a white man purely because I am married to 'one'? This is deeply offensive to me as I do have a brain and the ability to express myself.

As it stands at the moment, the coconut word is used to intimidate a black person as a means of showing them to have lost their roots. How? Long standing Yoruba cultural traditions are at threat. Not because of a group of wicked white men. They are at threat due to this ridiculous image that to be black is somehow synonymous with being a glamorous gangsta rebel. And yet English and American black youth culture buys into this self-deriding image, with its oversize underwear, its crotch-clutching, gold-chain-wearing stereotype.

If you don't believe me, just take a look at the magazine rack in your local newsagent. Magazine after magazine seems to have a surly looking blinged-up black man on the front, proudly showing off his macho attitude to any who view it. Why is this aggression always to the fore? Why can't we smile more at each other? This posturing is so idiotic and only serves to lure impressionable youngsters into a life of crime and perhaps an early death. I do not understand how we have allowed it to be seen as cool for black kids to be stupid in the classroom. This is not the way my parents or I were brought up. Who is the coconut now? Who is going to employ these kids when they grow up only knowing the language of 'the street'?

Ironically, the main group of people who benefit financially from this image is white men. The heads of these international global companies (normally all white) love an image that can sell. By slipping neatly into parody rap stars such as 50 Cent are holding back intelligent black children from developing their potential. You can just imagine them in the board-rooms: 'Here is another shot of a black man with a 9mm pistol. This should sell nicely in downtown Hackney.' It may well sell nicely but what about the trail of misery caused by gun crime on the same streets? I am not condemning this music, and do not want to be seen as an advocate of censor-ship, I just want to see black parents giving more positive examples to their offspring closer to home. This does not just mean buying them a book during 'Black History Month' it means educating them to be responsible citizens.

Surely the coconuts are those in our community who smoke drugs, get into crime and generally lead a lifestyle that is stereotypically labelled as 'black'. These are the people who drag us all back as they help to foster the image that many white people have of us. Why be a walking white man's stereotype? We all have brains – let's put them to use.

I may have laboured the point somewhat in this chapter but I, as a typical Nigerian, really do appreciate the value of education. It is education that defines a child's whole life. Only by getting maximum help from both parents can a child mature. At the moment, too many black kids' futures are being thrown away on the rubbish tip. Other people will not necessarily help us, we have to show the way forward and help ourselves. My own niece (13 years old) was at risk of being corrupted by the negativity of American black youth culture that force-feeds its way into black children. What did my sister do? She made a financial sacrifice by re-mortgaging her house and has managed to send her to private school. How many other parents would make such a selfless decision? It is time others followed her example.

Summary (by Margaret)

As Bobby mentioned this was a chapter difficult to write for him. Yes, we do have our differences regarding discipline, but both of us really believe in education and respect for teachers.

It is hard for him to cope but I cannot be too harsh on him as parent-hood is a new and continually changing role. He had no experience of bringing up children, whereas I had quite a bit through looking after younger siblings.

It would be remiss of me to acknowledge that we did not have problems once our children were born. These, though, were of a practical nature rather than they themselves being 'confused' about their dual heritage. As an example, Bobby did not know what to do with kinky Afro hair at first and he was bemused by all the lotions and creams that Joshua and Olivia use. He learnt though, and that is the key to this chapter and indeed the whole book. Throughout life you should not be put off from doing something because it is new. Anyone can learn, it just takes practice and effort.

We are both trying to the best of our abilities.

CHAPTER 9

Food

Bobby

Food glorious food! You may think it is strange to include a chapter about food but it really has been an area where we have had conflict.

First of all, a confession; I do not like Nigerian food. Not quite as bad as my self-doubts concerning parenting but you would not believe so, given the reactions I have had. Whenever I mention to Nigerians that I can't stand pounded yam, semolina, cassava or jollof rice, the response is always one of absolute horror. It is as if I have just insulted their mother or committed blasphemy. But I can't help it, Nigerian food does nothing for me and I can't swallow spicy things. Instead, I love food with little flavour that does its job and gets out so to speak. I do not like food that lingers in the mouth causing your skin to burn and your face to go red! And by golly, my face does go very red.

Unfortunately, this has led to problems for Margaret, as people often assume she hasn't 'educated' me in a gastronomic sense, a gross slight on her ability as a cook. Whilst it is correct to say she is no Rusty Lee (ex-GMTV chef) in the kitchen, her rustic charm serves its purpose. Certainly, she knows how to rustle up a lovely chicken stew with dumplings.

I discovered Margaret's cooking skills sometime into our relationship, as it took her nigh on six months to summon me to her flat for dinner. Indeed, it took her so long to invite me round, I was on the verge of thinking she ate all her food from McDonalds. The truth, when I eventually discovered it, was different. She was scared. Scared of what to cook an Englishman for supper.

So what was my first meal? Super noodles, frozen peas and chicken thighs! I am sure you will agree that a Marks and Spencer chicken pie and my own mashed potatoes were a better offering. I have never understood why,

75

when you are trying to impress someone, you would feed him or her thighs rather than breast. Margaret later explained that in Nigeria, thighs are considered more of a delicacy than breasts. I did ask her if she was talking about sex or food but she never got the joke.

Still, I shouldn't complain, it was tasty enough in a wholesome kind of way.

But even food such as this she has to abuse. Just about everything Margaret eats is covered by the Devil's own invention: Encona Hot Pepper sauce. Urgh – it tastes like something you put down the toilet after an especially heavy night on the cider. I really don't want to think what it is doing to her insides.

Looking at the bigger picture, I find it strange that food is seen as a pawn in the cultural battle for supremacy. I have lost count of the number of times Margaret has been told I am rejecting her 'culture' by not adapting my culinary tastes to suit hers. I always refute this as I do not feel that someone's culture is defined by their ability to eat potatoes or rice and peas. I view culture as an ethos that goes far beyond what we digest in our stomachs. Food to me is simply something to be enjoyed and to keep the body fit, regular and healthy.

Bizarrely, I have found that Nigerians, in this country at least, view it as a personal attack on them if you reject their food. How ridiculous. I wouldn't mind but I have tried to be diverse with my food intake. For instance, I have been to numerous Indian restaurants to sample their culinary delights. True, I haven't got any further on the menu than a chicken omelette with chips, but at least I have made an effort. I, too, can now swap stories about stained curry house tablecloths and patronising Indian waiters, who just cannot resist a smirk as they ask if I would like my omelette mild or hot.

Now that I am on a career break, the cooking duties have been passed on to me, so Margaret has to swallow whatever I concoct in the kitchen. This, unfortunately for her, has led to a barrage of potatoes. Mashed, chipped, boiled, jacketed and roasted. The potato is, for sure, the best foodstuff known to man and I can't get enough of the little bleeders: Maris Piper, King Edward, Charlotte, new potatoes, old potatoes and red potatoes – the choice is endless. Poor Margaret did not appreciate quite how many ways there are to cook the humble spud. It is fair to say she does now. I cannot state she is entirely happy with this – for she complains that a staple diet of potatoes is boring. I would have to disagree. I also cook pasta but that really is a boring food. No, for me, the potato is king. The King of excitement.

My potato obsession does, unfortunately, give us problems when Nigerian family or friends come to our house. It invariably means that two meals are cooked, with the exception of the Sunday Roast that everybody seems to enjoy. Our children, on the other hand, are a different story. They eat anything – be it English or Nigerian. Whatever food is dished up before them lasts for only a few minutes. This is especially the case with my son as he perfects his impersonation of a human dustbin. Surely this is how it should be? They are growing up with a Nigerian mother and an English father so it is normal they like a bit of both. I suppose you could call them bi-foodual.

But the food issue does not apply to us alone. If you ever watch one of the endless talk shows that discuss the 'mixed marriage' topic, I can absolutely guarantee at least one of the talking heads will mention food when it comes to cultural differences. I will never understand this. What does it really mean? Will you not go out with someone purely for what you put in your belly?

Another area that puzzles me is the constant put-down of English food, (normally by the French.) I do not understand this as we produce some absolutely delicious dishes. Who can hold a candle to such fantastic products such as pork scratchings, Cornish pasties, Yorkshire pudding, pork pies, toad in the hole, Cumberland pie, pork and apple sausages, fishfingers and the omnipresent potato? You can stick your snails, curried goat and yams back where the sun doesn't shine. Argh, it never fails to get me going when people ridicule English food. It may be heresy to write this but not everyone in England shares a passion for curries and rice.

I have three further complaints regarding the food problem. Why is it, whenever a group of people discuss where to go for a meal out, the choice invariably comes down to: Italian, the curry house or Chinese? No-one ever suggests: 'Let's go to a pie and mash shop.' Why is this? Because the media have infected the population of this country with the belief that English food is rubbish. As a consequence, people are embarrassed to admit to liking it. I write again; English food is the tops. I know I come over like a rabid BNP supporter in this chapter but I just want a fair deal for English food. Go on, give it a try, you might actually like it!

Secondly, why do some black people have no idea what English food is? Margaret told me a conversation she overheard at work recently – between two British-born black men of around thirty years of age. One asked his friend if he knew of any decent English restaurants as he wanted to take his wife out for a surprise meal. The guy frowned, thought for twenty seconds, and replied that he didn't know of any. He topped this off by admitting; 'What is English food anyway?' My God, going by this example it seems like English food has been erased from the history of our nation. C'mon Jamie Oliver, stop moaning about Turkey Twizzlers and educate these philistines!

My third complaint concerns the world of work. Whenever people are encouraged to bring in food for a communal lunch people opt to bring in, for want of a better word, 'ethnic' food – in the places I've worked anyway. Apart from a pile of sausage rolls (that strangely are always eaten first), the rest of the gastronomic assault course tends to consist of piles of jollof rice, pasta, spicy chicken and assorted samosas. By the way, it was always me who brought in the sausage rolls. I used to sit there munching away on a round dozen of them, being exotic only by the choice of a low fat butter alternative on my French stick. The other 'tempting' morsels were excluded from my diet, as I sat there in a version of food solitary confinement.

However, rather than respecting my ethnicity when it came to food, I was instead held up as a figure of fun by my 'diverse' colleagues, who tucked into whatever was on offer. And my word, did the stick go on and on. I must have been asked one hundred times why I don't like spicy foods, especially as my wife is Nigerian. This one always puzzled me. My stomach has always been the same; both before and during marriage. If my wife were American, Nigerian or Jamaican, it would still have reacted the same way. *I CANNOT EAT SPICY FOOD*. But I was made to feel a social leper – all because I stuck to English food.

Don't get me wrong, I am not demeaning these other foods; I just find it strange that I have to make an excuse for liking English food here in England. Truly, we have lost touch with our history when it comes to food. English, potato, punk and proud is what I stand for.

Well, I have put my case for the defence: it is now time for the prosecution to consider the case against English food. Over to you, Mrs Smith.

Margaret

So far in this book, Bobby and I have agreed on many issues. Here, though, I am afraid he is totally wrong and even on the verge of madness. How can anyone like English food? It is so...so....bland. It is like eating sawdust with the obligatory gravy dumped on top.

I always tell Bobby, 'If English food is so good why do they have to make it with additives, preservatives, and dump salt and tomato ketchup on it to make it remotely edible?' I love Bobby dearly but I really find it hard living with a potato head. Most people would come home from work and look forward to a refreshing meal whilst they unwind. What do I get instead?

Margaret: 'Hi honey, I'm home – what's for dinner tonight?'

Bobby: 'Hello darling, it's that family favourite; mashed potato, Turkey

Drummers and baked beans. I'll just put down my pinny and dish up for you.'

I ask you, is this what a woman really wants to come home to after a hard day at the office? Would it not be better to walk into the kitchen with a sense of expectation, as an aroma of fish stew wafted down the street? I do not understand how a woman can be satisfied with the junk food served up by the present generation of men that have learnt to cook via a microwave oven. I like real ingredients, real chicken, real yam, real rice, real....*flavour*. Is it, therefore, any wonder that the English are currently suffering an obesity epidemic given the food they eat?

I am afraid, though, the English will never understand the attitude of Nigerians to food – as confirmed by Bobby's comments. For us, food is a natural expression of our way of life. Yes, we like to eat, it is a pleasurable experience. Is eating mashed potatoes everyday a pleasurable experience? I don't think so!

I always remember when I came back to England the first time, being asked by my foster carers in Brighton what I would like to eat. I replied that I liked rice. What did I get for dinner? A huge plate of rice pudding! Pah! The English are so confused over the food issue, they even manage to bastardise a simple staple like rice. Rice pudding? What a peculiar concept.

To be fair to the English, I do admit that they come up trumps in certain food areas. I just love their desserts (apart from the above). What other nation in the world can list better afters than: cherry cheesecake, apple pie, rhubarb crumble, Auntie Doreen's chocolate cake, spotted dick (before I met Bobby I used to think this was English slang for venereal disease) and lemon cake? The list is endless. If only they could start and stop at the dessert.

As Africans living in England, we have to be careful to ensure our children are not corrupted by this decadent English food. We have to pass on a love of fresh ingredients to our children so their taste buds are not infected by this processed rubbish.

Sadly it has to be admitted that, in some cases, we are too late already. My good friend Anita's children already prefer sausage rolls to cassava. What a burden of shame for her family. But wait, it gets worse. Round the corner from us, there is a friendly Ghanaian family whom we have got to know well. They have a twelve-year-old daughter who does not like Ghanaian food. What does she eat instead? Burgers. American! In the name of Jesus, that is even worse than English food.

Being married to Bobby, I am wary of my own children growing up in this fashion. I could never look my mother in the eye if Olivia and Joshua spurned jollof rice for a plate of mashed potato. Ah ah, the public scorn and humiliation would be too much for our distinguished family to bear. This is where I vehemently disagree with Bobby, as, for me, food is definitely part of the culture that I come from.

Saying that, I do find it hard to understand why people jeopardise having a relationship with someone over it – despite my comments about potatoes. Food, though, is a really important sign to Africans, as it gives a clue as to whom we are as a people. This is why many Nigerians feel personally attacked when Bobby admits he doesn't like our food. By rejecting our food, it is as if he is rejecting our culture. Being married to a Yoruba woman, he should have picked up some taste for our food over the past ten years but, oh no, not my dear husband, for him yam is something to be avoided like the plague.

In many ways Bobby resembles the Eddie character from '70s sit com *Love Thy Neighbour* – as they both share the fear of being 'swamped' by 'foreign' food. It is fair to say that neither Eddie nor Bobby will ever develop diverse taste buds, as they both get the shakes if their dinner plates fail to contain a couple of King Edwards. Sadly, I have come to terms with the fact that England has more chance of winning the football World Cup than I have of seeing Bobby munch his way through a Yoruba fish stew. Poor man, he has my sympathy.

Bobby also always jokes that whenever he meets a Nigerian for the first time, they always ask: 'Do you like our food?' followed up by: 'Have you been to Nigeria?' Whatever his response, they also manage to bring up three other subjects within ninety seconds: their religion, their degree and their 'business.' Weird maybe, but absolutely true.

To compound my annoyance, I have found that many English men are adventurous with food. It's just my bad luck to have ended up with someone who thinks a potato is God's best invention. I should have married Bobby's friend, Julian Smith, instead, as he is far more exotic in the food department. Come to think of it, he also likes the same type of music and clothes so the transition would be relatively easy.

But I can't be too harsh on my husband, for it's not really his fault he doesn't appreciate good food. No, the blame lies on his '70s upbringing. Let's face it, kids in the Seventies were brought up on a combination of: Curly Wurlies, Peach Melba mousse and puffa puffa rice – hardly what one would call a well balanced diet. What I don't get is; how come the obesity crisis didn't strike earlier – given the above nutrient deficient menu.

Another food area where we disagree concerns fingers. By this, I mean the fingers on one's hand and not the humble fishfinger. Being Nigerian, I often eat food with my hand. To Bobby this is wrong and a sign of un-civilised behaviour. As a consequence, I have to listen to Bobby kissing his teeth at me whenever I scoop up a handful of pounded yam from my plate. I don't know what is harder to bear; Bobby criticising my eating with fingers or him trying to be black!

Lastly, then, I have a warning for black women who are considering dating white men; don't worry about the size of his penis, worry, instead, about his eating habits. Cultural barriers can be successfully hurdled but food could be a step too far, as not many African women have the willpower to successfully swallow the 'white man's' food. After ten years, I feel sick just looking at a potato, but I have to grit my teeth and remember my marriage vows. Dear Lord though, it is hard.

Summary

Here is a chapter where we appear at opposite ends of the spectrum. I love potatoes, Margaret loves rice and never the twain shall meet.

However, by our mutually entrenched views, we are merely demonstrating that we are both eating from the same cook book, albeit in a different language. Both of us, when it comes to food, are unwilling to bend to accommodate the other. This could become a major problem but we recognise the other's point of view (if not menu) and do not let it affect the marriage. How does it work out in a practical sense? There is an old English proverb: 'No Potato is wasted.'

That is certainly the case in our household. Bad luck, love – do you want them mashed or boiled?

CHAPTER 10

Hobbies

Bobby

Why have we bothered to write a chapter about hobbies in a book about cultural differences/similarities? Because both of us feel we are defined by our interests, rather than our ethnicity or the country we were born in. All of that is immaterial – as we had no influence in it – our hobbies, though, are personal and specific to us as individuals. They have shaped who we are as people and the way we interact with others.

At this point, people who know me already will be tempted to skip this chapter as most are aware of my passions. For those remaining, I ask you to hang onto your hat and come with me as we enter the mysterious, murky world of German punk rock!

For me it all started in 1984. I was calmly watching music programme *The Tube* when they appeared. Who? Slime – the first German punk band I had ever heard of. I remember the presenter introducing them as: 'for those of you who like your music a bit rough round the edges.' Well, that sold it to me. I will not bore the reader with tales of Dirk's (singer from Slime) raspy forty-cigarettes-a-day voice or Elf's melodic guitar playing. No, you will have to check them out for yourself. It is worth doing so though, as they are simply the best band that ever existed. Other German bands of note are; Loikaemie, The Shocks, Oi-Melz, Walter Elf, EA80, Hansa-Plast, Die Mimmi's, The Stage Bottles, 4 Promille, Popperklopper, Terrorgruppe and literally hundreds more. Sadly, most people around the world have never experienced Deutschpunk and this is a huge cultural shame. Certainly a record like *Brace...Brace...*, the new '77 style opus by The Shocks, is a gem waiting to be discovered by the discerning public.

I must admit, it was a bit of a culture shock for me to discover German punk back in 1984, as previously I had only associated German music with Nena and her '99 Luftballons'. Being a diverse kind of guy though, I soon opened my ears and discovered the crazy punk rock sounds that were sweeping Germany during the '80s. I should inform the reader that punk in Germany really took off at this time. It did exist in 1977 but most bands (The Buttocks, Male, Razors, etc) concentrated on singing in English. Only when the mighty Slime appeared, did singing in German become *de rigueur*. This, to my ears at least, was crucial, as punk sung in German just fits perfectly into the three-chord classic song structure of the music. The guttural language complements the angry buzz-saw guitar sound and leaves the listener in a state of musical bliss. What, you don't believe me? Many readers are now probably thinking: how on earth does Margaret put up with my music? A valid question for sure and one I cannot answer. Still, I put up with her religion so I guess it's a fair swap.

However, I would concede she does find it hard to cope with, as she will never understand the appeal of a musical genre that has no positive words for God. I have tried to explain to her it is my belief in punk that makes me want to fight the injustices in the world, but I cannot get her to believe this. Truly though, it is the case. Punk lyrics generally are not about picking up some hot bird at the local disco. No, they are far more socially conscious and politically aware.

Seeing as how I got into punk in the early 1980s, most of the big punk bands had split up to be replaced by bands such as Sham 69, Riot Squad, Subhumans, 4-Skins, The Fits and the Exploited. Bands not as instantaneous in the punk memory as the likes of The Damned or The Clash. As my old friend, David Nunn, always says; 'they weren't proper punk, they were Johnny come latelys.' In a chronological way I guess he is correct, but I would vehemently disagree. Is Wattie (singer from the Exploited) really in a punk band because it is trendy? Nah, he is into it because he still believes the world is a messed up place and he has something important to say. Granted, he probably hasn't the intellect to be an accountant or doctor but it is the spirit that counts. That is why I admire old punk rockers today; they have kept the faith in an era when slavish devotion to material possessions is the only thing that seems to matter.

Mind you, one of my own pet hates is when someone says: 'Oh, I used to be a punk when I was younger.' For some reason, this normally happens when I am urinating in a public urinal, not the best place to argue the merits of old style punk to new. The man boasting of his punk past is then always disappointed by my response, as I merely nod my head in a resigned fashion, reel in my big fish, and zip up my zipper. I am sorry but I find it hard to reconcile my passion with what, for them, was obviously just a passing fad. As my mate, Big Dave, always points out: 'If you used to be a punk then you never were one.' Spot on. I fail to see how you can profess to be a punk if you ditch it once the trendiness has gone out of the scene. To be a punk is to remain loyal to its beliefs. Wearing bondage pants, glue sniffing, or owning a dog on a piece of string is not the be all and end all of punk. No, punk means living your life the correct way, by being cynical and disbelieving of authority figures. Presumably, this is why I now subscribe to *The Daily Telegraph*!

Just about the only thing that has changed regarding punk, are the punks outside gigs who used to beg for admission money with the plea; 'Have You Got 10p?' – as the Ejected sang in the early '80s. Nowadays, it's; 'have you got a pound for me to get in?' What I'll never understand is, how come the money requested went up by so much, so quickly? Perhaps, more importantly, has this increase been noted by the Retail Price Index?

It is a clichè now, but punk really is about a way of life – a life I have embraced to the full. It was never about (from 1980 onwards at least) being fashionable; it was about being true to your roots.

Just about the only music that can hold its own to punk is its shaven-headed counterpart; Oi! Yep, I am also a fan of the most misunderstood form of music in the world. For those not aware Oi! has long been tarred with the brush of racism as it grew out of a mixture of the punk and skinhead scenes that were popular at the back end of the Seventies. Certainly at the time of its birth, it was a scene riddled with the politics of the right. I should remind readers here, we are talking about a Seventies Britain where a significant number of its white population sympathised with the extreme right-wing politics of the National Front. And, for the Nazis, their music of choice was Oi!

For a long time punk, Oi! and skinhead concerts were disrupted by riots as Anti-Nazi League members fought with white power skinheads. So, a music scene that was initially a working-class 'tell it as it is' type of sound, was rapidly transformed into a fascist recruiting ground. Oi! though, was not supposed to be that way. It was a genuine voice of disaffected youth – angry and confused by a cocktail of rising unemployment or factory fodder jobs. As Jimmy Pursey (of streetpunk stalwarts Sham 69) used to say: 'Just tell us the truth.' Truth is, working class kids were being fed into the system and spewed out the other end as disposable commodities for the ruling classes to play with. Oi! was a way the kids could fight back. Unfortunately, they (the kids) largely forgot about the movement's ideology and ended up fighting each other. This was wrong. Oi! was never about black versus white; it was about standing up for working-class communities and uniting against those who couldn't give two figs for the working man. At the risk of sounding like Garry Bushell (current day TV pundit and past journalist who championed the Oi! scene when he wrote for *Sounds* music paper in the '70s and '80s), I feel these are worthy sentiments that ring true even today. Sadly, the middle-class snobbery of the music and national press managed to kill Oi! off before it had a chance to show the world its true potential.

Looking back now, the strange thing is the members of Oi! bands said exactly the same things as the rap stars do today – whenever they were/are accused of glorifying violence. They all said/say they were just a product of the street, that they sing about the lives they lead. Songs like 'Evil' by the 4-Skins with its anti-social lyric; 'jump up and down on your head, kick you around until you're dead,' were excused in this fashion. I, personally, don't buy into that, as both movements know that violence sells and a lot of people have got rich on rap for this image. It is fair to say the Oi! bands didn't get to the same level of financial stability. It is also fair to say they never had the same quality of birds in their music videos!

I actually found it a shame that most of the Oi! bands resorted to such negative lyrics, as the music was normally rock solid. Certainly 'Evil' is a great slab of guitar driven angst and anger. Great tune, slightly dubious words.

Along with The Business and Cock Sparrer, the 4-Skins were the most culturally important of the Oi! Bands, their sound influencing a whole host of new American bands such as Rancid and Anti-Heros. The 4-Skins; often replicated, never replaced.

To the outside world, Oi! pretty much finished after the Southall Riot in July 1981 (when a gang of Asian youth's torched the Hambrough Tavern pub where a load of Oi! bands were playing.)

Oi! though, as a movement, did not go away. It reformed itself and came back underground. Without wishing to bore people about its infighting, it basically split into two factions: the Blood and Honour Nazi types and the Goodnight White Pride/SHARP skins (Skinheads Against Racial Prejudice.)

Most people now involved in the Oi! scene realise the danger that politics pose to music and, by and large, reject the political beliefs that soured the scene back in the Seventies. The problem is that society often views the current day punk rock/skinhead image as being anti-black, shocking and confrontational. The anti-black thing is actually quite sad, and blatantly wrong, as punk would not have existed without the ground breaking rock'n'roll of Little Richard and his like, whilst the whole skinhead scene would have been a non-starter but for Trojan records, reggae and singers such as the late Desmond Dekker. People normally forget but the original skinhead sound was ska and Blue Beat music from '60s Jamaica and not the white noise of Nazi bands like Skrewdriver. This is what skinheads are refer-ring to with their nostalgic lament for the 'Spirit of '69'.

It should be admitted though, that a number of skinheads are drawn to Oi! under the mistaken belief it is Nazi music and that you have to be racist to be a skinhead. You don't. The people who think like this do the whole movement a disservice and are acting like the 'Clockwork Skinhead', immor-talised by the 4-Skins song from the glory days of Oi!

Almost all the punks and skins I have met are anti-Nazi and just don't understand their image as a bunch of fascist inspired thugs. Punks are creative, friendly and basically just fun people to be around. The movement's political ideology is probably best summed up by the amount of punks at the forefront of the Rock Against Racism movement back in 1977. The ideology is pretty much the same even now.

And, as for it being shocking or confrontational – what a joke. It is about as threatening as an old episode of TV soap *Emmerdale*. Does anyone anymore really find a pink mohican disturbing? In these days of violent crime and rogue states, are bondage pants still a 'clear and present' danger to the nation's youth?

I honestly feel we need a 'Punk History Month' to educate the masses as to the real meaning of punk rock. As it stands at the moment, American flavoured power/pap, such as Green Day, passes as punk. It's not.

John Lydon and his band PiL sang about punks' poor 'Public Image' in 1978, but the Upright Citizens more accurately summed up the public's perception of us with their 1982 German masterpiece 'Scum of the Earth'.

Maybe things would have been different if Maggie Thatcher had adopted a 'hug a punk rocker' strategy in 1979? Perhaps, if current Tory party leader David Cameron is reading this, he may belatedly introduce such a policy? Who knows, the punk vote may yet swing power away from New Labour!

Whatever, it is time punks had a makeover. We deserve it.

Yoruba culture, although it may not have spawned much good music, does at least pass on its good manners to people. This is ably demonstrated whenever a Nigerian visitor comes to our house, especially if they are younger than me. Somehow, I always manage to put on some obscure German punk to make them feel at ease. I watch barely able to conceal my juvenile delight as they squirm at the sounds coming from my stereo. Of course, once the song has finished I politely enquire if the person liked it. Being in the company of an elder, the young person is compelled by their culture to answer: 'Yes, that was jolly decent, have you got anymore?' As I say, juvenile most definitely, but it never fails to make me laugh.

But, apart from music, what else defines me as a person? Well, I have been a Wolverhampton Wanderers football supporter since 1981 and a season ticket holder since 1987. Why do I support Wolves, given I live down south, is a question I am often asked. My answer is always the same: 'I liked the colour (old gold) of the shirts when I was growing up.' Not an original explanation I know, but at least I wasn't attracted to them because I was chasing glory. Still, saying that, I was once accused of being a glory hunter by a Wolves fan on the terraces at Barnsley years ago. If I remember rightly, it was a midweek match and a relegation battle at that. Glory? Wolverhampton? I don't think so!

I also remember picking Wolves at school, as all the other schoolchildren supported a football club, foolishly believing that if I too had a team I would not get bullied. I suppose I should have gone for Tottenham, so as to please dad, but that was too obvious. No, Wolves it was to be. Oh dear, what a mistake. I had signed up for years of abject misery via my erroneous choice. Unbeknown to me, Wolves were about to embark on the worse period of results over their entire rich history. Three successive relegations followed, as *the* team of the Fifties plummeted, by the middle Eighties, into the bottom tier of English football. Still, at least they were 'my' team, even though everyone else laughed at them.

I still go to football these days, but have become disillusioned with the way the game has gone and now attend only out of loyalty and routine. So why am I disillusioned after all this time? Because the modern day footballer uses fans as mere wallet-fillers. We are there purely to keep footballers accustomed to luxuries such as mock Tudor mansions and boob job blonde girlfriends. I get intensely irritated at the thought of my hard-earned cash subsidising their *nouveau riche* lifestyle. In many ways, it is eerily reminiscent of how the prog rock bands of the '70s, like Yes or Emerson Lake and Palmer, reached the end of their musical shelf-life. Thankfully, they were swept away in the trail of gob, vomit and vitriol that heralded the arrival of punk rock. We definitely need something similar to happen in the world of football today so as to destroy the 'greed is good' mentality that holds sway in the game.

What players don't realise is that many fans are having to make a choice; to have a family holiday or to purchase a season ticket for football – due to the ever increasing cost of admission. Admission that is linked to the salary increase of the players. And for what? Just so a player can see his ego fed wage increase from £30,000 to £60,000 per week? I may have led a sheltered existence but how can an individual spend this amount of cash? My feelings towards footballers in general are summed up by the words of the 1978 Big Balls & The Great White Idiot song 'Ain't Impressed': 'You drive in your cream-coloured sports coupe, you're friends with the rich kids all over the world – I ain't impressed.' Classic.

Where art thou Johnny Rotten when we need you again?

So, what is this loyalty that I referred to in my previous paragraph? Most definitely not to the team. No, my loyalty is to my drinking buddies in the pub, where I spend many happy hours supping the cider that makes the football a little less boring. Andy, Jon, Simon, Neil and Tars, binge drinkers to a man, I salute you. For me, the cultural side of football (the chat, the drinking, the falling over and the camaraderie) will always be more important than the performance of the team on the pitch. This is something not understood by people who never go to football. If it really was just twenty two men kicking a bladder around, it would be boring in the extreme.

In contrast to my music and football, I also enjoy more cerebral pursuits. It is a bit nerdy to admit it but I like military history. I must have around five hundred books on World War 2 (WW2) alone, covering every campaign from Russia to the South Pacific. So, the obvious question; why am I so interested in this period? Two reasons. Firstly, because I grew up on a diet of 'take that sausage eater' and *Achtung Spitfeuer* in my youth, via the comic strip antics of Johnny Red and Charley's War, as they battled old Jerry to the death. As a result, it was easy, via literary heavyweights such as John Keegan, Richard Overy and John Erickson, for this to morph into the more intellectual side of military history. Their expertly crafted words, dripping with respect and admiration for people who went through the pity of war, helped me immensely as I struggled into adulthood. Heavy reading for your average teenager I accept, but I also had the war porn of Sven Hassel to lighten my mood when faced with the misery of teenage acne. My adolescence was also spent playing with toy Schmeisser MP40 machine-pistols (from the *Golden Shot* TV show) and pineapple hand grenades. For me WW2 never ended; it just got bigger. For us '70s Tommies the 'var is never over'. I know I am not alone with this attitude. For instance, my mate Glen knows the words off by heart to the film *The Great Escape*! This is actually quite sad and takes the WW2 obsession onto a different level, but I can at least sympathise with him. I blame the Nazis; they were the best enemies a kid could have when growing up. None of this psychobabble rubbish, that suggests we take into account their feelings and how their mothers brought them up. No, they were complete bastards and therefore perfect for comic book parody.

It is sad to report most kids nowadays don't have this WW2 interest, their pliable minds preferring fantasy figures such as *Power Rangers*. Poor buggers. As the English Dogs so eloquently put it, in a line from their 1984 album, *Invasion of the Porky Men*, 'why doesn't anybody sing about World War

Two?' I honestly have no idea, because reality is always more interesting then fiction.

Secondly, I am drawn to WW2 because it was a time when being British stood for something special. It was a period of history when others really admired this country. Sadly, I feel the stoicism of its people during the 1939-1945 conflict is unlikely to be repeated today. Sure, we have the people that struggled into work after the July 7, 2005 bombings but nothing over a sustained period like the Blitz. Can you imagine Londoners struggling into work every day if 60,000 of them had been blown up by terrorists in the preceding nine months?

Writing this, I know I am at risk of over romanticising the wartime generation. For some, it is a surprising fact that crime actually shot up during the war, and the activities of the black marketers are legion. Generally though, the population did rally round during adversity and put on a brave face. Do we, as a nation, still have that strength of character?

I see so much to admire from people who went through this period. People like my parents and other family members. My own mother nearly died during the war and she vividly remembers hiding under a front room table as a V–1 doodlebug hit another house in the road she lived in. Those that went through experiences like this have a modesty that radiates affection and humility. They really knew what sacrifice meant and willingly did so with a fortitude that demands appreciation from everyone living in Britain today.

We may still buy our poppies once a year, but do we really understand the suffering others went through? I don't think we do. This is why I find it so hard to see elderly people struggling to make ends meet, what with the high cost of fuel and the *bete noire* of pensioners; council tax. This is one area that Margaret and I totally agree on – as you will see in her little rant later.

Aside from music, football and history, I also love cricket (way before Tony Blair clambered on the Ashes bandwagon), and going to the boozer for a few pints of cider. A healthy and mixed range of pursuits, I would argue.

Margaret, though, is more of a specialist when it comes to her interests.

Margaret

My number one interest has to be my passion for dolls and Gollies, or Golliwogs as Florence Upton originally named them before political correctness was invented. I just adore them and have a rapidly increasing collection of the little sweethearts.

Bobby, it is fair to say, does not understand my 'obsession,' as he terms it.

But I really identify with the dolls and the history encased within their fabric bodies. History? Yes. How many other pairs of hands have caressed and been comforted by them over the years? How many infants have drifted off to sleep clutching one of the dolls to their chest? This is what I find most appealing about the little darlings.

I should confess here that I'm not very diverse over my choice of dolls as for me only black will do. Why? I guess I am drawn to them because they resemble me more than the blond Barbie dolls – so popular with girls when I came to England. Strangely, when growing up in Nigeria, I never had such an interest. Indeed, my passion only started about three years ago when I was buying a black doll for our daughter. So, why do I buy black dolls for my daughter? Because I feel it is important for our children to see a mirror reflection of themselves with the toys they play with, although it is almost impossible to find mixed-race dolls. So, in our marriage we compromise. Joshua has white Action Men and Olivia has black dolls.

Bobby can't complain about my interest, as he confided in me that he had a collection of WW2 Action Men when he was growing up, whilst his sister also played with Barbie dolls. Apparently, his sister always wanted the dolls and the men to marry and presumably live happily ever after. Bobby preferred to use the dolls as innocent victims in his hostage fantasy game. Going one step further, he also had the bizarre habit of drilling a hole in the plastic bottoms of some of his GI Joes! I have no idea what was going on in his head when he was doing this and can only assume it was Bobby being plastic 'curious.'

Meanwhile, back in the real world, I confess to being the proud owner of a collection of over two hundred dolls and Gollies. A collection that is increasing rapidly and starting to become a bit of a nuisance to the rest of the family. To be fair, I do appreciate it can be a bit annoying when you reach for a can of baked beans and instead get a collection of Heubach dolls falling on top of oneself. But I just can't stop myself, I have to have more.

So, where do I go to buy all of these dolls? Antique shops and dolly fairs. This may come as a surprise to the uninitiated but these fairs are held up and down the country. When I first went to one, I found it was a relief to discover that I am not alone with my interest and, with the help of Ebay, I have since discovered that the whole world shares my passion for dollies.

One of the benefits of attending fairs is talking to all the lovely people who share my collecting habit. My friends Linda, Irene and Brenda have been especially helpful when it comes to tracking down obscure German composition black dolls. Strangely, I seem to be just about the only black woman who attends these fairs. Almost all are white middle-aged (or older) men and women, who have had the hobby for decades. I must say that, without exception, these people have totally accepted me for who I am. I never feel I am a token when visiting these fairs and I never feel out of place. This is one of the joys of liking dolls. It really does bring you into contact with groups of people you may not normally have mixed with. From these get-togethers I have gained a healthy admiration for these elderly citizens, who demonstrate the stoicism that my husband mentioned in his earlier comments.

This is where Bobby and I totally agree. We both respect elderly people and recognize that we are only here because of them. So many people nowadays have no time for old people, as witnessed by the all-too-frequent stories of abuse in care homes and by relatives. I find this extremely upsetting. In Yoruba culture, we value and treasure their wisdom and listen to their stories. In England, it often seems we write off a person once they reach the age of sixty-five. This is wrong. Luckily, Bobby feels like this as well, and, in addition, he has always addressed his aunts and uncles via their proper title. Not for him the sloppy first name calling that many in England tend to do.

Apart from the dolls, I also collect other antique items, as I like to surround myself with things from the past. Be it old toys or calendars, I just like the feeling that so much life has gone before from the items I touch.

Continuing the theme of old things, although a tad more recent, I also have an interest in Eighties horror films. Oh, how I lick my lips just at the prospect of watching classics such as: *Evil Dead*, *Cannibal Holocaust* and *Zombie Flesh Eater*. Quite frankly, if it has gore by the bucket-load I want it. Blood dripping from the ceiling, entrails across the floor, eyeball gouging, I love it all! In contrast, Bobby can't stand these types of films and, if forced to watch, he views them through clammy fingers as I get off on the gore. The irony is that, despite enjoying military history, with its daredevil tales of men fighting against the odds, my dear hubby can barely get through half an hour of *Casualty* before retching into his handkerchief! What a wimp.

For some reason, people are always surprised that a practising Christian like myself can enjoy these films. I am frequently asked why I prefer say, *Saw*, to religious films like the *Passion of Christ*. I always answer that I can divorce reality from fiction.

One of my other main hobbies is the basic human need for sleep. Yes, I just *love* sleeping. In my youth, I recall taking leave from work so I could have a whole day of unadulterated sleep. I know this sounds really weird but sleep for me is the same as a cup of tea is for Boy George. And, when I sleep I sleep big time. I am dead to the world whilst sleeping and unable to be woken, except by Bobby's farts that go off with a sound vaguely reminiscent of a shotgun discharge.

Prior to knowing Bobby though, my sleeping 'sickness' kept me in splendid isolation from the rest of society. Once, I recall the Fire Brigade being called out to attend a raging ball of fire in the flat above where I used to live. The whole block of flats was evacuated for the day whilst the fire was tamed. All, that is, except me. Yes, I managed to sleep right through a towering inferno and the screech of numerous fire engines. I woke the next day and thought my neighbour was joking when she complained about being put up in a hotel!

I also read a lot of books – generally true human-interest stories and African history. I have read some of Bobby's WW2 books and especially enjoyed his number one book: Guy Sajer's Eastern Front memoir, *The Forgotten Soldier*. Likewise, Bobby reads some of mine and he found Sista Souljah's *No Disrespect* an interesting read.

Apart from books, we also grew to love each other's films. I must confess that, prior to knowing Bobby, I would never have watched Joseph Vilsmaier's WW2 film, *Stalingrad*, through choice. Now, though, I can appreciate its war-is-hell reality. Bobby, whilst he doesn't understand my love of horror, did bend a little and also enjoyed one of my favourite films, *Imitation of Life*, the classic 1959 Lana Turner film about race and identity.

This is definitely a good illustration of how a mixed marriage can benefit the two individuals. Both of us are comfortable in learning more about the 'black' or 'white' half of our relationship – even in simple areas such as books and films. It does not mean Bobby is acting black or I am acting white. It just shows that each of us is prepared to learn from the other.

Leading on from this, Bobby introduced me to the German television series *Heimat*. For those not aware, it is a fictional account of life in a German village from 1919 – 2000. Initially it didn't sound very appealing but I sat down to watch it as Bobby insisted I would like it. Bobby obviously knows me better than I thought. *Heimat* was an absolutely fantastic programme that really showed the small-town mentality that existed in Germany during that era. What struck me about it though, was how similar (especially in the period 1919-1960) life was compared to a Nigerian village. Superficially you would have thought they could not be more different but they really were identical. You may find this puzzling, but the attitude of the people in it towards elders was totally how I was brought up. It was such an eye-opener for me that Germany used to be like that. In addition, the slow pace of life shown in the series is so typical of Nigeria even today.

When it comes to music, my collection pales into insignificance when compared to Bobby, in volume if not quality. I enjoy sounds as diverse as; Anita Baker, Whitney Houston and American rapper Tupac (or tooth plaque as my disrespectful husband calls him) but I just can't appreciate the more 'robust' sound of Bobby's Buttocks – however much he plays them to me. At least if we ever get a divorce it will be easy to sort out the CD collection.

I really can't get my head around Bobby's music. I can just about see the importance of the lyrics but I do not understand why they have to shout all the time. What is wrong with melody and soul?

And as for attending punk gigs? Well, I went to a few and all I can remember saying is: 'some people here could really do with a good wash and a one-night stand with a bar of soap.' It is sad but I guess we will never be compatible over music.

I do, though, understand why he goes to football. His friends in the Midlands really are a nice bunch of guys – especially after six pints. One of the reasons I like them is that almost every one of them has managed to find me a golly item in their loft. The social side of it is also something that I replicate with my dolly friends, albeit without the six pints.

Summary (by Margaret)

On paper we have vastly differing interests. Bobby with his punk rock, military history and football and me with my dollies, antiques and '80s horror flicks. Aside from the music though, the similarities are striking, if not immediately obvious. We both like things from the past. We both value honesty and integrity and the ability to speak the truth in a plain fashion.

This is one of the reasons for us liking our dollies and punk rock. The strange thing is both groups of enthusiasts act exactly the same with their passion. By this I mean, both the punkers and the dollists(?) trust you implicitly if you show an interest in their hobby. For example, Bobby and I have often had goods before we have paid for them. Likewise, we have given things away to other people from our respective 'tribes'. Would you get the same level of trust at the supermarket?

In a way, both of us are trying to escape from the modern world. Not by taking drugs or getting drunk every night, but by seeking out values from the past. Our lives are certainly running parallel when it comes to interests – even though it is hard to see the link between a golly and a Spitfire.

Despite this we still manage to have arguments.

CHAPTER 11

Arguments

Bobby

An interesting one this. Couples argue frequently: finance, time, the in-laws, whose turn is it for the washing up; all these subjects have a tendency to turn from an everyday discussion into a full blown argument. This is normal.

The strange thing is, Margaret and I rarely argue about the concerns I have just listed. No, we flare up over a topic central to the both of us; our children. What makes it worse is that our arguments can be heard halfway down the street. Indeed, our disputes are so animated that friends compare us to Jack and Vera Duckworth from *Coronation Street* – yes, that loud.

I don't mind the fact we argue, but what does irritate me is how Margaret is very quick to lay the blame for many of our arguments on our skin colour/culture. Personally, I would put most of our arguments down to the fact we are a man and a woman first and a black and white couple round about number thirty-two. However, I have lost count of the amount of times she has said: 'See, this is a cultural difference.' I am not in denial about any differences between us; I just don't see it as the root cause of our arguments.

So, why do our children start up so many of the rows? Because they act just like, err...children. Without knowing it, they subconsciously know the buttons to press to ignite their parents' fire over the most mundane of situations, such as who gets to receive their dinner first.

It may seem a bit unfair to blame a child for the actions of two grown adults, but it is surprising (to non-parents at least) how children can transform a relatively intelligent adult into a slavering emotional wreck, or in our case two emotional wrecks. This is best illustrated by what happens after our son misbehaves in the slightest fashion. I guarantee Margaret will shout at him first and me a mere nanosecond afterwards. Why do I get it in the neck?

Because my reactions are slightly slower than Margaret's. I, therefore, cannot discipline him as she has already done so. If only I was given the time to tell him off then things would be better. Margaret though, is too hot-tempered and rises to his bait immediately with that fearsome stare that one has to see to be believed. My wife is rightly famous for her Jim Carey *Mask* impersonation but I am more familiar with her Norman Bates *Psycho* look.

So, due to my inability to be a firm disciplinarian, I then get told that I am a wimp and not a proper man – generally because I am softly spoken and more considered with my voice. In contrast, Margaret is too governed by her hormones and demands I replicate her somewhat crazed style of parenting. Of course, if I disagree with her it is because I am English and that a Yoruba man would not say the things I do. This is partly true. My son even told me himself he is scared of his German/Nigerian Uncle more as he tells him off in a way I cannot do. But I cannot believe every Yoruba parent reacts in an extreme manner with regards to child discipline?

Another common theme that often leads to an argument is when Margaret tells me: 'You don't realise what I have given up for you.' By this, she is referring to those of her friends who no longer come to our house and use her marriage to me as an excuse. Rather than reflect that her friends now live further away and have children – both factors that hinder friendship – Margaret insists it is solely because I am in the home. I refute this because I am often out at football on a Saturday. This, then, leads onto her other favourite topic: that I do not communicate with her friends. This is true but normally it is due to them speaking Yoruba and excluding me from the conversation. Whose fault is that?

To back this up, many of her friends who speak English in our house have now become good pals to both of us. I would argue this is the way it should be.

Maybe, though, it is my fault? If I complained about Yoruba being spoken in our house it would probably stop. I have two fully grown legs so maybe I should stand up more for my 'human rights' and insist on English being used in our house? Maybe I am too compliant with Margaret's wishes? Perhaps she has worn out the doormat and secretly wants someone to answer her back in an equally fiery manner? Or maybe I should just bite the bullet and learn how to speak Yoruba?

Is this a 'cultural' difference or just the nature of two people?

My mum certainly reckons I am too quiet and should speak up for myself more. In all honesty, I find this hard to do; as I cannot pretend to be someone I am not. I was born a placid person and that is the way I will meet my maker. It is not in my nature to be ranting and raving, so instead I absorb the tension within. Not healthy in the long-term I know, but it is just the way I am.

Given what I have just typed, I am beginning to see why I was bullied so much at school. From outside, I must appear like a man with no backbone or gumption. I must confess I agree wholeheartedly with this suggestion and admit that I do need to confront my wife more often than I do. Oh well then, here goes.

I find it absolutely staggering how Margaret is quick to apportion blame for our disagreements on my nationality. Often she has said: 'If you were Nigerian you would know what I mean.' To my mind, it shows that she still has doubts being in a mixed marriage to occasionally allow this type of comment to rise to the surface.

In addition, during arguments, she sometimes accuses me of using her as a 'slave'. This is a very emotive word and is used primarily to wind me up. What makes it stranger is, I do more housework than the average man and have for a long time paid all the bills. Slave? I think Margaret needs to look again at how she responds to flash points in our marriage. She needs to look at me as an individual and not as an English man.

She also, bizarrely, thinks I use my military history knowledge on her. By this, she means that I adopt classic military tactics to outflank her and ensnare her argument in a pincer movement. This is peculiar with a capital 'P'. I am totally mystified as to how she believes I speak to her in the same fashion that, say, Eisenhower would have addressed Montgomery or Bradley prior to D-Day in June 1944. And yet, she is totally serious with this allegation. Mad. Still, at least I feel better now that I've got that lot off my chest.

It has suddenly struck me writing this book that I started out with the good intention of promoting mixed marriages and showing their positive points. However, I feel that readers who have got this far may come to the opposite conclusion. The more I re-read it, the more I feel we still have major issues to confront. I still believe, though, most of our problems are to do with our obstinate characters rather than our colour.

But, at least, we can categorically state that both of us are being honest with the practicalities of surviving the marriage minefield. If both of us thought everything in the garden was rosy it would be pointless, and maybe boring, to write about. To be fair to my wife, I do admit that I am at fault for the rapid escalation of our arguments, as I tend to clam up whenever conflict approaches. I know this infuriates Margaret and do so not with the intention of irritating her. It's just that I feel we would be better talking about any issue when we have both calmed down. I have read that this is a classic male tendency and females get extremely annoyed by this. Well, it's a fair cop guv', I have no defence.

However, I suspect that most people would be sympathetic to me if they could visually see Margaret when she argues. An argument with her is like trying to break in a wild horse as she bucks and brays before finally running out of steam. I have never known any woman who possesses such a temper. How on earth someone who attends church, who attends antique shows, who reads intellectual books, can suddenly go stark raving bonkers when we have a disagreement is beyond me. This is no exaggeration and I am left to wonder if this happens in most marriages.

Of course, this is where I am at a disadvantage by dint of my not having other relationships prior to Margaret. I will never know if what we argue about is the norm for all couples or if it is a madness only my wife suffers from. To balance this part up, I should confess that I have also been known to lose my temper but the difference is it lasts for only a few seconds. Margaret possesses the 'talent' to stay angry for days. I will never understand how she manages to do it.

Margaret, I am sure, will not agree with my comments. In fact, I am sure we will have another blow up when she reads this chapter!

Margaret

Bobby is right about one thing – we did have an argument over his words! I think Bobby's main problem with arguments stem from his all round lack of experience with women. I do not mean women friends (of which he has many); I mean proper sexual relationships with them. This is why Bobby is so quick to blame everything on my hormones. Yes, I admit I am fierier than Bobby. Yes, I do stay angry for a long-time. But aren't most women like this? Poor old inexperienced Bobby just thinks it is me.

Maybe, if he had a couple of affairs he would understand me better? To be fair, I have tried pimping him out to my friends but no one would have him. I can't think why!

His technique of handling arguments also doesn't work well with my character. I would much rather get everything out in the open when we disagree. I do not see the point in withdrawing until we have calmed down as this only gives me more time to get irate. Far better for us to air our disagreements and hopefully find a solution.

Bobby was correct, though, when he said most of our arguments concern our children. Why? Because he is so stubborn with regards to his dealing with them. Example. I have always given our children a 'bucket bath'. For those not aware, this is a typical way of washing for people of African descent. It involves washing oneself down with water from a bucket container as water 'back home' is sometimes in short supply. As a contrast, many English people have the habit of lying in a bath. I, however, can never accept this as a way to keep clean as a bath means dirty water is in constant contact with the skin – most definitely a cultural difference.

It is true that you can have a shower and this does fit my definition of being clean. Despite that I still prefer our daughter to have a bucket bath. Bobby cannot see the point and, although he gives her a shower in the morning, he sticks his heels in and gives her a 'proper' bath in the evening. His reason? So she can play with her ducks. The outcome? Conflict.

I also do not like the way he creams or scrubs her body, even though he insists he does it just like me.

Argh – the man is impossible; he just refuses to obey orders. Even the very act of typing these words irritates me, as I can see his soppy little smile as he innocently explains he has put her cream on. I will remain convinced until my dying days that he does it deliberately to wind me up. He refutes this but I know the books he reads. I have always suspected, because he reads books such as: *The Psychology of Military Incompetence* by Norman Dixon, he tries out the same tactics in our marriage. This allegation pisses Bobby off but I honestly feel he approaches me in the same way a General may confront a Major.

To give further proof, I offer the example of fishfingers. At first glance, this may appear bizarre in the extreme so I will explain further. Many years ago, as Bobby was struggling to make an impression at work, he informed his colleagues he existed purely on a diet of fishfingers. Why did he do this? He has told me before that he was demonstrating an old military tactic; letting the enemy (or, presumably in this case, workmates) underestimate you. I am still not quite sure how a fishfinger can be seen as a weapon of breadcrumb destruction, but I accept his point. Bobby was probing away to see if he could infiltrate his colleagues' gullibility defences, on the off-chance that one day he may genuinely need to pull the wool over their eyes. He was ensuring he had the element of surprise for when it was needed. A nice theory, I guess, but one that still strikes me as more than a little mad.

Good old Bobby, he honestly thinks of himself as the poor man's Basil Liddell Hart (famous English tank theorist knocking around in the '30s) always raging against the establishment with his superior military intellect. Sad. He really should have joined the army when he left school.

I notice Bobby complained about my mentioning of the slave word. What he doesn't understand is its meaning for Nigerians. Although we frequently tell people: 'Stop treating me as a slave,' it really just means; 'Do you not have a maid to do that?' It is everyday slang for us to use and not nearly as offensive as Bobby suggests. I also disagree with his comments about me referring to his nationality. Yes, I do often say 'your people this' or 'your people that', but I am really referring to British people and not white people in general. I can categorically state I have no underlying problems being married to a white man.

Perhaps Bobby's sensitivities over the slave word betray a hidden secret? Maybe he has researched his family tree and discovered that slaves were once owned by his forefathers? To be fair, I did put this to him and he retorted by asking me to check my own family tree. I got angry when he first suggested this, but he could have a point seeing as how my roots are in West Africa. Many like to forget it happened, but black Africans also played an active role in the economic exploitation of brother Africans during slavery. It is this exploitation that lies behind the modern day animosity felt by some Caribbean origin men and women towards Africans. Our ancestors are viewed as 'traitors' for selling blacks to the white man when he came seeking cheap labour. Some Africans, paradoxically, look down their noses at West Indians and blame them for having a 'slave' mentality. Sometimes, I can only shake my head in wonder at the historical hypocrisy of my fellow Africans.

Another problem I have with Bobby is his habit of undermining my authority with the children. I just cannot stand it when he calls me 'stupid' in front of them. In Yoruba culture, this is seen as a heinous crime. Children must not see another adult insult their mother or father. It is even worse if one parent disrespects the other. I am not denying Yoruba men and women insult one another. No, I am just informing the reader that they would do so in private away from children and their prying ears.

To conclude, I know our arguments have to stop and, slowly, they have become less heated. I guess, though, both of us will always wonder if it is natural for couples to argue as much as we sometimes do.

If so, it is not a good advert for the state of married bliss!

Summary (by Margaret)

Well, we both disagreed with each other over this chapter. I guess by definition that was always going to happen.

Arguments can be a good thing as long as both of the couple participate in the discussion. They also show children that an argument can be constructive if the dispute is resolved.

What they should not be is a continual war of attrition. If they persist *ad infinitum* they only offer a bad example to impressionable children. For the sake of both of our children we have to stop the arguing. Bobby just has to accept this and acknowledge he is wrong when it comes to the kids and their bath time.

I know he says he is just doing it different to me but I still say he is going about it the wrong way. He should just admit to being as stubborn as a mule and listen to his better half!

CHAPTER 12

Identity

Bobby

This one really concerns how each of us view ourselves. What is the mirror reflection we feel comfortable with?

As I have explained, I largely grew up in the cosseted, semi-detached, idyllic lifestyle of Broxbourne. Only when I left home and moved out into the urban battleground of Enfield Town, did I begin to appreciate that the world was a violent and prejudiced place.

So how do I define myself? First of all, I have never been one for nationalistic tendencies. The idea that because one is born English they have to support all its institutions is false. Why should you support the England football or cricket team just because your parents gave birth to you in dear old London Town?

As it happens, I do support the England cricket team as they embody everything that is good about being English. A man, such as left-arm spinner Ashley Giles, is the perfect embodiment of how the English used to be; well-mannered, with charm and all round good eggness. A more polite man in world sport would be hard to find today. The cricketers also like a drink (witness the riotous scenes the day after the Ashes victory at the Oval in September 2005) and can actually hold their alcohol content (apart from Freddie Flintoff), always an admirable quality in a man.

On the flip side, the characters in the England football team do nothing for me at all and I do not see why I should feel ashamed of this. I'll go further on this point as I really do struggle to understand how Englishmen feel represented by the ex-England Captain, David Beckham, a man who is famous for wearing a sarong! How can I relate to that in my world?

But it gets worse. The star striker in the England team, Michael Owen, is alleged to have never read a book in his life. Again, and not wishing to read like a book snob, how do I feel represented by this man? Sorry, but I don't.

And don't even get me started on the infamous football players WAGs (wives and girlfriends), as I am sure I'm not the only Englishman embarrassed by their antics whilst away from our shores. It may sell a few newspapers, but their reported behaviour (excess drinking and spending), is adding to the poor public image that Brits abroad have to endure. What a contrast between these women, who were alleged to have spent £10,000 on fake tans alone during the World Cup, and the more down to earth nature of some of their football opponents. As an example, it was claimed in the *Telegraph*, during the 2006 World Cup, that the Ecuadorean footballer, Ulises de la Cruz, gives 20 per cent of his income to charity. Money that has been used to install running water and electricity in the village he grew up in. In addition, he has also paid for a school and hospital to be built. Personally, I admire his actions rather more than those of the WAGs. His nationality is immaterial, it is behaviour that counts.

This is why I am so against this absolute loyalty to flag, nation or history. There are enough rules and regulations in the world that we do have to follow, so I don't see the point in adding to them by compulsorily supporting the country of one's birth. Surely, a key tenet of democracy is the notion of freedom of choice?

Sadly, I am beginning to realise the mentality of this country, with the exception of lippy teenagers and hunt traditionalists, is slavish acceptance of everything laid down by authority. Sometimes it takes a brave voice to say: 'Stop, you do not have to do it that way.' There is always an alternative.

This reminds me of when my dear Auntie Doreen discovered I was going out with Margaret. She said: 'That's typical of Bobby, always has to be different.'

Yes is my response to that. Yes, I am different because I do try to find alternative ways of doing things, to think for myself. Does this make me a social deviant? Whilst I would accept that both Margaret and I are a long way short of the stereotypical English man and Yoruba woman, I fail to see this as a problem as it adds to our characters.

So, do I see myself as an Englishman? No is my honest answer. I have always considered myself a human being first, a punk rocker second and a European third. I have no desire to wrap an English flag around my shoulders or wear badges declaring allegiance to the Queen.

Saying that, I do think it's a good idea that moderate Englishmen and women have made an effort to reclaim the English flag and traditions, such as celebrating St George's Day, from the far right. Why should emblems of freedom be adopted and misused by someone whilst the silent majority stand idly by? The flag denotes England, not the BNP. Sadly much of England has yet to grasp this point. Witness the cries of racism whenever English pride struggles to assert itself, with the loudest voices coming from those of a white middle class background. To be honest it seems at times as if being English is something to be ashamed of. The very words 'English pride' probably make me appear as a depraved neo-Nazi. Why is this? Why have we let the extremists and liberals destroy our cultural heritage?

Although I don't totally identify with the idea of being English, I do love certain cultural things synonymous with our nation. Such as our humour. You may laugh but I really do feel that English humour is the best in the world. What other country can take the piss out of itself as much as England? Self-deprecatory humour should be recognised as a cultural strength of the English, on a par with its tolerance of others and its (once) good manners. For those who don't send yourselves up, I say: 'Give it a go,' you may feel better about the world afterwards.

Of course, being a camp punk rocker, I have no choice but to embrace the self-abuse option. Yeah, it is true, I do sometimes look like a stupid little leather boy walking down the road in my bondage pants and big boots but at least I am free. If I want to look like a demented circus clown then surely that is my right in a democratic world? I will never understand why so many people have a problem with folks that look different to them. It really is akin to racism the way people shout abuse at you if you don't wear the correct pair of trainers or shirt. As you may well expect, I get this more than the average member of Joe Public, so much so that I have stopped recording the amount of times I am called 'batty boy' just because I do not wear baggy jeans or Reeboks. How on earth does that make me gay?

Margaret disagrees with me on this issue as she correctly points out I do not have to wear the clothes I wear. She, always, has to wear her skin. To me the principle is still the same. As a nation we were once tolerant of eccentrics, be they Quinton Crisp or Larry Grayson. These days anyone remotely different is looked down upon and ridiculed. How then, could I possibly be proud to call myself English?

At the same time, I have to say I do get mildly irritated when the English are described as a people without 'culture'. At Margaret's care workplace, she hears on a daily basis her African co-workers coming out with this nonsense.

No culture? Err, how about William Shakespeare, Elgar, Tony Hart, Charlie Harper, Captain Sensible.....Jeremy Beadle, the list is endless. I find this suggestion arrogant and insulting. I am fed up hearing English culture consists of beer-swilling binge drinkers whose whole lives consist of going to football, going to the pub and then vomiting on the way home. Oops sorry, I forgot the obligatory fight at some stage on the bus or train.

Hang about, I can hear you say, you must be a hypocrite as you listed going to football and having six pints amongst your interests. Well yes, for sure I like to go to football, and I can certainly binge drink with the best of them, but I do not vomit or fight on the way home. Perhaps, more importantly, that is not the only part of my life. As I have mentioned, I have my more intellectual/nerdy pursuits as well. It is easy to look at the drunken hordes on a Saturday night and assume these people are doing this all the time. I suspect they are not.

I guess this follows on from my earlier line about self-deprecation. Maybe as a nation we are too good at it? Perhaps we should stop it altogether and just be deadpan serious all the time? Margaret is forever telling me that Nigerians just would not send themselves up like this. For them an insult is an insult. Maybe we should stop it but if we do many of the conversations in an average pub will turn boring overnight. The ability to 'take the piss' is an enduring character trait of the English and one that should be defended to the last.

Another popular image of the English is the homosexual one. Why is it English white men are thought of, at best, as effeminate and at worst as a nation of raging homosexuals? This was brought home to me when I read the results of a recent international survey, a survey that placed English men at the bottom of the European league, when it came to providing satisfaction for 'their' women. The excuses for their poor performance were centred on their own relationships with their mothers and a desire to seek the company of other men. I find this disappointing. In my case, it is also wrong. No, don't laugh. I can do sexy – as any who have seen me on the dance floor, wiggling my flat arse, will testify.

Unfortunately, many people around the world believe this image. An image compounded by the absence of manly English role models. As a result we are seen as sexy as a wet fish. Oh, how I wish English men would assert their masculinity more. Hugh Grant is probably the most well-known English actor in recent years. I ask you – an upper-class toff! How is he sexy to women? The list goes on: singer Pete Doherty, is his waif-like body really sexy to women apart from Kate Moss? I doubt it.

These pseudo-womb men types may help to sell newspapers but they are stripping away the sexuality from white English men. Nowadays, English blokes feel the need to bombard their bodies with lotions and creams so as to look more feminine. My sister's boyfriend, Chris, has twenty-two different creams in his bathroom for his body. Twenty-two! I find this unnatural. Whatever happened to 'real' British beefcake like Ian Botham or Lewis Collins? They have been eclipsed by men trying to be women.

I think this whole metro sexual brand has been taken too far and needs to be dumped in the rubbish bin. Personally, I would go further and ban all men's aftershave, with the exception of High Karate (for reasons of nostalgia). This may be a tad tongue-in-cheek but we really are seen as non-sexual beings by a vast chunk of the world's population.

I have asked Margaret as to why this un-sexy image has persisted for so long – especially with regards to the way Nigerian women see English men. Her answer always comes down to television. Apparently, during the Seventies and Eighties in Nigeria, the most popular English TV shows were *Benny Hill* and *Some Mother's Do 'Ave 'Em*. Fantastic. This would explain our public image then with a lot of Nigerians. We either parade around in nappies all day (Benny Hill sketch), or we act as feminine buffoons who wear 'dirty old men' raincoats (Frank Spencer.) No wonder Margaret has a lot of Nigerian men offering her sympathy when they hear about her choice of husband.

I know, I know, before you start laughing. I can see the irony of my words – I have after all confessed to being a touch camp. But surely Nigeria must have its share of camp men? Not according to Margaret. Homosexuality (not that I am confusing camp with being gay) is a crime against the Church so, therefore, does not happen in Nigeria. You would not believe the amount of people that have told me this myth. I always reply; it obviously does go on but people are scared to admit to it, preferring to keep it underground. No, I am told, we leave that to the decadent perverse West.

Oh dear, it would seem that homosexuality and Nigeria are not compatible bedfellows. Certainly, the way the two countries approach the issue demonstrate how we are poles apart in our morality. This was highlighted by the minor furore that broke out when Communities Secretary, and staunch Catholic, Ruth Kelly, refused to answer a radio interviewer's question on whether homosexuality was a sin or not. I have to admit I chortled to myself at the sound of her getting all twisted up in knots, as she tried desperately not to offend homosexuals and, at the same time, remain true to her Catholic faith. By fudging the issue, she only succeeded in making herself look foolish. I daresay that, if the same question had been put to a Nigerian minister, the answer would not have been so vague. Something along the lines of; 'What a stupid question – of course it is a sin.' Say what you will about Nigerians, but they are certainly forthright with their opinions over this issue – seeing it most definitely as a crime before God. Sitting on the fence is not an option.

Is it any wonder then that gay Nigerians keep a low profile? The dangers of 'coming out' ensure that many gay men have to hide their sexuality from prying eyes, as for many 'coming out' means possibly being ostracised from your family and the Church, or even being killed.

Then again, it's not much better in Jamaica with the murdering of gay men being treated almost as an Olympic sport.

Scandalous.

I am also informed by my wife that masturbation does not happen in Nigeria. Hmm, not sure I believe that one. In my opinion, Nigeria has its fair share of tossers. Margaret informs me that Nigerian men don't have to do it, as they are too busy having affairs! Despite her explanation, I remain a cynic. Do young boys in Nigeria go to bed with their hands tied behind their backs? If not, then it happens. They are boys, it is natural, accept it and move on.

I've gone off on a tangent, as usual, but to bring the argument back to my main point: is it really a surprise, given all these negative images of English men, that I do not identify with being English? I really do feel we are dismissed as a nation of aggressive, drug taking, football hooligan, bad food eating pissheads. Oh sorry, I forgot the fact we wouldn't know fashion if it hit us in the eye. What poppycock! How anyone can criticise a nation that gave the world bondage trousers is beyond me.

The other stereotypes, whilst containing elements of truth, are not the whole picture. Many English people, the silent majority, live quiet lives, hidden away from scandalous newspaper headlines. These people, the much-maligned working-class/lower middle-class types, potter around on small lawns in the week and wash cars on crisp Sunday mornings. This is the romantic, idealistic England that still remains, albeit with its values sometimes questioned and held up for ridicule by certain sections of the press. Quietly, we get on with our lives not bothering anyone and welcoming all whom we come into contact with. This is the England I am proud of.

Sad to report then, that this is the England gradually slipping away. If you don't believe me, watch the house-for-sale signs that spring up whenever a few black, Asian, or punk rock families move into a street. These actions are obviously not in the same league as those who dump excrement through letter boxes, but the underlying trend of living in isolation from each other is spreading as rapidly as bird flu. So many white people are now leaving London for the suburbs, only returning to the city to watch their black football idols play for Tottenham, Arsenal or West Ham. It is integration at arms length. We should all resist this mentality to enjoy the benefits an open mind can produce. So, next time a punk rocker moves in next door, do not speed dial your estate agent. No, instead invite him in and ask him about his Buttocks CD collection.

Currently, the big debate is how British Muslims see themselves and how they identify with Britain. Looking in from outside, it seems to me strange that pressure is put on Muslims to be either 'moderate', or 'extremist'. Fine, label the obvious radicals, such as Omar Bakri Mohammad, but what about the majority who would reject both labels?

Another thing that puzzles me is the concept of one-size-fits-all when the press or television talk about Muslims. Despite the Muslim world being inhabited by all sorts of different types of beliefs and traditions, the media tends to label them as just 'Muslims'. Personally, I would find this offensive if directed at me, as it fails to recognise the varied strands of Muslim life. I can certainly relate to this because, even in the punk rock world, we have our own little sub-sections.

But, rather than delve into this interesting subplot, we instead get bogged down in the identity mire. I know it annoys my friend, Asif, when he is asked this identity question. Just because he has a brown skin he has to declare an allegiance to one side or the other. And yet I, a man who openly admits to not sharing an empathy with some aspects of being 'English', can get away with it. I am not criticised by strangers and asked to condemn suicide bombers and the like. No, my views are obvious because I am white English.

Right?

Wrong.

That is not to say I condone the actions of suicide bombers or directly link them with British foreign policy as I don't.

Right now, it seems as if the world is full of men searching for a cause to die for, with death a welcome release from the moral weakness of being a human being. I don't know about you but I can't come to terms with all of this; it's too much for a simple punk rocker to take in. I guess, at heart, I am just a regular bloke who doesn't understand the mentality of a person who sets off a bomb on a bus or a plane.

Frankly, I am also puzzled by the lure of the mythical seventy-two virgins these self-styled 'martyrs' are supposed to acquire when they reach heaven. If they want these virgins that badly, they would be better off packing their backpacks with cash and condoms and heading for fleshpots such as Thailand and Cuba. Apart from curing any sexual frustration, this would also demonstrate to the world their total assimilation into the sex tourism aspect of English society – thus killing two birds with one stone. Oh, I nearly forgot, and dozens of innocent lives would also be saved from a fascist ideology far removed from humankind or any sane version of religion.

So, why do I not identify more with England then? What is it that puts me off our green and pleasant land?

One of the main reasons is that I don't connect with the public face of England. By that I mean I don't watch soap operas or reality shows, or wear jeans or trainers. I know this is not unique just to England but it seems like everyone just wants to look and sound the same, leading sad identikit lives with narrow outlooks and closed minds.

If you don't believe me, take a wander down your local high street. Not only do the people all resemble each other, the shops are normally replicated, no matter if you walk through Darlington, Wolverhampton, or Kentish Town. The only difference concerns the various food shops that reflect the ethnic make-up of a particular area. Everything else is just homogenised rubbish.

Where is the individuality that the English were once famous for? It has all been subsumed by the brand name colonisation that has been allowed to ruin the appeal of our streets. Fancy a coffee? Go to Starbucks and not to the café over the road. Want a Danish pastry? Call in at Sainsbury's on the way to work. You may well argue that the shops are merely meeting demand and to a point you are correct. But have we no soul? Instead of treasuring Mrs Miggin's pie shop, we have let it go to waste. Everything seems to follow the 'consumer is King' approach, with dissenting voices relegated to a mere whisper in the wilderness.

The stupid idolisation of 'celebrity' status in England is another area of being 'English' that is absolutely guaranteed to drive me crazy. The amount of people who chit-chat about the lives of people they will never meet makes me pull my hair out in frustration. So many important things happening around the world and yet all you hear on the street is mindless babble about some famous person's new hairstyle or fancy clothes. I just want to get hold of these people, shake them up and down and scream; GET A LIFE! Is it only me that feels like this? Have we, as a nation, jettisoned our intelligence and ability to engage in decent conversation? Who actually cares if Paris Hilton has a new boyfriend/car/coat/hairstyle? Does she sit at home wondering her 'pretty' head if I have a new pair of bondage pants? I doubt it. Celebrities? F**k the lot of them!

These are the reasons then, why I feel at odds with this nation's population. This is why I prefer to look elsewhere for happiness. Maybe it was this sense of being different that, in my sub-consciousness at least, attracted me to Margaret? Maybe my Auntie Doreen was right all along?

I should add here that throughout the book up to date I have referred to Margaret as being Nigerian. Seeing as how she was born in England, should I not describe her as English or British? I would agree, I should. However, she likes to think of herself as Nigerian – despite having lived in England for her entire adult life. Confusion?

Still, on this point she is in agreement with my mother. Dear mother, despite welcoming Margaret and her family wholeheartedly into the Smith 'clan', still cannot grasp the idea of someone being black or Asian and English. Mum tends to label them all as 'foreigners', even though most have probably lived their entire lives in England. Doubtless she is not alone with this way of thinking, and I guess it can be confusing for people of a certain age to cope with a rapidly changing population. However, I don't think we should be too harsh towards those of an elderly disposition where race/identity is concerned. I am sure the rest of us have equal levels of confusion about the subject – only without the honesty exhibited by the likes of my mum. Gentle persuasion rather than the whiplash of the stick is the way forward for those at the veteran stage in life.

And of course, it is not just the elderly white English who have a problem with identifying who they are. It is often also a delicate matter for someone of Asian or African descent. How does one define oneself? By the colour of a skin, a parent's background or merely the land they inhabit? I always feel it is up to the individual to decide as no-one else has the right to tell someone who he or she is. So Margaret is thus described as Nigerian even though I may not agree with her.

The trouble is, she will never feel totally at home either in England or Nigeria. Despite her denial, she always seems to be on the outside looking in.

My mate, Asif, also experiences this feeling whenever he goes to his parents' country of origin, Pakistan. In many ways, he is doomed forever to wander from one culture to another held together purely by his religion. He feels a tug from England and yet cannot entirely shrug off the draw of Pakistan. This is an issue that, if you think about it too much, could tear you apart. I think it is better just to have an open attitude to this and concentrate on one's beliefs and morals rather than the country you 'belong' to. Surely, we belong more to our wives, husbands, families and friends than to the country we were born into or grew up in?

Yet, despite the conundrums I have listed above, the myth is still allowed to persist that it is mixed race children who are most confused about their identity. But, to me, they are the ones least likely to be confused as they have an obvious bloodline claim to belong to, in my case at least, Nigeria and England. I would always state that 'pure' black or Asian children living in

England have more of a problem than mixed race kids over this. As an example, Margaret's niece Whitney (13 years old) proudly wears Nigerian colours and thinks of herself as completely Nigerian. She has spent one month of her life in Nigeria and was born in London. I know I have just written it is up to the individual to decide who they are but I cannot help but type the word 'confusion' once again.

Talking of confusion I now pass you over to my wife. Just who are you Margaret Smith?

Margaret

Some people in my situation often have a crisis of identity, because they have grown up on two different continents. I have no crisis. I am 100 per cent Nigerian, simple as that. The fact I was born in England does not automatically make me English. My formative years were mainly spent in Nigeria and so it is that country I look to for my identity.

Saying that though, I do consider myself more a child of God than of a particular country. My religion has always been more important to me than the nation I live in. I am a Methodist who just happened to grow up in Nigeria and England. I have no truck for nationalism or for those who feel it matters where someone was born.

Whilst I have no issues over my identity, I do appreciate that some black and Asian people in England find the subject problematical. Like Bobby, I agree the identity issue is best left to the individual to decide. It is a personal choice no-one else can make. Because of this, I feel it is supremely arrogant of the government to ensure we fit neatly into whichever version of English is fashionable at the time.

That is why I can't understand why our institutions are so insistent upon a person's ethnic origin. Every time I complete a form, I have to find a label that fits me. Am I Black African, Black Caribbean or Black Other, etc. What good do these labels do us as a nation?

I would argue that this labelling just serves to segregate people even more. It is so divisive; mountains of tick boxes that one has to complete. How many more years do we have to do this for? How many more centuries have to pass before black and Asian people can break free from the box marked 'ethnic minority'? When will I simply be known as Margaret?

If we are not careful, by the year 2010 the tick boxes will have grown to unmanageable lengths. For instance, if my son was to marry a Jamaican/English origin black woman, they would need more than two boxes. My son's child could then marry a Polish woman and end up having children who would fit even more categories. By this stage, I suspect people from an Eastern European background will have a couple of dozen boxes of their own to tick. Frankly, it is all getting completely out of hand and needs to stop.

Patrick McGoohan, star of Sixties cult TV show *The Prisoner*, once famously declared 'I am not a number.' Well, I would equally like to declare 'I am not a tick box.'

Following on from this, I do not understand why so many black people in England like to specify they are black British. Why not just British? Our colour should be irrelevant by now. There is no need to keep mentioning it. Black British, White British, Black English, White English, why are we twisting ourselves into knots over this?

As an example, further afield, do white Zimbabweans think of themselves as African or European? The white Zimbabweans I have met consider themselves African. They have African cultures, manners etc. The fact they have white skin does not make them any less African than me. This surely is the way it should be, as they are comfortable with their African identity. Why then, are some black people so insistent on labelling themselves with the prefix black?

It must be admitted that I am slightly playing Devil's advocate, as I do understand this mentality. During my early twenties, around the middle 1980s, I used to have a few 'black' t-shirts. Whilst the rest of the nation was going Frankie Goes to Hollywood t-shirt crazy, my ample chest was busy proclaiming myself 'black and proud'.

Reminiscing now, I wonder why I felt the need to identify myself as black when anyone with a reasonable level of eyesight could see this for themselves. I would never have entertained the idea of wearing a t-shirt with the slogan 'look out big-breasted woman approaching', so why did I wear a 'black' shirt? I can only imagine it was connected with the racism I had suffered, for when your colour is emphasised by others, it is the brain's natural defence to grow more insular and withdraw into the part of you that is being attacked. So, rather than shy away from my colour, I turned the argument inside out and declared myself proud of my skin. At the time, this was a comfort to me, but the end result is just suspicion of others and a false pride in one's own colour.

I notice these days you rarely see such t-shirts anymore. Is their absence a good thing? Has society improved to the level where we do not seek to label ourselves to outsiders?

I still think we have a long way to go over this matter. This is best illustrated by a discussion I had with a Jamaican-origin man concerning football. I asked him why he talked about Arsenal football club all the time and not his local team – Tottenham. He answered that he supported Arsenal as they had more 'black players.' This saddened me because his words betrayed him as a man only able to identify with black football players and not a team in general. This man had lived all his life in England and yet still could not see beyond skin colour. Bizarrely, he felt he had more in common with Thierry Henry (the black Arsenal French striker) than he would with Michael Dawson (the white Tottenham English defender.)

It made me ponder that if Bobby had said he only liked Wolverhampton, because they were a predominantly white team, he could easily have been labelled a racist. My black colleague was under no such peer pressure and felt totally at ease in going public with his words. I daresay many black people reading this would have heard similar views expressed and not batted an eyelid at the reasoning behind it. The problem with this racial favouritism, though, is that it provokes an insular siege mentality and you see enemies where perhaps none exist. This partly explains the feelings I had regarding the white men who had approached me before Bobby.

Since I married Bobby, it has brought home to me just how confused many black people are about their identity. Luckily, at the advent of middle-age, I am now totally at ease with who I am as a person. If you had told me, in the 1980s, that I would be marrying a white man or that I would be going to dolly fairs with an almost exclusively white clientele, I would have laughed in your face. I feel I have benefited by this. How many other black or white people would benefit by opening their eyes beyond the restrictions of their colour? As it stands at the moment, too many just concern themselves with issues regarding their ethnicity. As an example, one of Bobby's old colleagues used to buy book after book about self-help black identity. The titles usually ran something like this: 'Ten ways a black woman can find a partner.'

Or; 'Ten ways for a black woman to achieve financial success.'

Or; 'Ten ways for a black woman to connect with her inner soul.'

What next?

'Ten ways a black woman picks her nose?'

The point I am making here is that we are all one people and these colour/ethnic barriers achieve no good at all. On their own they are perfectly harmless but, long term, they act as a stick to keep us apart from one another.

And the biggest stick currently being wielded by misguided idiots is that of religion. The current Islamicist terrorist propaganda that promotes the idea of the West's 'war' against Islam and a 'clash of civilisations' is luring Muslims onto dangerous ground. A ground all too readily lapped up by those in the right-wing press who have also fallen for the terrorist rhetoric. We need to be careful that this way of thinking does not further spread amongst young, vulnerable people, who are open to influence, and who really believe that the terrorists care about events in Chechnya and Iraq. I have news for you – they don't. They are using these as *cause celebres* to entice young minds into their plans for world domination. They are not Islamic in the true sense of the word. No, they are using religion as a shield for their own twisted means. It is largely because of the terrorist threat that Muslims are now having the same identity crisis black people went through in the early 1980s.

It should be added that religious inspired fanaticism is not unique to Islam. No, the very same logic applies equally to those Christians who welcome conflict around Israel as they see it as a prelude to the Second Coming of Christ.

Islamicist terrorists and Christian Fundamentalists both do a disservice to religion generally and their respective influence is too large amongst the communities that support them. Good men and women of sound character need to defeat 'extremism' wherever it originates from, if countries are truly to shake hands with their neighbours.

To do this, we need to divorce ourselves of loyalty to race or religion. This though is hard. For instance, I witnessed no mass Muslim demonstrations, but plenty of condemnatory words, after the July 7 bombing attacks in England. Calls for action over the on-going slaughter of innocents in the Sudan were also muted, apart from fundraising dinners for Islamic Relief missions and statements of sympathy. For some reason, both of these atrocities were largely ignored by organisations, such as the Muslim Association of Britain, whilst other issues, that supposedly bind Muslims together, like the Prophet Mohammed cartoons, picked up immediate support. How is this correct? Why were no people on the streets waving banners and flags in protest at fellow Muslims being killed in the Darfur region of Sudan?

Palestinians murdered and abused on a daily basis by American funded Israeli troops are rightly held up as examples of neo-colonialist oppression, yet state-sponsored genocide, by the Sudanese government, was allowed to pass with little or no condemnation. The best we had, by way of protest, was a September 2006 demonstration supported by the likes of Amnesty International, Christian Aid, Muslim Aid and the Darfur Union. Why were other big Muslim organisations not supporting this? This is not a matter of West v East, or Muslims v Christians. This is simple compassion for fellow humans.

Likewise, the Stop the War coalition have not organised rallies against these injustices to mankind – presumably as the anti-American lobby sees no mileage in the plight of poor black Africans.

I could go on and mention the non-attendance of the Muslim Council of Britain (MCB) at Holocaust Memorial Day – due to its specific commemoration of an event forever associated with Jews. I know the MCB themselves have called for a more inclusive day of remembrance, such as an EU Genocide memorial day, and this would appear sensible both on a moral and political level, but, this still strikes me as an obvious own goal. They have also issued statements empathising with the Holocaust but I still feel they are making current-day political capital by declining to honour past victims of Nazi terror. Those who died at Auschwitz/Treblinka etc, stand as a lasting memorial to man's inhumanity to man. Surely we can put aside the emotions prompted by the Israeli/Palestinian conflict for a day and mourn human beings killed purely for their religion? We owe them this small act of remembrance for their suffering at the very least.

Seeing as how we live in a public relations driven world, I also cannot understand the logic of this decision. If the MCB gave it its physical blessing, it would send a powerful message of peace and correctly show that Muslims are not dominated by hot-headed terrorists who wish to kill half the world's population.

However, by its refusal to attend, stereotypes and inaccuracies concerning Islam gather apace in the Western world and media. This in turn leads to more barriers between people and an increased feeling of alienation, on both sides. Peace is what the world urgently needs and a gesture such as this would send a more positive image of Muslims to the greater population of Britain. By attending, they could have claimed the moral high ground and given an example to other faiths and religions that we were all born out of a womb, whatever our religious differences. Life is not a competition to see which group of people can behave in the most vindictive manner. Just because Israel and America choose to ignore UN resolutions when it pleases them, should others replicate their intransigence? What better way could there be to combat the Islamophobic tendencies, real, perceived or imagined, that sometimes rise to the surface in the press? What do they gain by their abstinence? Absolutely nothing.

Perhaps, more importantly, what on earth have we got to lose by spreading love and unity instead of hate and distrust?

I often think this identity thread is unique to whatever country someone originates from. As an example, when I look at Holland it never crosses my mind that famous black footballers such as Ruud Gullitt or Edgar Davids are not as Dutch as Holland's white inhabitants. It is the same with Thierry

Henry. He is French. I am not bothered whereabouts his parents or grandparents came from – it is irrelevant to his ability on the pitch or the way I see him.

I can only wonder if other Dutch men or French women, who happen to be black, see 'Black Britons' as a separate entity or if they view them as just Britons.

It is a similar situation in America. I find it so divisive that black Americans insist on calling themselves 'African-Americans'. This achieves no useful purpose, and, instead, sends out a segregationist message to the world as to how Americans see themselves. Whenever I see the word American, it does not automatically register in my brain that the person is white – their ethnicity is irrelevant. I see them purely as being from the United States.

Bobby interviewed a black American woman named Cherlyne, during the writing of this book, and she also hates this description, seeing it as unnecessary and a needless emphasis of her heritage. Specifying one's ethnicity also makes people think more about race; a subject prone to more myths than any other.

To highlight this identity debate, I have a close mixed race relative in my family – my niece Yinka. Although she is half Nigerian and half English, she sees herself as totally Nigerian. This is despite the fact she has only lived in Nigeria for three of her twenty-five years. Is this correct?

It is up to her, as I mentioned earlier, but being Nigerian is not just what it says on your passport. It is about learning its customs and ways of life. The young lady in question cannot speak Yoruba and is not familiar with all of our culture. To my mind, she is British or English first, but she wants it the other way.

All of this can get confusing unless you are comfortable within yourself as to who you are.

I can give you a further example from my cosmopolitan family; my sister is married to a German Nigerian named Lawrence Dennison. Bobby always refers to him as German but to me he was Nigerian. It is only when he came to this country and I mixed with him more, that I realised Bobby was nearer the truth than I thought. Bobby is more familiar with Germans due to frequent trips to Germany to see punk bands and he spotted Lawrence's 'Teutonic' tendencies immediately he met him. My husband pointed out he was different to British Nigerians and that he acted exactly the same way a white German would. Although it hurts to admit this, Bobby was right.

Another puzzling factor regarding identity is the mystical and romantic notion that attaches itself to the word 'Africa', usually from British or American born people of African or Caribbean origin. These men and women, who probably have never been to Africa in their lives, see it as their spiritual homeland and a region deserving of its place on a pedestal. To them Africa is 'home' and cannot be criticised. This is yet another reminder of the experience of slavery and the fragmentation of the Black Diaspora. Africa as a continent has many faults and sweeping them under a nostalgic carpet will not solve problems such as fraud, AIDS, and corruption.

One interesting part of the 'identity' debate sprang into life during the recent football World Cup of 2006. For about a month before the tournament started, and for quite a few weeks after it ended, the nation was bedecked in a multitude of all things red and white. Flags, car stickers, t-shirts, just about everything one bought in the supermarket came in these colours. This led to furious discussions in the media, as they suddenly cottoned on to the fact that black and Asian people were comfortable sporting the very same colours the BNP have used over the years.

Interestingly enough, it was the left-wing newspapers that found this harder to comprehend. *The Observer* dated June 18, 2006, included this comment, written by a female Muslim journalist by the name of Urmee Khan: 'I was surprised to see little Muslim girls running around with their faces sporting a red and white St Georges flag.'

Personally, I am disappointed at her surprise to this. Why is it a surprise that a child, who has probably lived all her life in England, declares her nationality on her face? The fact she has brown skin is immaterial to her decision. If we continue to be surprised at children doing this then the segregating of races in England will continue, mainly because left and right-wing doctrine tends to categorise people via the colour of their skin first and their character second. It is surely time for this laziness to cease.

Staying in the sporting field, I can give you further proof of the left-wing problem over race and identity. In the winter of 2005, the England cricket team fielded the first Sikh to represent England; Monty Panesar. A good player with bags of potential, Monty slipped into the cricket team following injury to one of the Ashes heroes, Ashley Giles. Straight away, he looked at home in the rarefied air of Test Cricket and impressed all with his verve and vitality on the pitch.

What was perhaps more interesting to me was the attention he subsequently acquired from the nation's press. Article after article made an issue of his ethnicity. Questions like; 'Do you feel burdened by being a Sikh and playing for England?' These questions were especially prevalent in left-wing newspapers. Really, for such an inexperienced player he was interviewed out of all proportion to his talent. And, after the interviews, came the praise. I cannot recall a player of recent times who was lauded to the heavens as much as Monty Panesar. It seemed, reading the reports, as if England had discovered someone who was a combination of Shane Warne, Jim Laker, Derek Underwood and Abdul Qadir all rolled into one.

I got the impression that these ethnicity obsessed writers were trying to absolve themselves of the sins of empire by wetting their pants every time good old Monty got a wicket (quite often) or managed to catch a cricket ball (not often.)

These lefty liberal types may deny it but they were using his ethnicity as a brand. A brand for them to proudly boast of their pride in multi-coloured modern England. Who is exploiting who now?

Praise Monty, by all means, but leave his colour out of it. It bares no relation to his ability to play cricket.

So, how do I view my children's identity? Unlike me, they have not grown up in Nigeria, so they can only be British or mixed Nigerian/English. It would be damaging to them for me to call them Nigerian and faintly ludicrous.

That does not mean they will only have European culture inflicted upon them. No, they will also know and appreciate what it means to their mother to have lived on a different continent. That way they will have a better understanding of their distant family. That is why they have both already visited Nigeria and enjoyed the variety of life over there.

To close this chapter I will admit, despite my opening line, I am a mixture of Nigerian and English cultures, not in a blood sense, like my children, but in a practical sense. I will never be fully at home in either culture and yet equally I have two exciting worlds to explore. Am I blessed or cursed?

Personally I feel blessed, although anyone reading the book up to now may disagree!

Summary

Potentially a source of conflict, yet the reality is we both generally agree on this point. Neither of us believes in nationalistic tendencies and is not fooled into blindly following political instructions from either the left or right. We both look on an individual as simply that – an individual.

I have known many left and right-wingers over the years and they really are identical in the language and tactics they use. In our opinion, the world would be better off without those who try to exploit differences between peoples for their own purpose. A simplistic view, I grant you, but one more relevant today than ever before.

The interesting thing here is that neither of us is happy with the current state of England, as clearly illustrated by our reluctance to adhere to all things English.

Thinking about it further though, I wonder if growing up in a country that does not flaunt its nationality has made me turn out this way. I really do feel I would have more affinity towards being English if the history of this country was more predominantly displayed. As it is the English tend to look down at other countries, such as America, that constantly hark on about their nationality. I never used to think this was important but I am starting to change my mind. I am still not personally proud of being English but I would like others to recognise that England has often been a source of historical tolerance.

I feel that because I grew up in an education system imbued with left-wing attitudes, it has affected me without my even realising it. As a consequence, I now find it hard to identify with modern English ideals and character traits. I know I am not alone. I always remember a union representative being asked at work which team he supported in sport. He duly replied, 'any team that is against England'. I think this mentality is more widespread than we appreciate. In my opinion we have substituted a sense of national identity with a virulent strain of anti-Americanism – justifying our 'prejudice' towards the States because of one man; George Bush. I can only wonder if this attitude is unique to England. I suspect not.

At times it seems like each and everyone of us, white, black or Asian, are all as equally mixed up as each other when it comes to the question of identity; witness the debates over devolution, faith schools and English football teams with no English players in them as proof.

In conclusion, I guess we are both still searching for our own identity, for a place to call home. Will we ever find it?

Probably not. Should we be bothered by this?

I don't know. But I am beginning to realise how we found each other.

CHAPTER 13

Race, Racism, Ignorance or Curiosity?

Bobby

To an extent Margaret and I have largely avoided any physical racism directed at us, with two exceptions we will elaborate on later. The 'racism' we have experienced has been of a more subtle kind – the kind that many will not even recognise as racism.

In some ways ignorance is probably a better word for what we are about to describe, but ignorance is often the starter for ten that leads someone into developing racist tendencies. Where ignorance meets and overlaps with curiosity is also an interesting part of this chapter. I daresay each person reading this will have their own ideas on the subject, we can only write about what has happened to us.

What I will inform the reader first is, that the average black person (in England) talks about issues of race far more than the average white person. This is largely due to a white European history that, until relatively recently, deemed black as being of less value than white. It is, therefore, not hard to imagine why race continues to exert its influence over the everyday lives of black Britons. I guess if I too were black I would feel pretty much the same way.

For me, racist comments were something I may have heard when growing up but I never really understood the hurt they could cause. As mentioned earlier, the only ones I can recollect now were from my sister's boyfriend at the time. I presume there must have been others at school or at work but I cannot remember exact cases. It was only after I started dating Margaret, that I began to fully understand the real pain that could be inflicted upon someone purely for their skin colour. I no longer had the luxury of being colour-blind.

To add bulk to this chapter, I will now recount some of the stories that have happened over the years we have been married.

One of my favourites is when we had just moved into our new home in Hertfordshire. Like most couples, moving requires furniture and appliances, so we went down to our local electrical shop to purchase a few items. Whilst walking round the store, Margaret noticed a black lady of around forty-five years of age who couldn't stop staring at us. Indeed, the lady was staring so much she walked straight into a display of toasters and knocked the whole lot to the floor. Rather embarrassing for her but amusing for us.

I should add here that I was not wearing my punk clothes, just a grubby old pair of tracksuit bottoms and a plain t-shirt. To be truthful, I do acknowledge that a lot of the persistent stares we get are more to do with my clothes rather than our being a mixed couple. And, of course, I am not presuming her staring was prejudicial – I just find it strange that, in the 21st Century, a coupling of any group of people is viewed as different or something to be fearful of.

As a contrast, I should mention what happens whenever I go out with either of my two children. I referred in an earlier chapter to how stressful I find being a parent, well, it does have some advantages. One of these is that children are an absolute babe magnet! And, of course, mixed race children are especially babe magnetic to black women. The usual response, when I walk past a black lady is: a quick look at the child, then a longer look as they realise they are mixed race, finally a third glance at the Dad. By this stage, I normally cannot resist a slight smirk (apologies once again for my juvenile sense of humour.) What I find comforting is that some of the women smile back at me. I asked Margaret as to why I get this response. She answered: 'Because they can see you like a bit of black.' Well yes, that is true, but I don't want to be judged on what is only circumstantial evidence.

Men and women in mixed relationships just want to be left alone to make a success of their liaison, without the added outside pressures that can sometimes come to marriages such as ours. The key is that people in mixed marriages want to be judged under the same criteria that people in same race relationships enjoy. Equally, we do not seek someone's patronising 'tolerance' or 'acceptance' of our union. Unfortunately we have found that even tolerance is beyond the scope of some people.

On another occasion, Margaret and I were visiting a museum with our son in London. She walked past a group of young black women with me in tow. They, as one, all kissed their teeth at her as we walked past. Not appreciating Margaret's hot temper was a mistake on their part, and she rounded on them. 'What's your problem?'

The girls, no doubt taken aback by her ferocious Les Dawson expression, could only offer a dismissive glance in my direction. To this day I am amazed that Margaret, in the parlance of today's youth, never 'bitch slapped' them, but she managed to restrain herself with a glare and we left them to their own prejudices.

After the event, I explained to Margaret they were probably jealous of her for stepping out with such a sexy man, but I don't think she believed me.

Another of my favourites occurred during a shopping trip. After buying up all the bargains, we went to the check out. As is my way, I always say hello to the lady or man who serves us. I do like to play up to the English gent image but it really is the way I was brought up. In this case, the young girl was of Caribbean origin and merely kissed her teeth when I said good evening.

The check-out girl also totally ignored Margaret and our children – who were trying to make small talk with her. How rude. It is fair to say, I am not one for displaying anger in public – or at home. Nope, I normally rely on my finely tuned sense of humour for a witty response. Feeling this time that a one-liner would not suffice, I passed her my money and managed to slowly stroke her hand as I passed over the notes. I complimented this brazen act of flirting with one of my infamous campy smiles, as her horrified eyes met mine.

Her reaction was more than mildly amusing; she immediately pulled her hand away in absolute horror, in the process dropping the money. 'Allow me to help,' I whispered huskily to her, but she declined my generous offer with a brief 'no thanks,' her nose wrinkling up in disgust.

These things do not just happen to us. I remember my old friend Norma (who is black) recounting the story of how she was walking down Tottenham High Road with her boyfriend (who was/still is) white. A Rastafarian guy told her she was walking the 'wrong way sister.'

Whilst the above are relatively harmless examples of how prejudice can come into play, I have had unpleasant experience of a more physical nature.

It was just last year when I had problems on the train home from Wolverhampton. My friend Andy (white male of approx forty-five years of age) got into a dispute with a black guy of similar age. After an initial verbal confrontation, I sensed the two of them were about to park their brains in the multi-storey and engage in fisticuffs. Being somewhat squeamish, I decided it was time to act and attempted to separate them. In my somewhat naïve way, I imagined the sight of me dressed in leopard-print Doc Marten boots and matching top would stop the bloke who was haranguing my mate – whose only crime was in wanting to use the toilet. I was wrong, as my presence served only to exacerbate the problem.

Leaving my friend alone, the stranger proceeded to whack me several times around the head whilst shouting 'white bastard' as he landed his blows. I must confess that, as I raised my puny fists to defend myself, the number one thought in my head was; 'this will fit perfectly in my racism chapter'. Weird or what? I know that, by typing this, I run the risk of trivialising what was a scary incident, but it honestly was my first reaction. The next day, I sat down to analyse the attack in a more mature way and tried to gauge my feelings.

The main emotion I felt was frustration, not at my lack of manliness in response to his abuse, but the fact he kept emphasising my colour. What can I do about it? It is this frustration that I guess is shared by all those who suffer racism. A feeling of helplessness, as we cannot help the colour we are born into. For me, I just find it totally depressing that this guy couldn't see beyond my race; it was like my entire life history had been reduced to a pinky skin tone with the rest of my identity immaterial to him. I was white and nothing else mattered.

Just in case people think I may be mistaken about the racial element to this story, I was not called just a white bastard. Oh no. Basically everything he said to me had the prefix 'white'. 'Get away from me white man' was another favourite line of his as he bashed my head in. A truly sad situation for me to write about.

Another incident that has stayed in my head was when I was cycling home from Tottenham. My attention was taken by two young Asian youths gesticulating wildly at me from the safety of the pavement. Thinking they needed assistance, I slowed down. It was then I realised their gesticulations were of a somewhat rude nature, compounded by a barrage of naughty words.

Being somewhat taken aback by their insolence, I responded with a rude word of my own and cycled on. I know I should have ignored their comments but I was gripped by 'cycle rage' and felt compelled to answer back. Shortly after, I meet my nemesis in the shape of a red light. Unlike a lot of cyclists, I stopped and patiently waited for the light to turn green. The youths then caught up with me and shouted once again in my direction. I looked at one of them with an expression of utter distain. Enraged by my barefaced contempt for his behaviour, he threatened to give me, and I quote, 'A Paki slap.' I must confess, at this point I didn't know whether to laugh or cry, so I merely shook my head at the bizarre situation. Why bizarre? He was around eight years of age. Eventually, I did admonish him for using racist language and duly cycled on, once the lights changed. I did wonder, though, as to the level of education he was receiving in the borough of Hackney. I guess MP Diane Abbott was right when she insisted her kids were educated privately.

At this point, it is only fair I mention that cycling on the streets of London seems to attract unwanted attention from all manner of people – regardless of racial origin. Over the past few years, I have had the following thrown at me: eggs, a big chunk of boiled bacon (I kid you not), a lump of ice that was big enough to sink the Titanic and numerous cans of drink. A volley of oral abuse invariably accompanies these from the thrower. So why are these objects hurled at me? I honestly have no idea. For some reason, the sight of a skinny, tracksuit-wearing, late thirties guy seems to trigger a Neanderthal response from less enlightened members of society. Suffice to say, I have learnt to keep one eye on the pavement whilst dodging the never-ending barrage of flotsam and jetsam.

I have listed these few incidences here for the reader to see that ignorance of a couple's relationship comes in many forms. The number of black girls that do kiss their teeth at Margaret (normally they are teenagers or in their early twenties), or give her the benefit of a 'how dare you' type of stare, is quite high but I put this down more to plain stupidity than outright racism.

We now come to the segment of the book that relates to transport, especially the ordeal that is public transport. I was tempted to write a whole chapter just about my experiences coming back on the number 279 bus from Seven Sisters tube station, but on second thoughts I will lump all my experiences together. This is the 'avoid public transport unless you are feeling brave' part of our story.

Exhibit one: I was returning home from football around 9.30pm on a Saturday night. I boarded a busy 279 bus and sat down. Opposite me were two Somalians (a teenage boy and girl). After about thirty seconds the boy scowled at me and demanded that I move. 'But why?' I politely enquired, comfortable in my cheap but cheerful bus seat.

'Because that seat is for Somalis only.'

What? I thought to myself. I know Ken Livingstone is in favour of encouraging diversity on the buses but is this not a step too far? My response, as usual, relied on my smart-arse type of humour: 'Really, I can't see any signs to say that?'

This, as you may well imagine, only infuriated the guy. He then accused me of 'not liking black people.'

Hmm, I ruminated again, just by sitting down and cracking a one-liner, this guy has me down as some kind of rabid Nazi. Realising that another flippant comment was probably not the best course of action, I changed my angle of attack and outflanked him. 'Here is a picture of my wife and kids,' I proudly said, as I showed him the passport sized snapshot of my family that sleeps in my wallet. As if by a miracle the man was cured of his prejudice. Instead of remaining angry, he answered: 'Respect man.'

To be honest his apology actually pissed me off more, as he was once again presuming to know me – this time on the basis of a picture. A picture that could have come from a magazine.

So, why did he level an offensive allegation towards me? Because he could not see past the punk rock clothes I was wearing.

Moving swiftly on to Exhibit number two: I was riding the same bus, on a different night, and a white man of around thirty years motioned to me as he was about to get off. Being an approachable sort of chap, and expecting an innocent exchange of pleasantries, I inclined my head in his direction. Instead of a pleasantry, he said: 'I don't like Nazi types like you.'

'Like me?' I replied.

'Yeah,' he slurred, as he pointed at the badges on my leather jacket. I should explain here that the six badges I was wearing were: Anti-Pasti, The Fits, Oxymoron, Slime, Blitz and Oi! The first five are all punk bands for those not familiar with the punk scene. The sixth one denotes the music I like. Oh dear, I sighed to myself, here we go again. Reaching once more for my picture of the family I brandished it before him. 'I must be a bit confused then?'

After my comment he looked fuzzily at the picture. Expecting him to apologise, I stared at him straight in the eye. Instead, he shook his head a few times and stumbled off the bus. Maybe I was silly in expecting an apology, but it does annoy me when people freely cast aspersions towards people with no evidence. Each and every one of us, including me, is guilty of this to a degree. It is human nature for our brain to process the images our eyes see, but at some point intelligence and the 'innocent until proven guilty' line has to stick.

Exhibit number three: Another trip home from football brought an unfortunate incident with a white guy of around forty years of age, at the time I was formulating this chapter. I was on the bus as usual and quietly minding my business. Next minute, this bloke asks me if I am Scottish, on account of my tartan bondage shorts. I replied in the negative and then tried to explain I'm a punk. He couldn't understand the concept of a punk rocker being around in 2006 and politely asked me 'are you some kind of a c★★t?' He followed this up with; 'you're as bad as the niggers'. I don't get this. I'll never understand how people can come out with this rubbish at the drop of a hat. By associating me with such an offensive word he was, in effect, calling me a 'Rock and Roll Nigger', as Patti Smith sung back in 1978 when she empathised with the plight of the racially downtrodden. Going by his comments, perhaps bed and breakfast owners should update their advertisements to include; 'No Blacks. No Irish. No Dogs...and no Punk Rockers?' It seems we are all deemed suspicious these days.

When I told him off for using such language, he also didn't comprehend why I was upset, due to my being white. To be fair, he was probably also wondering why I wasn't upset at being called a c★★t, but a discussion as to why English manners have declined will have to wait for another day!

Why is it when racists come out with comments such as these they automatically assume you will agree with their racism just because you have the same skin colour?

Exhibit number four: This time I was on a Victoria Line tube on the way to Seven Sisters – again returning from Wolverhampton – when I overheard a group of young girls abusing (as I later discovered) a Nigerian lady. The three girls were complaining about her skin tone being 'too dark' and 'ugly' because of it. They carried on for a couple of minutes and I could see the lady was getting upset. Feeling morally superior, via my six pints of cider earlier in the day, I leapt to the lady's defence: 'Leave her alone, you are so rude and ignorant.'

Boy, it was as if I had lit the blue touch paper. The three girls got to their feet as one and started berating me with comments like: 'What do I know about it?' and how I should 'Shut up mister, before we start on you.' Personally, I thought they had already started on me by the act of standing up and shouting, but I let the technicality pass. Instead, I tried to explain how their words were stupid and ignorant, but they wouldn't have it. By this stage I was sobering up rapidly and my courage was going down the pan!

Luckily, the lady whose assistance I went to started to speak up to defend me, and told them off for not respecting elders. Unfortunately, her words didn't do the trick and the girls were becoming steadily more irate. Thinking quickly, I resorted to the only option I could think of – I brandished my picture.

This time it failed to do its magic, and they merely knocked it from my hands. It did, though, buy me some time and the tube pulled into Seven Sisters. Both the lady and myself got off and we made our way to the over ground train platform (I was too scared of the bus after past experiences) shaking our heads at the stupidity of the girls.

It was whilst we waited for the train that the lady told me she was Nigerian. She went on to tell me she found the girls' attitude towards skin colour deeply disappointing, especially as they were so young.

The supreme irony of this story is that all the girls were mixed race!

Maybe, then, I am wrong, if this snapshot of our times is anything to go by, maybe mixed race children are confused about their colour?

The whole issue, though, of skin tone is shown up by the depressing habit of skin bleaching. Margaret told me about this many years ago and I now realise it is quite a common occurrence in Africa. I find this very strange and yet another sad legacy from the days of slavery.

The mixed race girls on the tube were merely echoing words from centuries ago – when 'mulatto' children were allowed to live closer to their slave master's house on the plantation. What on earth happened to their education that they hate that part of them, that part of their heritage that has coloured their views on life?

Margaret's niece Whitney also confirmed this fondness for light colour skin when she told me our daughter Olivia was 'lucky,' as she has the colour that 'black boys go for.' Lucky! I am sorry but I do not consider the prospect of my daughter being treated as a trophy as something to look forward to. Having dark black skin should not be seen as a negative – although that is easy for me to write as a white guy.

To classify someone as inferior because of their skin is corrosive and damaging to the mental well-being of all black people. And yet, this colour 'grading' continues to invade many different areas of life. Take the issue of dating; a black female friend of mine once told me she refused to go out with a man because he was 'too dark.' She went on to say 'imagine how black the children would be.' I have no idea as to the percentage of people who share her opinion, and can only hope she is in the minority. Unfortunately, though, ignorance and denial are hard obstacles to overcome.

Then again, is not liking dark-skinned black men/women something to be concerned about? Surely, it is the same to my admitting I do not find mixed race, Asian or white women attractive? Actually I think there is a difference. Although I have expressed a preference for black women I do not hate my own or anybody else's skin colour. I may not 'self-love' but I am a long way from self-hating.

In contrast to this, I give you the example of Rodney. Rodney is a Zambian colleague of Margaret's at the care home. A polite man, Rodney is the type of guy who exudes good vibes and friendliness to anyone he meets. Margaret naturally gets on well with him, so well in fact that she has managed to convince him to laugh at her jokes and impersonations (this truly makes him an ethnic minority!) As a result of their developing friendship she showed him a picture of our children. With barely a second glance at the picture, he congratulated Margaret on their avoiding the 'curse' of being dark skinned.

Surprised by his words, Margaret pressed him as to why he saw black in this negative way. Rodney explained that his opinions were formed during his childhood in Zambia. Whilst at school, he witnessed black children fighting and dividing themselves over ethnic and tribal groupings. However, the mixed race kids at the school were not part of this and instead got on with everyone. Rodney, therefore, mistakenly came to the conclusion that black equals trouble. As a result of this, he turned against his own skin. He went on to tell her she should never 'go back' now she has mixed race children. To compound this, he added that, if I was to die early, she should find another white man to live with because her life had progressed so much by her marrying me.

Whilst I would agree Margaret has had a bit of luck regarding her choice of husband, this is not due to my race. Margaret was deeply puzzled by his words, as Rodney is black himself. He saw blackness, his mirror reflection, and viewed it as something to be ashamed of. How peculiar, you may be excused for thinking, but this was only the start of Rodney's confession. When Margaret informed him that I only find black women attractive he was dumbfounded and told her I should stay away from them – for my own good. He also told her that our children should marry white people if they want to progress in life. Developing this theme, he boasted how all his cousins had actively sought out mixed race or white women to have children with or to marry – just so they could remove the 'blackness' from their family tree! Poor Rodney had allowed his self-consciousness to be infected by this self-loathing to such a degree that he sees black as something to be eugenically eradicated. Even the BNP aren't this radical when it comes to race!

When Margaret told him he was stupid to come out with such nonsense, he retaliated by pointing out she was doing the same thing by marrying me. This did not go down well with my dear wife; she found it bizarre in the extreme that she was presumed to be with me just so she could have some nice brown babies. What a crazy, mixed-up world we live in. What is worse, is that when Margaret informed Rodney of our intention to write about this incident, he was proud of it. Proud! How very strange.

Then again, can we really blame people like Rodney when the media bombard us with negative images of black beauty in general? I would wager that the self-loathing felt by some black people has its roots in the number of surveys done that list the world's 'one hundred best looking babes.' Every time these come out, I study such lists with interest hoping to see the divine sex goddess Serena Williams included. Every time she is ignored!

Instead, the list always comprises of ninety odd white women, a handful of Asians and Naomi Campbell. Can we really be surprised if a percentage of black people hate their skin when this image of beauty is constantly fostered onto us? I have heard numerous black women complain about these surveys, as they rightly feel let down by the inference that their race is inferior to white. I am very sympathetic to this line of thought, for obvious reasons. Then again, my sympathy soon evaporates as, more often than not, the very same women label white men who seek black partners as 'sexual perverts' or 'exotica chasers'. Sorry love, but you can't have it both ways.

It is truly depressing that, in 2007, so many of us cannot see beyond simple skin tone. What is equally depressing is that I would not have been aware of these issues before I met Margaret. By marrying her, I accepted that I would need to learn more about where her family were from and the culture that spawned her. This does not mean that I want to be black. No, I just want to understand her more.

Another point regarding skin bleaching is that the men and women who do it are trying to fit an image of European beauty. The idea seems to be; the whiter you are, the more accessible you will appear to a white audience and/or employer. The irony here is, whilst black people are bleaching their skin white to resemble caucasians, white people are injecting collagen into lips and buttocks to look 'blacker'! Well hello, someone has got it wrong. I suppose, in some ways, we should view these developments as a positive, as each is admiring the other's appearance. Who knows, they may eventually understand more about the history behind the skin/collagen, but it still strikes me as somewhat peculiar.

To continue the theme, I have a number of white friends who are married to black women. Like Margaret, all of them are dark-skinned. Yet still the myth persists that white people prefer light-skinned black women. Doubtless some do but broad generalisations, apart from the ones I have used myself in this book, are often wrong. To balance this up though, I have noticed how most non-white models in clothing brochures tend to be mixed race these days. Maybe there is some truth, then, in the idea that a light-skinned 'black' image is easier on the eye, for the ad-men at least?

I think the rationale behind this is that a mixed race person perfectly demonstrates how integrated we have become in England. It's not true, of course, but having a plethora of mixed race people on display puts off the debate of how 'integrated' we are for another day. Until that day our organisations can pretend we live in a multicultural melting pot where we are all 'colour-blind'. Oh, if only life was so simple.

A much neglected part of 'racism' in England is the degree of animosity towards those of mixed race – the fastest growing minority group in the UK. Whereas before they were classified as black, they now have a racial identity all of their own. As a consequence, they seem to suffer prejudice both from the white racists, who lump all non-whites together, and black people who view them as competition – due to their dominating of 'diversity' positions in jobs or adverts. This is so hurtful, as children cannot help having the colour the advertisers like in their ads. Mixed race people, subsequently, are more likely to suffer racism from society in general, helped, no doubt, by this misguided intolerance towards them.

This prejudice is kept under the skin and displays itself in ways not immediately apparent. For instance, I frequently hear comments regarding mixed race children with white mothers, who are sneered upon for not knowing how to cream their child's skin or braid their hair. However, when I see black children with untidy hair they are allowed to go about their business without the same level of scorn. Fair?

I, myself, am very conscious of this, and always make a big effort to ensure my kids are not looked down upon purely for their appearance. Sure, they have a white father, but this should not single them out for abuse.

Another area that strikes me as a bit strange is the hostility towards black celebrities. I will never forget when I heard a friend of Margaret's berating BBC newsreader Moira Stuart for 'selling out'. What did she mean I wondered? Margaret informed me it was because she spoke in a voice that carried no hint of where her ancestors came from. In other words, a typical BBC newsreader's accent. What on earth was the poor lady supposed to do? Perhaps it would be more 'street' if she said: 'Dis is de news at 6.00. De word on de street is dat Gordon Brown is newly elected in da house.'

Nah, can't see it, can you?

I don't see why your voice has to reflect your heritage. If it means you can get on and develop a good career, why should you be penalised for having the talent and strength of character to escape 'ghetto mentality' culture? I will never understand the unwritten law that says black people can only succeed if they stick at what they are perceived to know about. Why should black children have this put on them from an early age? Just because you are a black boy your choice of occupation should not be just footballer or rap artist. You should have the support of both your teacher and peers to be anything you wish to be. Instead, it has become a modern trend for certain black 'communities' to ridicule individuals, who escape poverty via their talent, drive, or ambition. A trend largely imported from America.

And, of course, the number one insult would be the 'coconut' slur. This is so wrong, for these people are not acting white. No, they are acting clever. Barack Obama, the mixed race USA Presidential elect candidate, is the latest high profile non-white person to face this abuse. Golfer Tiger Woods also had similar problems a few years back, when he refused to be labelled as black.

So why, then, are these black men and women who achieve something with their lives subject to ridicule from others? Part of the reason is the self-loathing I mentioned earlier in the chapter and part of it is economic jealousy – the politics of envy – historically the preserve of the working-class. The perception seems to be that to be poor is to be black. Granted many black people are poor but, rather than denigrate those who escape from the bottom rung, we should instead celebrate their achievement.

God knows it is hard enough for black people to overcome white racism in the world, without adding to it with these self-imposed barriers to success.

I am also puzzled why famous black men who have white partners are sometimes looked down upon by black women. The usual comment I hear is that they have lost touch with their 'roots'. Sad. So what if they marry or date white women – it is their life.

I have read elsewhere that a lot of this animosity is down to basic sexual jealousy. The argument goes that, because black men are seen as home territory for black women, these females get upset when 'their' property is broken into and 'stolen'. Whilst I accept this is a contributory factor, I don't think it tells the whole truth, for, if sexual jealousy was the prime mover for this attitude, why is it that Margaret and I get the same put downs and problems from black women? If it was a simple matter of jealousy then, surely, it should be white women who would be angry at me for dating outside of my race?

As it happens, neither of us have ever had any problems from white women. Likewise black men, whilst they do tend to give Margaret some nasty looks, have also generally stayed silent. Why black women react in this way I just don't understand. It cannot be sexual jealousy in our case as I would not be seen as 'their' property. At best I could maybe qualify as a weekend holiday home. Logically, they should be happy that a black woman has found a white man to go out with, as it takes Margaret out of the equation when it comes to available black men.

Sadly, Margaret and I have discovered that logic has no bearing on the level of hostility meted out by black women to black people who date outside of their race. Yet again, I feel it is the 'selling out' idea being applied to the world of relationships. Black people are wrongly criticised for 'abandoning' their colour by finding personal happiness elsewhere.

In my humble opinion, I think this mentality betrays a lack of collective self-confidence in the black women who express such views. I shall explain. If all you can see is rich and famous black men going out with white women, it probably has a subliminal effect on the brain, by telling you that white equates to beauty and that black is the opposite. Conversely, the numbers of famous white men who date/marry black women are notable for their absence, with the likes of David Bowie, Boris Becker, Billy Bragg and Bob Dylan very much in the minority.

It is a sad fact that successful and powerful men generally have the pick of the female gene pool. If you don't believe me, how many less than stunning wives have you seen in glossy magazines like *OK!* or *Hello*? So, because these stars tend to go for the stereotypical blondie type, physical attractiveness is, therefore, associated with white, leading to negative opinions of black skin. This is ably shown via Margaret's discussion with Rodney just a few paragraphs before, or the girls on the tube train who associated black with ugly. Now, this idea is obviously stupid to anyone with half a brain but it is a belief that slowly, imperceptively perhaps, creeps into people's thought processes. Doubtless, no-one would admit to this, and it is only a half-baked theory I have dipped my toe into, but I personally feel it has some validity.

Racism and ignorance comes in many shapes and guises. I sometimes wonder, though, if our law enforcement organisations/Trade Unions/media are aware of them all. I pose this question because of an experience my Muslim friend Asif had at work, just after the September 11 attack on America. He was involved in an incident whereby he felt his religion had been verbally insulted by another member of staff and duly complained to the union. Bizarrely, he was told they could do nothing about it as the person who made the comment was black and, therefore, 'It is virtually impossible for a black person to be racist.' Aside from the sheer stupidity of this answer, is it not worrying that blinkers often come down when anything of a racial nature is mentioned?

Quite clearly the union official has not done his homework on this complicated subject. Margaret informs me that most Africans she knows admire two black historical figures; Idi Amin and Robert Mugabe. Why? Idi Amin for his expulsion of the Ugandan Asians in the 1970s and Mugabe for his land reform policies in Zimbabwe over the past few years. Both policies had their roots mired in pure racism and yet both policies have been largely marginalized or excused by those leaning towards the left.

Even I have heard complimentary words regarding 'affable' old Idi from those Africans I number amongst my friends. I tried to explain he was a dictator in the mould of Pol Pot or Stalin but they have none of it. Basically, he put Uganda on the political map so his crimes are acceptable to many black Africans – whatever the consequences for innocent people. Still impossible for a black person to be racist? Another example of this racial confusion was found in *The Observer* dated March 3, 2007. Richard Stone, one of the

131

panel from the Stephen Lawrence inquiry, was quoted as saying that 'Racism is not in the head of black people, it's in the head of white people.' Wrong, everyone possesses this disease; it's just that some are in denial of its presence. The difference is that white people are more likely to be in positions of power. A power that gives them the means to exploit this racism. Black people can generally only affect individuals such as Margaret and I.

I repeat my statement from the opening page of this chapter: black people talk about issues of race far more than white people do and are acutely aware of the harm it can cause. I actually think this can be a double-edged sword. It is fine for people to discuss/write about the issue just like any other. What it should not be used for, though, is a debating vehicle for the reiterating of stereotypes. I appreciate that, within these pages, I may have contributed to this, but I am only trying to show readers how it affects the everyday lives of people who are in mixed marriages in England.

Up until now, I have largely concentrated on the black side of the racist/ignorance thread. I would be foolish to think the opposite does not happen. Again, I will now recount some of the experiences I have had over the past few years.

On the way to football, I overheard a group of white men talking about how they find it wrong that they cannot refer to people as 'Niggers' and 'Paki's' anymore. They were only around twenty-five years old.

Another tale of racism, I can remember, happened around six years ago when I was sitting in the stands at the Crystal Palace football ground. I noticed a group of ten Wolves fans gesticulating at the Palace fans with a full range of Hitler salutes. The police, fans and stewards did nothing. Were they blind or merely turning a blind eye?

Staying in the football field, Wolves used to have a South Korean inter-national winger called Seol, a moderate player who had flashes of brilliance but who sometimes looked lost in the helter-skelter world of Championship footie. The problem is I lost count of the number of times I heard, 'Give it to the chinky' or 'chinky chonky' or 'pass it to the dog eater' at matches. For some reason, the football authorities ignored this, despite their long running 'Let's Kick Racism out of Football Campaign.' It seems to me that racism aimed at South Koreans is just accepted as part of the game. A game that cries foul when racism is directed at black people – such as the Aragones racial slur on Thierry Henry – can still be relied upon to bury its head in the sand when needs must.

I also feel that white racism has now become more devious, more cunning and is, therefore, more underground. Just as how the BNP changed their tactics and tried to become respectable; the same method is largely being adopted at a lower level. I think this is because the white racists accept they are racist and know their views to be abhorrent to the majority population. They then have no option but to hide their prejudices within. The tragic murder of the Liverpudlian black youth, Anthony Walker, in 2005 reminds everyone that this cancer still exists.

So why do these white racists hate enough to kill? I have always felt it is jealousy. The white underclass, (and normally it is the underclass class who kill – middle-class racism is more benign and sugar-coated) I think, feel that they are being left behind in a constantly changing world where their 'identity' is under 'threat' from new arrivals. Whereas, traditionally, this community had a passion for education and hard work, this is now sometimes replaced with hostility and anger towards outsiders. As a consequence, they are at risk of believing the far-right poison that spreads the idea of immigrants gaining better jobs, housing and cars, and feel disenfranchised. They see themselves as the losers in the game of wealth being played out on our streets. Any misconceived resentment they may be feeling could easily be triggered by an innocuous sight – the judge in the Walker case said the two white murderers were 'affronted' by the sight of a white woman in the presence of two black men. To the detriment of all, women are often seen as the 'property' of the male from whichever race they come from.

I mentioned earlier in the book a white female colleague of mine who generally only dates black men. She has had to put up with the racism that the learned judge referred to. Many a time, she has been labelled a BMW (Black man's woman). She also told me a story about a white male friend of hers who was dating a black woman. They were sitting in a pub having a quiet drink when a white male threw a bag of peanuts at the man shouting: '..and they are for your monkey.'

I write again: generally it is the working/underclass who commit such offences. A generalisation I know, but it is the working class who suffer most from a lack of decent education.

Rather than acknowledging the value of studying, and trying to improve their own lot through blood, sweat and tears, the white underclass would rather attack perceived enemies i.e; anyone who does not resemble them. Given their economic poverty, this is often the only way such people can fight back against class-driven British society. And, oh yes, despite the protestations from government, we are still a class-divided society, ruled by a coterie of middle-class do-gooders.

And what seems to fascinate the middle-classes more than anything else? Race. Especially when it's kept at arm's length. This is best highlighted by the type of white, middle-class dinner party guest, who is intrigued by anything of an 'ethnic' nature and who elevates it onto a higher plain. Until, that is, they move in next door to them. Then, they replicate the upper working-classes, sell up, and move to predominantly white areas to preserve their 'liberal' whiteness from ethnic 'contamination'. What a bunch of patronising BBC jerk off merchants! How far will these people go to avoid genuine black and Asian people? The sea? I guess it is alright to read about Bangladeshi people via Monica Ali's *Brick Lane* and Yoruba people through Helen Oyeyemi's *The Icarus Girl*, but something else altogether to mingle freely with the subject matter of their books. Wankers, as even Margaret has learned to say.

Of course, this racial emphasis on where to live also works the other way and I have heard many black people say they will not live in a white neighbourhood, as it must automatically be 'racist'. Strewth! House buying is hard enough without having to worry about all these outside factors.

And what about the black middle-classes? Are they as fascinated by white working-class culture? Do they sit down of an evening and debate the cultural merits of the skinhead movement over a glass of claret? Or perhaps they discuss Slaughter and the Dogs English punk song 'Where Have All The Bootboys Gone?' and wonder as to the nostalgic feel of steel toe capped boots? Then again, in the PC language of modern day England, they may see the song as a yearning for white cultural identity from spotty kids disenfranchised from our 'inclusive' society?

I have begun to realise, though, that black and Asian racism is not frowned upon to the same degree as white. It is almost as if the very act of being racist or prejudiced is seen as a white only issue – as demonstrated by the Asif incident or the Richard Stone quote. However, the examples I have listed confirm everyone has the potential to be as racist or ignorant or prejudiced as each other. Why, then, do I get the feeling that when black and Asian people utter offensive words, they can be passed off as just that – offensive – without being condemned for the prejudice that lurks beneath?

Numerous times I heard comments at work along the lines of 'these Asians, they don't wash' or 'these Jamaicans are a bunch of criminals'. No-one, including me I shamefully admit, said anything to the people expressing such views. Why the silence? Because the people that came out with these comments were invariably either black or Asian. Because of their ethnicity, I was scared to confront openly bigoted views. Views I would have questioned if uttered by white tongues.

So, because of our one dimensional, ingrained attitude as to who can be racist, we condone black or Asian people who come out with such comments

– normally against one another. The people that spout such rubbish know that their words, if censured at all, can easily be dismissed under the banner of being 'hot headed' or 'outspoken' – arguments I have heard Margaret use herself.

Then again, does this line of thought have credence? For years, I have heard Italian/Spanish/South American footballers excused excesses on the football pitch due to their having 'Latin' blood and being temperamental because of this. Are footballers really so different from the rest of us?

Whatever, I do wonder if we, as a nation, are ready to confront the differences that are slowly beginning to come to light in our sometimes fractured communities – especially as we continually emphasise the differences within them by promotion of multicultural political dogma.

Personally, I feel the multicultural agenda has been hijacked by both the Left and Right of British politics, as each tries to assert its authority over the other. The Left believes that other cultures are superior to England's, whilst the Right feels hostile to 'alien' influence and of being 'swamped' by hordes of immigrants. Unfortunately, they have both forgotten that innocent people, such as Margaret and I, are caught up in their stupid 'robust' debates. Too many people are using the multiculturalism topic as a vehicle for spreading their respective political views. Real divisive issues, such as faith schools, are allowed to progress relentlessly whilst our elected leaders waffle on about 'rooting out' extremism and the like. This kind of political rubbish needs to be ditched and replaced by good old common sense.

But does anyone really think the government is genuine about wanting to tackle the difficult and broad issues as to why people hate each other despite living in the same city? I don't, because the answer would be unpalatable for them. But to be fair to the government, what can they do to change the minds of people who exhibit blatant racism? How on earth can they change the attitude of the Polish Nazi skinheads, as witnessed by me, who get their kicks out of abusing black people at Seven Sisters train station?

Multiculturalism can and does work in Britain, but on a personal not political level. This fact is blatantly obvious to any who mix at grass roots. However, by attempting to impose multiculturalism on people who often don't want it, our politicians are ignoring a fundamental English character trait; we are stubborn and resent leaders telling us what to do. This point was rammed home to me on August 25, 2006, when an ITV teletext poll showed that 97 per cent of people thought diversity bad for Britain. It may be unpalatable for the 3 per cent who welcome diversity, but we have to understand why 97 per cent feel this way in order for society to progress. It is time to talk.

Margaret

For me, this is the saddest chapter to write as it reminds me of how stupid human beings can be to one another. It hurts me even more to admit I used to be one of those stupid people. Although, after reading the next few pages, you will begin to realise why I began to feel the way I did about white people. It is not an excuse, just a small mitigating factor.

Whilst I was living in Nigeria, racism was never an issue. Sure, we had a few white people living there but to the best of my knowledge, at least, there were no problems of a racial nature. In Nigeria, we like it and consider it flattering that a person chooses to live with us side by side. If they genuinely like and respect our culture, we warm to them even more. Bobby is a living embodiment of this, as West African women immediately take to him once he tells them he loves the African way of life. I guess I stirred his pot but Bobby really does have an empathy with African women. Sadly, I was not given the chance to develop an empathy with the English.

When I returned to England in the middle 1980s, I was disappointed and shocked at the hostility shown towards me. For the first time in my life, I had to look in the mirror and see how the majority of English people viewed me – a black woman. I had, almost overnight, lost my identity of Margaret and my colour was now my single most defining feature.

It is sad for me, even today, to list the racism I endured when I came to this country, but I like to think that England is now a better place for the suffering people such as I went through. You want proof? I will now take you on a journey through some of the most miserable days of my life.

When I returned home to England, my sister Anne and I went to live with Mrs Anderson in Brighton. All was pleasant for a few weeks. Then, out of the blue, her natural son Brian announced he was having a party. He told Mrs Anderson he could not invite her because, 'If she came she would invite those two niggers.'

This was very upsetting for Mrs Anderson, as she really did treat the two of us like her own. I remember her crying at length over Brian's comments. Suffice to say, she never went to the party. The 'funny' thing about this is that I really did not know what the word 'nigger' was. Growing up in Nigeria, this word is not used at all – a lesson for America and England to take heed of, I feel. I really don't understand the recent phenomenon of black people calling other black people 'niggas'. For me, this is disgusting and the word should not be 'reclaimed' just because it is fashionable to use in rap circles. It is offensive pure and simple and should not be used under any circumstance.

So, if nothing else, England has managed to broaden my vocabulary. I now know what the words wanker and nigger mean. I was better off being innocent.

Another time, I recollect Mrs Anderson's son-in-law visiting us in Brighton. He said to me, 'you sort of people smell.' He then went on to ask 'can you read?' and 'do you have newspapers where you come from?' At the time, I was bemused that someone had the nerve to ask such questions of me, and, in actual fact, I felt sorry for him as his attitude was so alien to what I had been told to expect from the English. I realised not everyone walked around in bowler hats and pinstripe suits, but basic manners and politeness I had taken for granted. This was not to be the last of my disappointments. I was finding every month that complete strangers would yell 'nigger' at me in the street, from the safety of the other side of the road. What petty, ignorant people, I thought, as I struggled to come to terms with their vindictive racism.

One of the worst cases I experienced was during my spell as a cleaner at the Iranian fish and chip shop in Brighton. Everyday I walked to work. Everyday the same gang of white children verbally abused me by calling me 'blackie' and telling me to 'go back to where I came from.' I put up with this for two months. Then, I snapped. Rather than turn the other cheek at their words, I instead chased after the group and cornered one of the boys in an alleyway. 'Who are you calling names?' I demanded.

This member of the master race responded by bursting into tears and whimpered, 'please don't hurt me.'

Bobby doesn't believe me as he types this, but I really did just let him go without further comment. Thankfully, after this the abuse stopped. I was learning in England that you had to stand up for yourself as no-one was going to come to your rescue.

I also remember another cleaning job I had, where my white colleagues abused me on a daily basis. They were at least a tiny bit more subtle than the young boys. During my break I used to sit in the canteen listening to them talking amongst themselves. The conversation normally went like this, 'did you see that TV programme last night, the one about the blackies climbing the trees?' Or, 'Did you notice their tribal marks when they danced round the pot.' Or, 'Those savages on the TV.'

It was all too much for me – a young girl studying hard and doing menial jobs just to survive. I broke down in tears. Luckily, a white woman from head office happened to notice my crying and asked what was wrong. In private, I confided to her and confessed to the abuse I was receiving from the other employees. To her credit, this lady consoled me, talked to the other cleaners, and ensured that the comments ceased. Despite this Pyrrhic victory, I continued to suffer, only this time my abuse was psychological, as I was 'sent to Coventry' for being a 'grass'. I was no longer just a nigger, I had moved up a level. Of course, nowadays, you would expect an employer to sack the people responsible for such behaviour but in the Eighties that response was still someway off.

On another occasion, I went to my local shoemaker. He was a pleasant enough man but he shocked me with what he must have thought was an innocent comment, 'It must be a great experience for you – to wear shoes for the first time?'

What can one say in response? Why did he ask such a question? It turned out that a documentary had been on TV the night before. The subject was a tribe of pygmies in Papua New Guinea who happened to run around naked – so presumably shoes were not an option. Just because I was black, he was lumping me in with them, despite Brighton being on the south coast of England and not the South Pacific.

I also had some bad experiences when I worked as a cloakroom attendant at a Brighton club called the 'Pink Coconut'. Whilst there, I worked under a white supervisor who was friendly enough, but who used to get close to me, just so he could ruffle my Afro hair. When I questioned him about this, he joked that he liked touching it and was curious to its feel. Indeed, he seemed fascinated by it – despite my pleas for him to stop. Around this time, Michael Jackson was very popular, so I was re-Christened 'Michael' purely because we shared an Afro hairstyle. The fact I was a woman and Michael a man was irrelevant, we were both black and that was all that mattered to him.

I mention these relatively trivial matters as it shows the environment I was working in. Although these people had the prejudices, it was me that was made to feel unfriendly if I didn't play by their rules and make fun of my own colour. Why should I have been compelled to tolerate *their* ignorance?

Matters at the club came to a head when a drunken white woman called me a 'stupid black', as I was working behind the counter. I responded to her: 'What did you say?'

She repeated her comment.

Showing my now legendary burst of anger, I leapt over the barrier, no mean feat as I am barely five feet tall, and chased her down the corridor. Unfortunately for me, she complained to my supervisor (the hair stroker) and I was dismissed on the spot for rudeness to customers. She, of course, was allowed to stay in the club.

All of the above events happened in Brighton, a place known for its tolerance of gays, but a tolerance obviously not extended to humble blacks. It was all too much for me to take in. I was becoming totally disillusioned with life in Britain and pined for my family. Unfortunately though, I had no option but to stick it out, as my studies came first. Gradually, my subconscious was beginning to see white English people as the enemy. They were calling me names, abusing my skin colour, and generally being disrespectful to my whole outlook on life. Slowly, without my even knowing it, I was withdrawing into myself. I was starting to hate white people.

The strange thing is, I had a lot of non-African female friends. But even amongst them, stereotypes and prejudice ran wild. I remember three of my white friends discussing the virtues of black men – especially their penis size. They used to tell me 'once you go black you never go back'. I know this is a popular saying but these women really believed it. They were using black men purely for sexual gratification, and didn't see a problem with this.

No doubt some black men would be perfectly happy being used this way, but what about those who are not? Why should black men be stigmatised with this sexual burden? Pity the poor black man who is more intellectual with regards his interests, and who would rather read a book than search out new sexual conquests. He is most at risk by this lazy stereotyping and prone to being called 'batty boy' because of it. What is so good about just being a piece of meat?

So I was a paradox; I disliked the English and yet socialised with them. I found nothing in their culture to respect and yet lived in their midst.

Reading this now makes me realise how confused I must have been. Bobby will never appreciate just how lucky he is that I managed to come through this stage of my life. If he had asked me out at this time, he would have probably got a punch in the face and a volley of abuse.

Please don't think I was an isolated case. When studying at university, I had a lot of Nigerian friends. We used to get together and bemoan the state of the white people in England, for to us the English were a nation of liars who had done nothing, apart from religion, for black people. We referred to them as 'uncooked chicken' with their 'pink skin'.

I should point out at this time that I was studying race, as part of my Economics and Social Policy degree, so most of my textbooks dealt with racial matters. I was also reading Malcolm X and beginning to see that black achievements had been airbrushed out of history by, as I saw them at the time, devious whites. For example, Mary Seacole has only recently been put on the same level as Florence Nightingale for her sterling humanitarian work in the Crimean War, despite both being around at the same time. The only difference is that one was white and one black.

Another example that registered with me, was a German explorer in the 1920s that discovered a sphinx in Egypt. Believing in the twisted ideas of the Thule Society – that white people were superior – he was horrified to see the sphinx had 'Negroid' features. He, therefore, chipped away at the nose to make it more European.

Everywhere I looked, it appeared white people were showing their true colours – a race of fraudsters who had got where they were on the sweat of others. Why was history allowed to be distorted for so long?

So there I was, discovering historically what being black meant, and, at the same time, having to fend off abuse from the street. Is it any wonder I was turning into a racist myself?

To make this situation even more bizarre, I remember being with a group of Nigerian students who were discussing Chinese people. I should explain that in Nigeria we often use the derogatory term 'chico people', when referring to the Chinese. My friends couldn't see how anyone could find a Chinese person attractive as they 'all looked the same.' I argued against this line of thought, and said we should not be so disrespectful towards another ethnic group. By denigrating the Chinese, another victim of white colonial aggression as I saw it then, we were distracted from attacking the real enemy: white people. The sheer hypocrisy of my thinking is hard to write down now, but it is important to confess one's sins and move on. I just give thanks to God that he helped me realise how stupid I was.

It should be admitted, though, that this anti-white sentiment still exists. Many of my African colleagues, at the care home I work in, still echo the prejudices I once displayed. Indeed the level of African hostility is so bad, I am amazed that white people in England still send their elderly and infirm relatives to such places.

Elsewhere, even well known black authors, such as Sista Souljah, refer to white people as 'devils' in their work. This is wrong and should not be excused just because we are part of a fragmented Black Diaspora. Respect goes both ways.

It was respect, too, that I was after and so I moved away from Mrs Anderson in Brighton and went to live in London for what I hoped would be a better life. The racism I had begun to experience moved with me too.

In London, I continued my studying at Middlesex University and developed many of my attitudes towards white people there. I was introduced to black book shops and started reading about the achievements that black people had achieved throughout history, such as Lewis Latimer (who perfected the light bulb filament) and Charles Drew (who developed the blood bank system in WW2.)

Up until this point, I had only ever been told about how Africans had been saved by the white man. Our inventions were watered down at best or, at worst, blatantly ignored. The fact that, even now, this may be news to some people, shows we still have a long way to go before we are treated as equals.

I did study history in Nigeria but, to my annoyance now, I found the subject boring as it concerned the ancient kingdoms of centuries ago. So I now attempted to catch up and cram centuries of black success into a few short months. With all this 'black power' knowledge flooding into my body, I found myself identifying purely with black people. For me, Black History Month didn't end on the last day of October – I was living it the whole year round.

Then again, my white peers at university didn't help matters much with their cynicism towards Africa as a continent. I can recall a fellow student commenting, 'I don't know why Africans complain about the West ripping off Africa. They had the resources yes, but they didn't know what to do with them until white people helped them out.'

To compound this attitude, I was also reading books confirming how the West ripped off Africa, by stealing its ancient artefacts and statues.

And what have we, as a continent, received back as way of compensation?

Live Aid.

Not enough to recompense us for centuries of abuse.

And even Live Aid is a controversial subject for Africans to swallow. Many Africans I know were annoyed at the attempts to alleviate suffering in Africa by Bob Geldof and his Live 8 shows. Some viewed him as a patronising colonial figure from the days of Empire – as if Africans could not help themselves, without him and his friends waving their guitars in the air.

For myself, I see him as a compassionate man who just wants to help fellow human beings. In the past though, I too would have looked down my nose at his efforts to help us as he came from the despised West.

When I was studying, I also read extensively about the slave trade and shed tears of anger at accounts of black slave women being raped by their white 'masters'. I was so angry. I just associated white people with violence and oppression against blacks. Everywhere I looked, such as in South Africa, I saw blacks being traumatised and subjugated by whites. The eyes of the world watched on in silence as 'my' people suffered.

During the '80s, I genuinely felt that white people were born in someway different from the rest of the population. It may come over as a bit

141

weird now, but I really thought they had hate genes inside of them that made them think they were superior.

At the time, I honestly couldn't understand how some black women voluntarily slept with white men – seeing it as an act of betrayal against our race. I used to stare and look down at black women who dated white men and pitied their families for the shame they had brought upon them. Reading this now it is an absolute miracle that Bobby and I came to be married.

So how on earth was I transformed from a white hater to a white lover? God, as you may expect me to say, played his role, as the scriptures do not teach racial superiority of any race over another. To be true to God, I had to be true and fair to everybody I came into contact with – irrespective of his or her colour. By harbouring evil thoughts, I was slowly slipping into the hands of the Devil.

During this earlier period of negativity, I am ashamed to write I lost my religious zeal. This is the wrong kind of book to discuss why, but I was let down by a family acquaintance, and so mistakenly took my revenge on the good Lord by ceasing to visit church. I was angry with God for making me feel this way and so was easy pray for the dark thoughts in my mind concerning race. I still believed in God and continued to read my bible but the passion had temporarily gone. I found myself looking at people for their colour alone and not their actions. It was only when I rediscovered my faith in God (around 1995), that I managed to shake off the prejudice I felt towards white people.

At the same time, I was becoming more politically aware. In Nigeria, our leader General Abacha was systematically ripping off ordinary Nigerians for his own benefit. In essence, he was displaying the same arrogance we had suffered under colonial rule, yet he was black.

I also read more about Uganda and was horrified at how Idi Amin treated both Asian and black Ugandans. He also was black. I started to realise it was individuals, and not necessarily races, that were evil.

In addition, western governments, prompted by a groundswell of opinion at grass roots level by both black and white, put pressure on South Africa to end its apartheid system. I was being forced to re-evaluate my negativity towards white people, as some genuinely seemed upset at the abuses committed against black South Africans.

Even when I looked back in history, I saw black leaders oppressing their own skin colour for the advancement of themselves. For instance, in Nigeria during the 1970s we had a 'problem,' as it was termed, with Ghanaian 'economic migrants' – owing to our booming economy at the time. Although millions had entered and lived peacefully in Nigeria, it was decided they should be forcibly deported from the country, with only a couple of months notice. This led to scenes of chaos as Ghanaians fled the hatred from fellow black Africans. Even today, the saying 'Ghana-must-go bag' applies to the particular type of bag they used to pack their possessions in, as they rushed to the borders.

How, then, could I logically hate white people with all the black v black aggression going on around the world?

As you can see, when Bobby came into my life, I had a lot of issues raging around my head. It was just his good fortune that he asked me out after I had re-found God. God helped me to re-evaluate life and, perhaps more importantly, he cleansed my soul of hate and made me open up to others.

And, let's face it, if God intended for races to live apart he would have placed black people on Mars, Asian people on Pluto and maybe left Earth for the whites! Instead he lumped us all together on the same planet. Without wishing to appear too simplistic, maybe it was a message from him for us all to mix in as one? Stepping out with a white man, therefore, held no fears for me, as my conscience with the good Lord was clear.

Poor old Bobby. He cannot understand how I could be such a swinger: one day I hated white people, the next I married one. I loved God, fell out with him and then considered being a nun! Where was my consistency? It appeared to him that I was being governed entirely by my emotions. Bobby, in contrast, is stable and just plods along with hardly any mood swings. I, however, like my raging emotions as they add depth to my character. For all that, I am glad my anger towards white people has now stopped, as there is no peace in being constantly angry, especially if that anger is directed at a whole race of people.

I have found, though, that some Nigerians, even today, still have this anger. An anger that can see a whole continent (Europe) written off as being decadent and morally depraved.

Of course, many Nigerians are perfectly willing to extend this ignorance when dealing with their fellow countrymen/women. I have an old friend – Sylvia – who is from the Ibo ethnic group (the biggest three in Nigeria are: Hausa, Yoruba and Ibo.) Despite Nigerians having a high level of education, some Yoruba people ask her if it is true that Ibo people 'eat each other?' I absolutely despair that this question is still asked. Why is this myth still knocking around? Education I guess has its limits. The answer can only come from the adults who spout such rubbish in their home. We all have a duty to tell our children that insults and myths like this are not acceptable anymore.

I also find it worrying that a lot of Nigerians are obsessed with the idea of people having light skin – as shown by the skin-bleaching epidemic. Having a mixed race child, I have had to get used to Nigerians complimenting my daughter on her 'lovely light complexion.' This always rankles with me.

I was also informed, by the mother of a friend, that she was disappointed I had married a white man. The reason for this disappointment was due to the highly likely event of my giving birth to mixed-race children. The lady in question told me she found their skin colour upsetting. I was tempted to ask her that, if she felt that bad about it, why on earth was she bleaching her own skin! The hypocrisy I have encountered is unbelievable at times.

On another occasion, I overheard two Nigerians in Nigeria, just a few metres from me, discussing if I was my daughter's mother, as I looked 'too dark' to be related. They were so wrapped up in their conversation, they seemed to forget I had ears and could hear their every word. They were rude, ignorant and plain stupid.

Yet another instance was when I went through passport control in Lagos. The passport checker asked me if I was married to a white man – on account of our daughter's light skin. I replied in the negative just to avoid any further questions. What relevance was it to my being allowed entry? He should have stopped being so nosy and 'minded his business' to use a popular Yoruba expression.

When I recounted this story to Bobby, he couldn't understand why I didn't answer truthfully to the clerk. He said he felt airbrushed out of the creation of our daughter. However, if I had confirmed the clerk's suspicions, I would probably have been asked for a bribe – as white equals money in the one dimensional mind of Nigerian passport checkers. I also did not desire the condemning look from the guy in question.

Bobby mentioned quite a few examples in his chapter about black racism/ignorance directed at him or us. This is an important part of our story that should not be neglected. I can give another incidence here. I was getting my hair done last year – at the lovely Phabs salon in Hertfordshire. One of the customers, a French lady of Senegalese origin, commented that '*all* white people are racist.' The owner of the shop and I replied that her statement was ridiculous. No, she insisted, she was correct.

'How do you know this?' I persisted.

She answered 'Because I only date white men so I know how they think.'

Err, hello, is Mr Brain in the house, or has he gone on a permanent vacation? How on earth could this woman, without a hint of sarcasm or irony, state that all white people are racist and yet, at the same time, choose to date them? We put it to her that if 'they' were that bad, why did she not date black men then? She didn't respond.

144

I state again: the myth is that mixed race kids are confused but this lady was more confused than any I have met.

Confusion over the role of black people, who live in predominantly white countries, is also an issue that needs addressing. It has become fashionable over the past few decades, for black to have acquired 'victim' status; that we are 'cursed' by having the black skin that Rodney was so against in Bobby's part of this chapter. It is noticeable that both whites and blacks have propagated this idea, in the vain notion that they are helping 'us'. How stupid. Instead of helping, this 'victim' idea has eaten away into the psyche of black people and acts as a ready made barrier and excuse for a person's own failings. Granted we still live in a racially unfair world, but I was not brought up to view my skin as a hindrance to success. By the same token, I am not a box for some lefty type to delve into whenever their 'diversity' points tally needs topping up.

My middle-class sister Kemi also had racial problems when she moved to Maryland, America, round about a year ago. Not, as you may imagine, from local red necks. No, her problems came from the black underclass who consistently labelled her 'jungle girl', purely because she came from Nigeria. Even now, people still ask her what it was like 'living in the jungle?' These people are obviously not aware that the standard Nigerian home is substantially larger than the average American one.

Of course, this has echoes of my own experiences when I returned to England in the 1980s, only my suffering was at the hands of white people and not fellow blacks. My poor sister has also been told that she doesn't speak proper 'American' as she has an African accent.

The irony is the very same people who allege this, litter their vocabulary with 'nigga this' and 'nigga that'. What is perhaps worse is that black Americans insist on calling themselves 'African Americans!' What a joke. My white husband knows far more about what it is to be African than these people do – and without the prefix 'English African.'

Quite frankly, this type of attitude shows that they have absolutely no idea of what it is to be African. They seem to assume that black American culture is the only black culture throughout the world. This is a perfect example of American arrogance – only this time from ordinary black folk and not the white neo-cons.

Because of her middle-class Nigerian background, dear Kemi also finds it hard to relate to these poor Americans as she aspires to more than a life on welfare. Again, they don't understand her for this and think she is acting white. What utter lunacy.

And yet, some black people still subscribe to the belief that we are 'one nation' with our 'brothers' and 'sisters' dotted throughout the world. It is time this belief was questioned and exposed for the lie it is. If anything, we are more divided over ethnicity than any other group in society. Hard to swallow maybe, but it is the truth nonetheless.

Strangely enough, the racism I had encountered in England came to a halt around the time Bobby asked me out. I suspect it had something to do with better race relations in society generally, but a small part of me thinks it is God's reward for my finding him once again.

However, just as I was being lulled into a false sense of security about the lack of racism around me, came an event that knocked me for six.

I was at a local petrol station, getting my tyres pumped, when I had a little dispute with the white attendant concerning where I had parked my car. I had apparently parked it in the way of a car waiting to get out – not that I was aware of this at the time. After complying with his instruction to move my car, despite the offhand nature of his request, I left the station to collect my children from school. Whilst I waited for my son, I silently seethed at the way this man had spoken to me. Feeling more and more frustrated, I decided to return to the petrol station on the way home with the intent of lodging a complaint against the attendant. It was whilst I was doing so, that the man lost his temper and told me to 'go back from where I had come from.'

At his words, I felt myself transported back to my cleaning job days and tasted bitter anger in my mouth. Understandably, I retaliated and said: 'Is that the level of education you have had?'

He then, unbelievably, did a reasonable impression of a monkey and asked me to 'look in the mirror.' I should stress that all of this happened in full view of two of his white colleagues, who did nothing.

Pissed off by his racism, I left the petrol station fuming and vowed to take the matter further. I opened my car door and calmed my now distressed children. Unbeknown to me, the man followed me and threatened: 'I will kill your kids if you go to the police.'

Being concerned for the welfare of my children, I quickly left the station and went home. Despite his warning, I called the police and they finally came round to see me the next day (after my MP had become involved).

After an internal investigation, the man was suspended from work and has since left the company's employment. I have not been told if this is because of my complaint or not but, I feel at least partly vindicated – even if the Crown Prosecution Service were unable to prosecute.

When I told Bobby about the abuse and threats, he offered to go round to the station and give the man a 'knuckle sandwich.' I was touched by

Bobby's response but I declined, as Bobby's fists would struggle to make much impression on a plate of strawberry blancmange.

I thought back after this event and tried to compare it with the experiences I had had as a cleaner. Whilst I was pleased my complaint had been taken seriously, I do wonder if we have really moved on as a society?

Racism nowadays is of a far more subtle nature than the 'Paki' or 'Coon' bashing that took place decades ago. These days, a smile is often the first defence of the racist minded. But what really lies behind the smile?

Summary

This has been a long hard slog of a chapter.

It is hard for Margaret to recount stories from her past – as we all like to leave skeletons locked away in the cupboard. It was also very brave of her to write about the person she once was – with her prejudice and hatred glistening in the sunlight.

Look beyond the depressing stories though, and a glimmer of hope shines through. It shows that however wrong a person may have been in the past, the future can be a totally different story.

This chapter has also demonstrated the strength of human character to overcome irrational hatred of people for the colour of their skin. Yes, it is fine to be curious of someone who does not resemble you, but, another altogether, to hate and distrust them for that reason.

What is striking to both of us, is that racism and prejudice are not left-wing versus right-wing issues. Everybody is prejudiced to a degree but some are just better at the art of camouflage. Some of those on the Right have a tendency to believe that black people are not as intellectual as whites, whilst many on the Left label black people as 'victims' – because they are black. Although diametrically opposed, both attitudes are demonstrating racial superiority theories that are odious and downright hateful, by viewing black as a hindrance.

Black people do not want to be patronised and have white liberal types pat them on the shoulder and pity them for having black skin. No, they just want a level playing field to compete in when it comes to jobs, housing or relationships. Margaret and I honestly believe that these liberal types are the biggest obstruction to healthy race relations in this country – with their outmoded, flawed and old-fashioned approach to matters concerning race. They need to see black people as people first and not causes to hang their hats onto.

Unfortunately, organisations such as The BNP and Socialist Worker, will try to exploit any differences between groups – be they race, class or political. Each group uses the same tactics to ridicule the other, each are quick to resort to violence if any dare question their views. Each is exactly the same. What I can't work out, is how come one (Socialist Worker), is not seen quite as bad as the other (BNP)? I don't understand this. The heroes of the respective parties; Hitler and Stalin, truly led parallel lives and were responsible for millions of deaths in Concentration and GULag camps. Majdanek or Kolyma, the end result is the same; starvation, forced labour and death.

It stands to reason, therefore, that Stalin and Hitler should both be listed in a dictionary as a definition of the word evil. The only tangible difference between the two of them is the speed with which their regimes were discredited. Hitler lost the war and the plot in May '45 whilst Stalin, for his actions in the war years, largely remained a heroic anti-Nazi figure for the Left until *glasnost* and *perestroika* under Mikhail Gorbachev in 1990.

But, as I say, it is deemed relatively acceptable to declare oneself a communist. Even in my circle of friends I have noticed this. I have a Wolves mate named Gareth who is proud of once being called a 'commie c★★t.' How ridiculous. People should be sufficiently aware of past history to feel embarrassment at being labelled either a Nazi or a Communist.

The fact is, Commies (Socialist Worker) and Nazis (BNP) exist only to oppose one another. Both ideologies are morally bankrupt and merely spread hatred and jealousy around the world. Oh, how I wish they would both go bust and leave the rest of us to get along without them. Failing that, maybe we should send the Socialist Worker members to Russia and the BNP types to Wales?

A crass and simplistic view of the world, I grant you, but one we firmly believe in. Our one hope is that others join our happy band and disregard the political dogma that serves no useful purpose other than to make lives miserable.

Whatever may happen in the future, Margaret and I genuinely feel that life in modern day England is better than it used to be, despite all the problems/stereotypes we have debated in this chapter. We can only hope that our children enjoy further improvements.

CHAPTER 14

The Roles of Men/Women in Yoruba and English Culture

Bobby

For years it was so simple; English men and women courted, married, had kids and accepted their roles in an average marriage. There was no discussion or soul-searching, as each was comfortable doing what seemed natural. The man went to work and earned a crust whilst the woman stayed at home to rear the children. This applied to both working and middle-class families – one of the few areas where the class divide didn't apply.

This type of marital relationship worked for decades but is now becoming less common. Many factors have influenced this: financial empow- erment of women, single-parent families, same sex couples, the list is endless. Whatever, families are now finding different ways of sharing the burden of parenthood.

Margaret and I will always believe that being part of a married couple is the best environment to bring up a child but it is a choice that only a parent can make. Increasingly though, we are finding more and more couples who are rejecting the traditional approach. This is proved by the startling fact that, according to the Social Trends report of February 2006, 42 per cent of children are now born outside of wedlock in England.

I suppose on this point my *Daily Telegraph*, rather than punk rock, leanings, show through. You would have thought that I, Mr Anarchy, would have wanted to destroy the marital status quo that has existed for so long. Not so, for I can see how two parents, rather than one, give a child a better chance in life. That is not to denigrate the one, just to emphasise that parenthood is a dual responsibility.

So, in our modern English society men and women now have these roles that are constantly changing, constantly in a state of flux. Are we any better for these changes? Let's take my parents and I as case studies. My dad worked full-time all his life whilst mother looked after the children and worked only part-time after she was married. She knew her main responsibility was to her children and acted accordingly. On the flip side, my dad knew he had to financially support his family and did so to the best of his abilities. Crucially, both were happy in their respective roles and appreciated one could not cope without the other. They complimented each other. My parents were nothing special in this regard – their lives being duplicated millions of times over throughout England.

However, Margaret and I have done things slightly different since the advent of children. When our son was born she was off work for around six months, believing that no one could look after him as well as his mother. Regretfully, she returned to work full time, leaving Joshua with a child-minder. I will always remember Margaret suffering from persistent guilty feelings at this point as she felt our son needed her around him at all times. I, however, disagreed, as I didn't want to raise a mummy's boy.

In the end, financial concerns won the day, so she bit her tongue and re-entered the nest of vipers that is the Civil Service.

Margaret also felt pressurised to return to work as she was expected to send money 'home' to Nigeria. By being out of the workplace, she was neglecting her duties under Yoruba culture – where women are not seen purely in the role of the stay-at-home mother. To this day, I can still hear her mother's cry of joy when she found out Margaret was returning to work – knowing that money would soon be flowing more regularly into the family coffers. In some ways, Margaret was seen as a 'cash cow' with her large udders ready to be milked by distant relatives.

Please do not misunderstand me here. Margaret wanted to help her family and understood her obligations, even if she does find it a bit demanding at times. I only mention this to illustrate the difference between the two cultures.

Of course, many white English women also return to work soon after birth but this is normally due to their *own* financial necessity and not for their extended family.

The child-minder arrangement we had for our son was satisfactory, but we couldn't shake off a nagging fear that we should have looked after him until he attended reception at the age of four. Therefore, when our daughter Olivia was born, we decided on a different approach. This time, Margaret had three years off work and we sacrificed little luxuries like holidays to enable her to do so. Then, from August 2005, I gave up work to become a househusband – a role I am enjoying even as I type these words. Margaret returned to work full-time and now supports me and occasionally her family.

Now I am off work, it is interesting to compare my experiences with that of my own parents. Margaret and I are not so constrained by the traditional roles of parents and are lucky enough to have the financial willpower to match our lifestyle to our income.

The reaction from family and friends to our changing roles has been fascinating to observe and it shows how regimented English society still is, despite the proliferation of different types of families. To start with, my family thought it a little odd, and I sometimes think my mother wants me to confess to being unable to cope with looking after the kids.

My sister also thinks I am strange (still, she has thought this for the past 39 years) and feels sorry for Margaret. She needn't worry, as Margaret just feels sorry for our children and their potato diet.

So, if my family think it's a departure from the norm, what do Margaret's parents think of our decision? Strange in the extreme! In Yoruba culture, it would be completely unheard of for a man to stay at home in the 'woman' role whilst the lady-of-the-house earned the cash. They just do not understand how I can do it. It also means that any financial gain they may have incurred, with both Margaret and I working, has disappeared for the next two years – the duration of my career break.

To be fair, Margaret's sister Anne and her Auntie in Brighton fully support our decision, as they could see the demands work had placed on me and the character changes I subsequently suffered from. They also recognized Margaret was fed up in the child-rearing role and needed a break.

Personally, I feel more couples should do what we have done as it gives the child/children the chance to experience both parents. I do not see why father should remain a figure that children see just for their bedtime story. Daddy should also be able to take them to school and help with their homework when they return. In reverse, a woman should not have to sacrifice a worthwhile career just so a man can keep his pride intact by being the main breadwinner.

On this issue, I do feel that Yoruba men need to be more relaxed about the way respective roles are assigned in marriages. I will never forget my ex-colleague Adebo who, when I informed him that I had to leave work early to prepare dinner for the children, said: 'Ah ah, that is why your wife married a European.'

Margaret, of course, was not impressed by this allegation. He should have said: 'Ah ah, the poor little mites, potatoes again,' a far more understandable comment.

Unfortunately, his attitude is sometimes replicated by African men in general. Our near neighbour Sheena, a pleasant, well-mannered, long-legged, Ghanaian woman, also told me, on this point, that an African man would not stay at home looking after the children. I find this sad as men have a very important part to play in the upbringing of their children. They have to be more than just portable sperm donors.

My not going to work has many advantages, despite what I said in the earlier chapter about the trials of parenthood, and I now enjoy being able to spend time with my children. I appreciate I am lucky to be able to do this and just feel sorry for those men and women who are not in our position.

So, now I spend all day in my pinny, cooking, cleaning and washing, do I feel that my manhood is under threat? I suppose I should say yes, given my earlier yearning for traditional male role models such as Bodie from *The Professionals* and Ian Botham. The bald truth is, I don't. I am perfectly happy playing the woman – although we haven't, at time of writing, exchanged underwear. Saying that though, the way I am putting on weight her pink bloomers may soon fit.

As an aside to our little story, an interesting cultural clash often rears its fat head whenever my weight is discussed. Since I gave up work, I have put on half a stone. A member of my family, seeing me for the first time in six months, remarked I was on the way to becoming obese. This is a distinct contrast to my father-in-law, who commented how healthy I looked because of my extra pounds. I wouldn't mind, but twelve stone is hardly over-weight for a man of six feet.

Many of my married male friends (in the Midlands) also think it is weird I have given up work, and cannot imagine doing the same thing themselves. They would much rather have control over any financial decision-making – due to their bringing home the bacon. I think they feel I am under the thumb for 'allowing' this to happen. Maybe I am, but the truth is I love being off work.

It does raise the interesting point, though, as to who rules the roost in any particular home. My male friends, as demonstrated above, really do identify purely with the earning role and, therefore, believe any financial decision-making is theirs to make alone. My dad also concerned himself with all monetary matters and left my mother to sort out only secondary issues – such as laying the dinner table.

The whole issue is one of control. The woman, via the experiences of my family and friends, is dependant on the man as he controls the income and expenditure.

But money is only one aspect of control. In my family the women, apart from matters to do with finance, are the dominant force. Superficially, it is the man who exerts control but, look beneath the surface and the illusion breaks down. To illustrate this, I give you my dear Auntie Doreen and Uncle John. My Uncle John, now retired, worked all his life and earned enough to enable my Auntie (who also worked) to enjoy her creature comforts at home. You might think then that he would have total control in their marriage. Not so. He barely has control over what goes in his stomach. By this, I refer to his habit of sneaking out into the kitchen, un-observed, to gorge himself on biscuits. The reason for his sleight of foot is that Auntie Doreen watches him like a hawk and restricts him to a biscuit a day. How depressing. You work hard all your life, retire and are then told off for enjoying a jammy dodger!

Even my own father has to constantly be on his guard when mother is around, in case she spies him snaffling a cream cake or two, although, in fairness, my dad wouldn't stop at two.

I find it so sad that English men have been reduced to this level of subservience. Where has the backbone of these men gone? I reckon it is all down to the evils of National Service. Where once they did what the Regimental Sergeant Major ordered they now jump to the tune of their wives.

Margaret can never imagine a Yoruba man having to do this. If a woman told a man that he could have no more yam, she would be laughed at and held up as an idiot. It is certainly true that, in Yoruba culture, the man is the head of the household and the woman's role is merely to support the man.

Sex is another area where the roles of Yoruba men and women are set in stone. Seeing as how Yoruba men are the dominant force, a Yoruba woman is unable to turn her husband down if he wants to 'get physical'. She can plea 'darling I have a headache,' but her plea will normally fall on deaf ears.

This is something that, for whatever reason, my wife neglected to tell me. I had to glean this interesting tit-bit of information from her dear sister. Whenever I mention this to Margaret, and advise her she should be doing more to regain her cultural roots, I am given one answer. She looks at me in disgust, rolls her eyes and says, 'I was born in London. I am English. If you want a docile woman like that you should live in Nigeria.'

I cannot win. Mrs '100 per cent Nigerian' is quick to change her nationality when it pleases her. Maybe, I should do the same and decree myself an honorary half-Nigerian? I would get more sex, true, but I would have the problem about what to put in my belly. And, let's face it, the number of times I eat in a week heavily outnumber the occasions I have sex. So, it's not a viable option; I guess I'll have to remain English.

The influence of other Yoruba family members also has a heavy bearing on our marriage. A good example of this happened just last year. Margaret was informed that her cousin Joyce was coming from Nigeria, and would be staying with us until she found somewhere of her own to live. The lady in question was twenty-seven and had not been back to England since she was a baby (she left for Nigeria when very young.) Neither of us had ever met her, and yet we were expected to share our lives with this person for sometime (for three months as it turned out). I am not necessarily against this, it's just that I would like a say in decisions that affect me. However, as they had already offered to help Joyce, we had no option but to comply with our instructions. Margaret's parent's reputation was on the line if we had refused.

So, I conceded, and had only one question to ask the young lady. 'Hello Joyce, do you like potatoes?'

Margaret

The role of a woman, in a marriage, is laid down by God. In the New Testament bible it states in Ephesians Chapter six, verse twenty-two: "Wives, be subject to your husbands, as to the Lord. For the husband is the head of the wife as Christ is the head of the Church, his body, and is himself its saviour." By taking this quote literally, some men are using the bible as a way of dominating a woman in her own home, knowing full well that one cannot argue with God. This is not what God intended.

So, how can modern-day Nigerian men and women comply with these biblical instructions and at the same time recognise we live in the 21st Century?

This is a difficult question and requires a lot of deliberation. Some of what I am going to write will doubtless be seen as controversial. This is not my intention. Being a proud Yoruba woman, I am very conscious not to offend my family and yet, at the same time, feel that elements of traditional Yoruba culture need to be questioned.

My motivation to debate this issue comes from seeing so many female friends/work colleagues of mine buckle under the pressures of living in England and also having to do all of the housework. In addition, they have to care for their children and all the responsibilities that this entails. They are all of Nigerian origin.

To give substance to my allegation, I give you the case of my Ghanaian friend Mammy. Upon completing a fourteen-hour shift at the care home, she returned home to find clothes strewn around the floor and dirty dishes piled high in the kitchen. Tired after her exertions at work, she asked her husband to do the housework as she wanted to go to bed. Without a word of complaint he complied. She told a Nigerian colleague of mine this and his reaction was one of horror, 'What? You asked your husband to do that!' After shaking his head at this 'unbelievable' story, he told her, 'I am so glad I am married to my wife.' I pressed him on this and he answered that he did not understand the concept of a Nigerian man doing housework if he was married.

My problem is, that by pointing this out, I am automatically dismissed again as being the mouthpiece of the 'white man'. Any opinion I have regarding the role of man v woman is influenced by my being married to Bobby. It is the 'Ah ah, that is why you are married to a European' argument again. Well no, it is not actually. I recollect many years ago a Nigerian man asking me if I was a feminist. I answered no at the time but maybe I am? Perhaps I am fed up with women being seen as the weaker sex and want us to be treated as the 'head' of the household as well? Surely two heads are better than one?

The problem with some Yoruba men in England is that they forget their wife does not have the support of the family – family in many cases on a different continent. So, whereas in Nigeria she may have numerous people to help with domestic chores, in England she suffers alone. It is this burden that needs to be addressed. In Yoruba culture, the woman also has a duty to work. Very few are content to play the role of the docile house wife who wiles away the hours, watching *Richard and Judy*, waiting for her husband to return. No, they are too busy slaving away cooking, cleaning, etc. Even if they work full-time, they are expected to do a wife's 'duties' in the home as well. Please also remember that Africans like three square meals a day and are not satisfied with merely a BLT sandwich. Nigerian cooking is time consuming and takes a lot of effort.

This is unfair and needs to be challenged.

To be fair, I know some Yoruba men do accept this and have modified their behaviour to make allowances for living in England. My sister Anne's German/Nigerian husband, Lawrence, often does the cooking, as she works long hours. Does he feel his masculinity is under threat by operating the oven? No. He recognises he has his part to play in keeping a family home happy and does so with a willing heart. The fact his dad brought him up alone may have something to do with this. He had no problems seeing a man doing 'woman's' work around the house and so is comfortable himself within this role.

He certainly married the right lady, as sister Anne is against the male control element of Yoruba culture. Although proud of her Yoruba roots, she is very much a modern lady with her attitude to men v women positions. She would not tolerate a man who expected her to jump at his every beck and call. Oh how I wish every Yoruba woman were like her.

Unfortunately, her husband's example is not one that all Yoruba men follow. Some feel their male pride is under attack, when asked to perform tasks traditionally done by women, and resent doing chores around the home. The 'face' concept comes into play here, as Nigerian men need to be seen as being in control of their marriage. This is why many of my Yoruba friends find our decision – to allow Bobby to stay at home – impossible to understand.

My old friend, Matthew, ably demonstrates the controlling element of male Yoruba culture. Despite his Yoruba wife being in England for around ten years, he has not encouraged her to learn a word of English. The reason for this is that he wants control over her. If she could communicate properly with others, she may realise her life does not have to revolve around her husband.

Matthew also told me, many years ago, that he could never go out with me as I was 'more intelligent' than him. He realised I would be able to answer him back and feared not being seen as the dominant force in a relationship.

I contrast this Nigerian male chauvinism with the comment made to me by a middle-aged white colleague of Bobby's – a lady named Tricia. I always remember her words of advice to me when she discovered Bobby and I were stepping out as a couple. She said, in a very friendly and motherly tone, 'Make sure you get rid of his clothes now that he is going out with you – you have to be able to control him.' She then pointed out to me, some years into our marriage, how disappointed she was that I still let Bobby wear his punk clothes, because 'it may cause trouble for our children at school.'

Oh dear, if I had wanted someone to lick my feet and control, I would have bought a dog! I just do not see the point in marrying someone if you see them purely as a computer to feed data into. I married Bobby because I like his character and his reluctance to follow the crowd – not for his ability to fetch a bone!

I am afraid it is attitudes like Tricia's that provoke English men to spend night after night in the local boozer, drowning their sorrows in a deluge of cheap beer. These men have no gumption and are merely running away from the control 'freak' at home. This is no good to anyone in the long run. If couples throughout England are constantly having these 'control' battles, it could be a reason for the high divorce rate. It is far better to accept one's partner for who they are, rather than the person you think you can mould them into. Both Matthew and Tricia are motivated by the same desire: a desire to control their partner.

Following on from this, it is quite obvious to me that white English men are repressed too much by white English women. They should stand up more for their rights and start to use their masculinity. Perhaps, and this is only a hunch of mine, this is a contributory factor as to why many white women have black boyfriends? The stereotypical image, rightly or wrongly, of black men, is more aggressive than that of white men. It is surely true to write that, even in the 21st Century, most women want men to be *men* and not just male versions of women. As it is at the moment, too many white women that I see have total control over their men and like nothing better than to boss them around.

Bobby's friend, Andrew, is proof of this. For his sins, he has had a season ticket at Wolverhampton Wanderers Football Club for over twenty years. For presumably committing murder in a past life, he also has to sit next to my husband whilst watching the match. A vision of hell, I quite rightly agree, but it is a hell he has brought upon his own head.

However, over the past couple of years, poor Andrew has often been forced to stay at home on match days and attend to more useful hobbies, such as decorating. The reason? His long-term partner objects to his trips to the footie and wants him to spend more time with herself and, one imagines, a paintbrush. So, the happy gang of alcoholics, that Bobby is part of, are one less on a Saturday afternoon. For me, as a woman, this is wrong and very un-masculine. I feel so sorry for men like Andrew, for they are not far removed from the little boy in the classroom who has to put his arm up in the air when wanting to go to the toilet. I am all for consideration of one's partner but this is not consideration. It is not even negotiation. No, it is utter subjuga-tion of his masculinity.

Mind, I shouldn't criticise his partner too much as at least his non-atten-dance leads to my husband drinking less, on account of Andrew being the pacemaker and beer Fuhrer, when it comes to alcohol consumption.

My dear husband, in direct comparison, insisted on buggering off to Wolves v Derby County just four days after I gave birth to Joshua. I was annoyed by his actions at the time but, thinking back now with the benefit of stretch marks, I am glad he asserted his testosterone. I would not want to be married to a pansy however nice he may smell.

I feel that part of my parents' confusion, over Bobby giving up work, stems from this idea of control. His role, as a man, is to work for the family and provide money. Due to his working and earning money, he would then have control within both his marriage and house.

Of course, they were perfectly happy for me to augment Bobby's wage –

by working part-time, and saw both of us going to work as the perfect solution. However, on our relatively low wages, this was not a viable option, given the high cost of child-care in England. Their response? I should work nights. Yes, I could work nights but this would be a recipe for disaster for any marriage. If couples have no time for each other, the end result is a slow drift apart and eventual alienation. Please don't get me wrong, for I am not criticising their advice here, it's just that they are viewing the world through nostalgic glasses. Sometimes, I wish they could be more flexible and see things from my point of view.

In Yoruba culture, though, the role of the family is paramount and everything else is secondary.

This is one of the reasons why some Nigerian men are allowed to treat their wives in a shabby way. Back home in Nigeria, the extended family would put their foot down and have a word, if a man was abusing his head of the household role. In England, away from such influence, many Nigerian men are not under such family pressure. Many of my friends are suffering the consequences.

It is only correct to mention that a lot of Nigerian women are actually supportive of these men v women roles. Many meekly accept, without complaint, that their lives will involve long hours at work and domestic duties at home. For many, this is the way they feel God intended them to live. To me, this is wrong, as God wanted men to earn their right to the head of the household position. If a man becomes dictatorial with his wife, he should be told to stop – by the wife or family. Sadly, too many Nigerian women blindly accept bad treatment from their partners, as they feel their role is secondary to the man.

This was demonstrated to me by what happened to a relative of mine, named Loretta, who left Nigeria for America. She departed Nigeria due to her husband physically abusing her, not to mention his penchant for the ladies. Quite rightly, she divorced him and has now made a successful life for herself in the USA. However, a lady who is very high up in the Nigerian government, recently met her for the first time and asked why she didn't live with her husband. Loretta then told her about her background.

'Ah ah,' she exclaimed horrified. 'That is no reason to leave your husband.'

The logic here defies belief. The woman must stay married to a wife beater purely to attain respect in our culture? Sorry, I love my culture dearly, but this is blatantly wrong. This mentality is akin to a woman being raped and then getting the blame for the evil act.

In our culture women are looked down upon if they are not married.

As a consequence, many Yoruba women grow up totally focused on the only objective that really matters: pleasing men. This is leading to women having no initiative of their own. They are becoming docile and often exist only to give service to the male sex. This peer pressure exerts enormous pressure within Yoruba culture and is ensuring that women struggle to be taken seriously.

For some reason, this is a subject hidden within our culture and is largely kept from outsiders. Any who do question this are slapped down, normally via a few quotes from the Bible. Whilst I have professed my love of God, it pains me to see his word distorted by mere mortals. The way some Nigerian Christians interpret his instructions – as to the roles of women – is similar to how Islamist terrorists have hijacked the Koran for their own ends.

For Yoruba men, this cultural dominance is the perfect scenario and they are happy for this to continue. It is, therefore, up to women to point this out and demand change in cultural beliefs.

Doubtless, Yoruba men reading this would dispute my allegation and point out that women (in Nigeria) are encouraged to be educated and to go into the world of work. Equality in the field of work, yes, but in other areas we are very much second-class citizens.

Our views on marriage also contrast starkly with those in England, what with its spiralling divorce rates and marriage not being seen as a fashionable lifestyle choice. As with most things in life, the best way forward would be for a merger of the two strands of thought. On one hand, you have the Nigerian belief in the sanctity of marriage; on the other you have the Germaine Greer influenced feminism women have taken for granted in the West. A marriage made in heaven you could say.

As a nation, Nigerians are very well educated. What we lack, though, is the Enlightenment phase that Europe went through in the 18th century. However, African attitudes are beginning to change. The election of Ms Ellen Johnson-Sirleaf following the Liberian elections of 2005 – the first female President in Africa's history – shows the way forward. Women are waking up to the possibilities of change and are appreciating that they, too, can play their part.

When it comes to sex, Yoruba women are also in, pardon the pun, the missionary position. I remember, many years ago, when an electrician came round to my house to fix a minor problem I had with my TV. He was a pleasant Nigerian man so I was shocked when he offered to fix *me*, free of charge, after fixing the television set! Shaking my head at his barefaced effrontery, I politely declined as I had already given him cash for his primary role. I suppose he had me down as someone fresh off the 'banana boat', who didn't understand that in England money was the preferred form of payment. At my rejection, he looked dismayed and called me a 'lesbian.' He then topped this off by adding I was 'lucky' he had offered sex to me and that I would struggle to find another man to sleep with. Whilst it is true I do not resemble Serena Williams, that doesn't mean to say I jump into bed with any Tom, Dick or Adebo!

In some ways though, I like the traditional roles men and women tend to have. Most women surely look to their man to be big and strong, to be able to protect them if their house was broken into? It is fair to say, Bobby has many qualities, but physical attributes are not high amongst them! In part, he resembles the man from the *Mr Muscle* advert – you know the really puny one with the arms and legs of a sparrow.

If we were ever burgled, Bobby would probably send me down to confront the burglar, whilst he went to the toilet to unburden his bowels. Oh, how I have wished for Bobby to be a Mike Tyson figure, all rippling biceps and thrusting hips. Instead, 'What Do I Get?' A buzzcock of a man who runs around like a constipated bird!

Traditionally, English men are also supposed to be good at DIY. Well, not in our house. In all our years of marriage the best Bobby has managed is to assemble a wardrobe from a flat pack.

Oops, sorry, I nearly forgot his *piece de resistance*. Bobby also managed, on October 2, 2005, to fix our washing-machine. I remember the date well, as I was amazed he could do this. Unfortunately, he now mentions this every time I criticise his DIY ability. Bobby, if you are reading this, enough is enough. Congratulations, you fixed it, time to move on to something else.

Still, I suppose I could learn a few things around the house myself, if I am so fed up with his efforts. But why should I?

It is the man's role after all!

Summary

This is an area where we are both in agreement. Neither of us feels constrained to adopt the traditional role of the man or the woman. If one of a couple is good in one area, and not in another, then why should they not change roles? Why should they conform to the way society would have them? Couples should be more flexible, if circumstances allow. For many, though, culture acts as a blocking force that restricts a couple's ability to do this.

I have always thought culture should be a means of showing how a person ended up at a particular point in time; rather than be used as a vehicle to imprison someone within its tight constraints.

So, here we did have a cultural difference – with regards to my giving up work. Luckily we managed to sail past it without too much of a problem, as we were both able to see the benefit of our joint decision. Our experiences also show that, whilst you should respect a family's opinion, you do not necessarily have to obey the letter of the (family) law. That is not to say that Margaret is disrespectful of her Yoruba traditions. No, it merely shows she is willing to improve them in a way that generations before her could not.

Margaret was very nervous when it came to this chapter, as she does not want to be seen as anti-Yoruba. She was reluctant and scared to criticise elements of Yoruba culture she feels genuinely unhappy with. I don't feel she is 'anti' her culture. To my mind, she is being brave by writing about issues that she knows many women, especially, will castigate her for.

But, as she is fond of saying: 'The truth is the truth.'

CHAPTER 15

UK 2007
A Segregated Society?

Bobby

This is a central issue for both of us, as we have felt for a long time that voluntary segregation is a major problem for the UK to address. It is precisely because we have been able to appreciate the benefits of living in a mixed marriage that we object to this unnecessary evil.

The first thing that strikes us is that whenever segregation comes up in the media, attention is always focused on Muslims. You could be forgiven for thinking it was a non-issue for the rest of the population. This is wrong. As we will show throughout this chapter, segregation extends to all groups in modern day England – although many deny the problem exists.

As I explained in my childhood chapter, I grew up in a world where black/Asian people, to a large degree, did not exist. My only dealings with them were via the pages of the newspaper my dad bought, *The Daily Mail*, and TV programmes. I don't mean the *Black and White Minstrel Show* here, I refer to good old cops and robbers shows like *The Sweeney*, *The Professionals* and *Dempsey and Makepeace* (I was still in my Glynis Barber phase.)

And, let's be honest, black people were never portrayed in a positive light in these programmes. Black people in *The Professionals* were consistently portrayed as pimps, gangsters or smack heads. They could not escape even in the credits. I remember one black actor merely being described as the 'handsome Negro.'

In the interest of fairness, I should point out this was 1978 and the credits were equally blunt about others in the show. For instance, Pamela

Stephenson was normally listed as the 'busty blonde.' Yes, it really was that bad.

But at least *The Professionals* did try to tackle the issue of racism. There was an episode called 'Klansman' where Bodie suddenly discovers he has racist tendencies himself after interviewing a white lady married to a black man – presumably an 'affront' to his Caucasian masculinity. To compound his sexual jealousy, he is then stabbed by a group of black men and is hospitalised. A shocking story that at least has a happy ending, as Bodie recovers and ends up going out on a date with the nurse who assists him. And yes, surprise surprise – she's black! He realises the error of his ways and everyone lives happily ever after.

The only problem is, in reality they don't – although this country has a degree in pretending everything in the garden is rosy.

So, how on earth did I end up marrying an African woman given nothing but negative media images of black people? Well, it all stems from my belief in the punk doctrine of thinking for yourself. I thus had no pre-conceived idea about the type of woman I would end up dating and lustfully grabbed hold of the one who landed in my lap. I realised it was stupid to base an opinion on whole groups of people from what you read or watch on the screen. Stupid and dangerous – for once you start demonising someone, it is easy to go one step further and end up murdering them.

What happened in Rwanda during the 1990s is a clear and recent example of that. For despite having a high rate of inter-marrying, Hutus slaughtered Tutsi with gay abandon. Why? Because they were labelled as 'cockroaches' and described as non-humans.

Jewish citizens in Germany, prior to 1933, also heavily married out of their faith in the years leading up to the Nazi takeover. Indeed, the percentage marrying out had grown to 28 per cent by the time Hitler came to power. In addition, many Jews fought loyally for Kaiser Wilhem II in World War One. Tragically, their loyalty towards Germany was ignored as the gas chambers and *Einsatzgruppen* slaughtered all whom society had labelled as Jewish, whatever their level of assimilation.

So what exactly am I arguing for? As I hope is obvious now, I am a passionate believer in different races coming together as one. It is only when one can truly love thy neighbour with a willing heart that a society can rightly claim to be civilised.

But surely, the two examples I have given show that the mixing of different racial groupings to benefit a country as a whole is merely an illusion, a panacea forever out of reach? Possibly, but what happens if we do not at least try? If we are content to live in our own little racially divided worlds, events such as the Holocaust may occur again.

The 2005 car burning riots in France are an obvious reminder to everyone that we cannot go on living separate lives from our neighbours, just because they have a darker shade of skin. It may come over as extremely simplistic but, if a higher proportion of people married away from their 'norm', then knowledge of the ways that we all do things would increase. I know, for I have learnt so much from being married to Margaret. I just wish others could share the benefits we now take for granted.

Please don't misunderstand me here, I am not suggesting everyone should run out on the street and grab hold of the nearest person who has a different colour skin to them and greet them like a long lost brother. No, I just wish people would be more open to anyone who happens to cross their path. Max Hastings, the esteemed military historian, received much praise by admitting he had never had a Muslim round to his house for dinner. His is an admission the vast majority of the population could replicate, if they felt contrite enough.

So why do people not mix more? The answer from many people I have asked is 'fear of the unknown.' I guess this is natural – the herd instinct is strong in humans – but it is still wrong. Trevor Phillips, then chairman of the Commission for Racial Equality, suggested, in 2005, that we are living in a segregated society, that we are 'sleep-walking' into segregation. He argued there was a lack of integration between various racial groupings in England. I remember many prominent organisations condemning his words as 'alarmist' and 'damaging' to race relations. He was accused of stoking a fire where none existed. Then we had the London bombings.

To those of us who truly believe in an integrated society, and who desperately wish to avoid the American experiences of 'white flight' to the suburbs and ghetto slums, his words have more than a ring of truth. It is only by speaking to those who are, superficially at least, different to oneself that we progress as a nation. That is why it is depressing so few choose to do so. It is easy and complacent to think we all live happily side-by-side, just because the inhabitants of a street now include a Patel, an Ali, a Brown, an Oshindele or a Smith. How much, though, does the individual really know of its neighbour? Not much – in my experience anyhow.

To demonstrate this, I have a Ugandan friend who has lived in England for twelve years. I am the only white friend she has.

In addition to this, my dear old friend Nikki recently celebrated her 40th birthday with a bash at a local drinking establishment. It was a pleasant occasion and involved people from all walks of life mingling together. However, of the eighty or so people who attended, Margaret was one of only two who were black. By writing this, I am not suggesting my friend is deliberately segregationist in any way. No, I am merely illustrating my point – that people mix socially with their own skin colour. Most are unaware they do it but it happens nonetheless.

Margaret's friend, Sade, also helped to confirm the point I am making when she had a birthday party for her delightful one-year-old girl. Sade is English born of Nigerian heritage. As a result, the party included all the usual traditional English games; musical chairs, bouncy castle, etc. However, out of approximately one hundred guests, I was the only white person. To make matters worse, I was gobsmacked when a young cockney speaking black kid asked me at the gathering, 'Which country do you come from mister?' Feeling somewhat bemused by the question, I looked around the mini Lagos environment of Hackney Town Hall, noted the bevy of black beauties swaying their hips to Stevie Wonder and replied, 'England, sonny Jim, the same as you, I guess'.

I could only marvel afterwards that this young pup was so unused to seeing white English, as opposed to Eastern European people, that he automatically assumed I was foreign! My God, are we really that far apart from one another?

Whilst this was a relatively amusing incident, I fail to see this segregation as a good thing. If we do not even party together how can we cope with more serious issues?

I can give other examples. In the care home my wife works on some weekends, most of the staff are black African. A colleague of hers at the home was bemoaning an old friend of a white patient who recently told her she was a 'nice' woman and how he had belatedly realised 'nice' people can also be black. She mocked him for his words as it had taken him sixty years to come to this conclusion. Nodding her head in agreement, Margaret asked her how many 'nice' white or Asian friends she herself had? The answer?
None.

How has this been encouraged? This parallel-lives society that never crosses over. So many people are seemingly content to stay in their own little boxes never dreaming for their world to change. If you don't believe me, look at an average ethnically mixed place of work for confirmation. Sure, people work alongside different skin colours but look again when the clock ticks round to lunchtime. Ethnic barriers are erected and people tend to eat with people generally of the same skin. No-one today, with the honourable exception of Mr Phillips, seems to bat an eyelid over this voluntary segregation – a segregation that is allowed to continue un-challenged. Un-challenged, that is, apart from government talk about 'inclusiveness' and social 'cohesion' (whatever that means). Civil rights leaders of the Sixties would surely recoil in horror at the world we have created.

The saddest part of this is, when different ethnicities do mix, they find, more often than not, that they can communicate and empathise with one another. It's funny but once you start talking with someone their words, and not their race, becomes the main focus of attention. At the moment, we are obsessed with the race part and therefore not giving communication a chance.

If you put this allegation to most UK citizens, though, they would deny they live in a segregated world. Most would say they mix happily with black, white or Asian people.

Truth is, most white people's view of 'mixing' would involve listening to R & B music, going to an Asian owned newsagents and ending a night out with a slap up meal in the local curry house. Is this really what we mean by integrating with people different to ourselves? Is it possible to learn every facet of Asian culture merely by eating a chicken korma or watching comedy sketch show *Goodness Gracious Me*?

I don't think it is. By laughing at its Asian/English ineptitude and culture clashes, we are papering over the very real divisions in society. It is sad to note, but an awful lot of white people like 'their' minorities in their 'natural' habitat: on the sports field, cleaning the toilet or laughing at themselves. In England, we are good at tolerating one another, so long as people stay in their 'place', but that is all. We have confused the idea of being tolerant with that of integration, mistakenly assuming one follows the other. If that was the case, then where are the friendships across the colour line? I remember reading an article in the March 2004 issue of *Pride*, a magazine aimed at black women, that asked a pertinent question: 'Friendship across colour lines: can black and white women really have meaningful bonds with each other?' Really, it was being serious. I found it truly staggering that such a question was still being asked in 2004. Even worse was the number of readers who replied to this question and answered in the negative.

Oh please, get real. If you like someone and they like you become friends. Colour does not have to stop friendship.

I also find it weird how magazine racks in newsagents are full of glossy publications like *Black Beauty*, *Pride* etc. These mags concern themselves with purely black issues and are directed at a limited clientele – black women.

Argument in favour for such magazines often highlight the fact that more mainstream 'white' publications, such as *Woman*, very rarely cover issues specifically relating to black people. Surely this is an admission of defeat? I would have thought a more concerted effort to get in the pages of the 'mainstream' would be a more desirable course of action? Why should white or Asian women not read about more diverse issues? By ignoring the concerns and interests of non-white readers, the publishers are helping to ensure that we live in our own little boxes, hostile to other boxes.

Another 'box' of note is the number of black or Asian themed award shows. There are so many that I can only list a few: Music of Black Origin (MOBO), Asia Sports Personality, Asian Business Awards.....it goes on and on. How long before the Black Oscars are awarded? Now, I appreciate that these awards are mostly just harmless fun and a way of celebrating 'diversity' but are they not a dangerous sign of how we are content to live segregated lives – often without realising it? By labelling these tacky gold statues as 'black' or 'Asian' surely we are yet again confirming the idea that we are colour first and nationality/personality second? The stupid thing is that it doesn't have to be this way. Let's take the MOBOs first. Rock'n'roll is a music of both black and white origin. Why, then, is it excluded from the MOBOs? The likes of Chuck Berry, Little Richard and Fats Domino – black one and all – are seminal players in the history of rock'n'roll. So why is rock not included?

Well, the obvious answer is that 'rock' is now seen as a predominantly white form of music. This is lazy stereotyping and actually wrong. Off the top of my head I can think of Lenny Kravitz, Bad Brains (US hardcore band), Jimmy Hendrix and Phil Lynott as 'black' music rock stars from the past thirty years or so. Country and western is similarly excluded despite black singers such as Carl Ray, Vicki Vann and Sunny Daye. The Asia Sports Personality gong, won in 2006 by England cricketer Monty Panesar, is even more bizarre as the main sports award show – the BBC Sports Personality – is open to all and the 2006 short list included dear old Monty! Given his appearance in the BBC final, surely the 'Asian' award is superfluous?

I know the counter argument to this is that the likes of Halle Berry winning her Oscar in 2002 was decades late in coming and that Monty could be seen as a one off, but why stop just when doors seem to be opening?

So how can we reverse these trends? Apart from writing and talking about segregation, we should encourage a higher percentage of ethnic minorities into our infrastructures, as it would help immensely if black people were more represented in the boardrooms and corridors of power. I am fed up with reading the business pages of the *Telegraph* and being greeted with the faces of smiling, slightly overweight, balding white men. I hate to sound like Greg Dyke (who famously complained about the BBC being 'hideously white'), but it does show a glass ceiling still exists. This is ably demonstrated by the disturbing statistic, provided by the Cranfield School of Management, that, whilst ethnic minority people make up 8 per cent of the population, they fill only 2.5 per cent of the membership of FTSE 100 companies.

Again, whenever I attend museums, football matches, gigs, just about the only time I ever see black people is in the tearooms, the cloakrooms, or acting as stewards. Segregation by occupation/wealth seems to carry on regardless of any edict given by the government. No-one cares that we live apart – until a catastrophe happens. Why wait for our Hurricane Katrina to arrive before doing something about it?

But, supposing we do open the way to the gates of power, will more ethnic (how I loathe this term – we are all belonging to an ethnicity) minorities come forward? To give but one example, until this year I was a School Governor at a local nursery school. Of the children who attend, 35 per cent of them speak Turkish as their first language. Every year the school runs a survey to gauge parents' opinion of its services. As the percentage of Turkish speaking children has risen dramatically over the past two years, it was decided to publish the survey in Turkish as well as English.

After some expense, that the nursery could ill afford, the survey was duly translated and given out to the Turkish parents. We sat back and waited, eagerly anticipating any issues that may have been neglected by the nursery up to that point. The result? Not one Turkish-speaking parent completed the survey. The black/white/Asian response of people who returned the survey was around 40 per cent. Using this example the integration argument has a long way to go before it can be said to be working.

As a nation, we have sat back whilst the world changed around us – the London bombings being an obvious illustration of a far deeper malaise. It is a complacent attitude that is causing all sorts of problems.

The language barrier, for instance, is often mentioned when talking about integration – with the sensible demand that English is spoken by all who settle here. But what about those who cannot speak English? What problems does this cause for society? Let us take education. Some of the schools experiencing the linguistic problem get around the issue by teaching children in their mother tongue. Seeing as how schools are under such pressure to meet government exam targets, this is understandable. However, it is also wrong as it reduces the need for the children to learn the host language. Children then often leave school with only a rudimentary grasp of English to take into the outside world. This is frustrating for both employers and other citizens of this country. To our eternal shame, it is the elderly who are affected more than most by this, with often devastating consequences for their social lives. Why?

Imagine the little old lady who may be widowed, infirm, and generally frail on her feet. Her children may have moved away and she is effectively trapped in the small world on her doorstep. For many in such a situation, their neighbours take the place of absent relatives and provide a comfort of sorts against loneliness. What, though, is the 'little old lady' supposed to do if she cannot communicate with the people living next door? Nothing. She can't move, as she probably hasn't the economic means to relocate to a different neighbourhood, and she is unlikely to want to enrol for Kurdish/Urdu/Polish language classes at such a late stage of life. So she sits, alone, waiting for the phone to ring or her body to expire. What a way to leave this world.

Of course, the language argument applies with equal logic to both the host and the incoming population, as being able to communicate with each other is surely the starting point for integration. And yet go to any local council/benefit office and you will see a myriad of leaflets in different languages. How is this helping to integrate people? All it is doing is keeping them locked into their own 'tightknit' communities. Superficially, the leaflets may help but at what long-term cost?

I would argue that people are naturally lazy. After all, why put yourself out to learn a language if everything you need is printed in words you are already comfortable with?

In all honesty, why would any sane person bother learning English, especially given the quite ridiculous amounts of public money spent on interpretation services for those who cannot, or will not, learn the lingo. Plain nonsense and a mere sop to the PC brigade.

It appears to me that at times our public services are obsessed with helping people to stay in their 'own boxes,' rather than encouraging them to branch out and make a decent life for themselves in England.

To counteract this, the government should do more to advance the cause of integration. Maybe if Gordon Brown invented a new form of Tax Credits (the mixed marriage tax credit?) people would mingle more?

Leading on from this, I feel strongly that our institutions should ensure the ability to speak English is the number one priority for their customers. I have found this is often not the case. This was brought home to me when one of the teachers at my daughter's nursery asked if Olivia spoke any other language. I answered no as she is still struggling to speak sentences in English. The teacher was surprised but went on to proudly inform me the children were learning six different languages to celebrate 'diversity'. I was not impressed.

The thing that irritated me the most was her facial expression being similar to a two-year-old that has spent an hour drawing a picture only for an adult to ridicule it. Presumably the teacher expected me to congratulate her on the school's idea of teaching 'diverse' language skills to children. She does not know me, or Margaret who was equally appalled by her boast, at all. I find it totally remiss of a school to branch out into other areas like this.

Surely the ability to speak English is the first thing any child should learn? Fine, learn other languages, but only after you have a good grasp of English. To compound this I noticed many of the nursery teachers greeted other youngsters in their native tongue. What type of message does this send out to those who were not born British? They are not learning anything about the English language if they are welcomed in Kurdish, Urdu or Punjabi. My objections here may come over as trivial but small incidents, such as the ability to say 'good morning' in the same tongue, can only help society as a whole as we struggle to reduce the alienation expressed by so many.

Compare this with schools in Berlin, Germany. Six schools have now banned the use of other languages in the school classroom and playground – so as to ease integration for those schools that have large percentages of foreign children. This strikes me as an entirely sensible idea. Talking to and understanding one another has to be the base before any culture can success-fully mix. It is obvious that speaking German should be the number one choice of communication for children in Germany. It may seem a tad harsh but how are people going to mingle if they cannot communicate?

As a contrast to the German system, Margaret recounts one of her Ghanaian friends, who, despite living here for many years, has not taught her three-year-old daughter one word of English. Instead of teaching her English, she sticks to educating her of her Ghanaian roots. Her reasoning for this is that 'the school can teach her the English language but not Ghanaian culture.'

Well, yes, they probably can, but why pass the buck for your child's learning onto someone else? For me, this is a socially irresponsible way to behave, as schools have more pressing priorities. Surely it should be possible for a parent to teach both?

I also have first hand experience of language barriers where I live. Margaret and I have always got on well with our neighbours and have gradu-ally got to know the majority of those who live nearby. However, a couple of years ago a Kurdish family moved in three doors down from us. They seem a pleasant family but I will never know for sure, as they cannot speak English. I get a nice smile from them whenever I say hello but the language barrier stops me from taking this relationship further. I feel we both lose out because of this.

Only, when we are able to communicate, will friendships develop. As it stands at the moment, they are as much a mystery to me as I am to them. This cannot be healthy in the long-term. Personally, I couldn't care less who lives next to me as long as we speak the same language. Surely this is the way ahead?

I have also witnessed language 'problems' whilst at work. I will never forget when a Yoruba colleague of mine was told off by her non-Yoruba supervisor. She immediately went on the phone and spoke at length to another Yoruba colleague. Now, she could have been discussing the weather forecast for the next day but she might also have been slagging off her boss. This must have been the hot favourite as I heard her say the *jabajantes* (rubbish) word every few seconds, alongside a glaring look towards the man who had admonished her. How is the boss supposed to react when the woman he has disciplined is speaking so animatedly on the phone – in a language he does not understand? I suggest his authority is undermined.

However, if the workforce was restricted to just English at work then this kind of incident would not happen and everybody would be treated the same. If this was the case then the supervisor would have felt confident enough to tell her to stop talking in a different language, with no unpleasant consequences for his career. Although I am of a gullible nature, I realise this could never happen, as our 'multicultural' political masters would say she is merely keeping in touch with her 'identity'.

I probably come over as a loony righty with this view, but my objection is based purely on the practicalities of workplace harmony. I am arguing this from a common sense angle. Is speaking English in England really a controversial subject? It shouldn't be.

Actually, come to think of it, why am I apologising for coming over as right-wing? If an idea makes sense does it really matter from which side of the political spectrum it comes from?

To be fair, Brits abroad also frequently fail the language test and most of us have experienced the enclaves of Spanish based Britons whose cultural awareness is limited to knowing the cost of the local plonk. They, too, should make more of an effort to learn the lingo and be more integrated into the Spanish way of life. It is rank bad manners to assume you can travel to another country and remain in ignorance of its history, culture and language.

I now come to the sticky subject of 'diversity', in particular the somewhat mixed message where employment is concerned. These days, if you read any job advert, it will normally include the sentence 'the workforce should reflect the community it serves.' On the surface, this sounds like a reasonable sound bite but what does it really mean? I have asked this question and I'm always told an area which is predominantly populated with black people should be staffed by a similar percentage of black workers, in order to aid diversity. Again this all sounds reasonable but.........

If I take myself for instance, I now have a fairly good grasp of Nigerian etiquette/customs when dealing with elders/strangers. 'Reflecting the ethnic population of the area', though, might mean I could be cast aside from a potential job. The irony is, a black man or woman with Caribbean ancestry would be deemed as having more in common with a Nigerian than me, purely due to the colour of their skin. If you mix with Nigerians, you would know they would laugh at this suggestion!

In addition, how far do we want to go with diversity? If an office is staffed by mainly Yoruba Nigerians should steps be taken to ensure that other Nigerian groups are represented? If we halt the 'diversity' agenda halfway through aren't we discriminating against Hausa or Ibo people?

Even though I am writing this, I accept that this will never happen – as it would be far too difficult to enforce. No-one admits to it but diversity is actually longer than a piece of string and very easy to get tied up in knots over.

The peculiarity here is that, by encouraging 'diversity', we are ensuring that the workplace mirrors the local population. I may be a touch stupid but how is that 'diversity'? It just means that people will stay apart in a kind of ill thought out apartheid. An Asian man in Blackburn, for instance, may have no dealings with white people apart from Mr Jones behind his local Post Office counter. If Mr Jones is replaced by Mr Patel is this increasing or reducing diversity?

By enforcing this 'diversity' mentality we are adding to segregation and, effectively, admitting that different races cannot get on. Sorry, but this is nonsense. The flag of surrender should not be raised without a fight.

Just because a person is white, does not necessarily mean they cannot relate to a black or Asian member of the community, or the reverse. If a white person is placed in a job say, for arguments sake, in Tower Hamlets and was worried about how to deal with Bangladeshi people, they could buy a book and read up about Bangladeshi customs. Maybe not a perfect solution but at least it would show a willingness to broaden one's mind. Instead, by adhering to the 'reflecting the community' misnomer, organisations are using race and ethnicity as a barrier to progress. It does not have to be this way.

On this point, I see even the pinko left-wing types at the BBC are getting in on the act. By this I mean an interview that was reported in *The Observer* of August 13, 2006, with the 'editorial executive of diversity', a lady by the name of Mary Fitzpatrick. In it she stated she preferred to see non-white journalists reporting from places such as Africa because 'I would prefer to see somebody who understands that culture'. She went on to say that 'what's really important is that BBC News reflects the audience that it's serving'.

The first issue here is that the vast majority of people watching the news would not even notice the reporter's colour. They are interested in the news and not the 'diversity' agenda of the BBC. Does this, probably well meaning but misguided woman, not realise how insulting this could appear to journalists of impeccable standing such as John Simpson? Secondly, she is presuming that only black Africans live in Africa. Surely white Africans understand what is happening in Zimbabwe more than a black guy who has lived all his life in Brixton?

The supreme irony is she then recounted a story of when she was mistaken for a cleaner, all on account of her being mixed race (although she describes herself as black). Rightly upset by this, she commented that 'it made me understand how some people can simply not get beyond the colour of your skin'. I presume this woman does not understand the meaning of the word hypocrisy.

This is a classic case of how we are in a diversity muddle in this country. Everyone has become so used to the word now, that it is trotted out without anyone stopping to think what it actually means. Just have a look in your local paper as evidence of this. Almost all job adverts now include the slogan 'we embrace diversity', or other vacuous words such as 'positive about disability'. Great, so that will put a stop to all the racism in the world then! Exactly what do these bland statements mean?

My suspicion is that many employers now feel it is enough to mutter a few glib words about 'equal opportunities,' as they consider an 'ethnic' CV, before they nevertheless dump it on the pile labelled as rejected. Is this really progress?

Please do not misunderstand me here, for I am not against 'diversity' *per se*, I just don't see how sloganeering helps anyone in the long-term. It seems that, in today's climate, diversity training is suggested as a knee-jerk reaction by companies to prove they are 'inclusive' of all groups in society – whilst prejudice continues unabated. Rather than sack racist employees, they are instead sent on courses to learn about being nice to blue and red people.

The other point that always puzzles me, when diversity is mentioned, is how limited its remit is. Surely, if we are truly to be a diverse society, the workforce should also have a percentage of under/working/middle/upper-class people as well? Why is this never applied or discussed? If the workforce mingled more, then maybe Margaret's middle-class sister, Kemi, wouldn't have to put up being labelled 'jungle girl' by underclass Americans.

The answer, of course, is that the diversity chiefs can ignore class in the way they cannot with race. Skin can never be made invisible.

Much the same principle applies where ethnic 'cleansing' is concerned. Crimes against humanity, such as the Nazi Holocaust, are rightly held up as acts of demented terror that are impossible to justify whatever an individual's political leaning. However, when crimes against people are committed for no other reason than their class – the obvious example being the oppression of the *bourgeoisie* in the Soviet Union under Stalin in the 1930s – they are conveniently brushed aside. This has to be wrong. Genocide or 'classocide' are both based around the idea of killing people purely for their belonging to a particular group. Why then further discriminate against victims of class aggression by not (in historical terms) treating them the same way?

Even today, we place a higher level of importance on someone's race than we do on their class. If you don't believe me, I need only refer to the way homicides are logged as proof. Racially motivated murders now attract a higher custodial tariff than 'ordinary' murders – a good idea that few fair-minded people would find objectionable.

Supposing, though, someone decides to murder all the chavs in their locality, would they be found guilty of class motivated murder? I doubt it. Or how about the street mugger who deliberately targets middle-class people because they have more money. Is he showing discrimination or merely being entrepreneurial?

So who in the marbled corridors of power decided on this yardstick of selective diversity? No one asked me, or you, or the bloke round the corner......

No one ever does.

It may strike the reader as bizarre that I link genocide with the diversity tzar's agenda at work, but I am merely trying to show how 'diversity' is not as straightforward as it first appears. We need to think it through a bit more – especially in the workplace.

Mind you, the world of work can be a veritable minefield to safely overcome. For instance, I have a good (white) friend who is a branch manager at a well known building society. The branch he works in is in Brixton so, somewhat predictably, all his staff are either black or Asian. This makes my friend slightly nervous as he feels it gives out the wrong message to customers and staff alike; that black people can only reach a certain level. To an extent I can see his point – going back to my earlier comments about glass ceilings. But if he, as an individual, is competent in his ability to do the job why should it matter?

By misinterpreting what 'diversity' actually entails, firms are slipping into the danger of defining people via their skin colour and not their suitability for a perspective job. This is both patronising and demeaning. Black and Asian people have origins from all over the world and are not just black/Asian entities. Each person is unique and enjoys a history that goes far beyond their immediate appearance. Of course, this also applies to white people in England (Welsh, Scottish, Irish, English, Cornish, etc.) It is ultimately insulting and dismissive of someone's rich roots to categorise them purely by skin tone.

At times, it seems as if this racial profiling is becoming the obsession of the 21st Century, with legions of people using it to justify their continued employment as 'diversity' advisers. The stupid thing is, via our desire to ensure that everyone is represented in every aspect of life; we are reducing not increasing diversity. It is *Gleichschaltung* – the enforcement of standardization – in its purest form.

This is best demonstrated by the desire of the government to ensure that 'ethnic minorities' (or is it minority ethnic now? I just can't keep up with the times) are evenly spread throughout the job market – *even in those occupations they choose not to do*. Whilst on one hand this is a laudable concept, it is also impossible to enforce. For instance, if black and Asian people are reluctant to join the Police force why should we insist that they do? If white people don't want to get up at four in the morning to run a corner shop, should they be coerced into doing so?

The last time I checked the constitution, this country was still a democracy with individuals free to choose the occupation of their choice. Has this changed without a national referendum?

Lastly, I come to my final point about diversity. Has anyone ever seen a non-Asian waiter working at an Indian restaurant, or a black member of staff at a Turkish supermarket? Or how about a white barber – the white guy from *Desmond's* doesn't count – working at a black hairdressers? No, thought not. Diversity, it seems, is a one-way street.

I also read, on Ceefax, that the government is studying why ethnic minorities are failing to recycle as much waste as white people are. How on earth do they know this? Does a man with a clipboard stand at the recycling plant noting people's colour and ethnicity each time they empty their tin cans into the bin? Presumably if I dispose of our household rubbish it is labelled as 'white'. However, the very same rubbish could be emptied by Margaret and then be described as 'black African'. Apart from being completely barmy, what purpose does this achieve?

On a similar theme, I now refuse to complete tick boxes that relate to my children's ethnic origin. I am constantly asked to tick who they are for the most ridiculous of reasons. This was brought home to me when my daughter wanted to join the nursery's toy library. Now, you may think a toy library is a good idea and free from prejudice – toys are, after all, inanimate objects without emotion. But...

Before I can borrow a toy, I have to complete a form with my daughter's details, including her ethnic origin. The form lists seventeen ethnic groupings for her to choose from. Err, excuse me for being stupid, but what relevance does this have for her wanting to borrow a toy? I can only surmise it is to see which racial groups tend to use the library the most. But what can a school do if one group is under represented? Are the teachers expected to go out onto the streets and frogmarch into the toy library half a dozen black or Asian kids? If they do not pick a toy will they get detention?

Really, such a thing baffles me. We are getting to the stage where you will have to state your ethnic origin if you want to use a public convenience. You can just imagine the jobsworth attendant if this came to pass: 'I am sorry, sir, but the toilet is reserved for black and Asian people today – as they are under represented in this mornings urine count.' He could then go on to advise 'but don't worry sir if you take a trip down this road you will find a toilet able to take another fifteen litres of white English urine this afternoon.'

I may be taking the piss but this could well be the case in another twenty or so years time.

Another incident happened when I was writing this book. Unfortunately, my daughter was involved in an accident where she was knocked down by a hit and run driver. I called the police to report this and, ten minutes later, the copper turned up. He was extremely polite, helpful and genuinely sympathetic towards our predicament. But, as is the way of the world now, he had to describe my daughter for his incident report. He swiftly produced a little brown book and asked me to pick my daughter's ethnic origin. The brown book itself was quite bulky and contained enough combinations of ethnicity to fill half a dictionary. I know I should have been more concerned about my daughter, she was physically unharmed apart from a superficial cut to her lip, but this really irritated me. What difference does her ethnicity make to her injury?

The policeman explained they have to do this every time they attend the scene of a crime. I sympathised with him and said I would rather not specify her ethnicity as I find this labelling divisive. He agreed with me but insisted I did. By now, I realised I was banging my head against a brick wall so I quit trying to make a point and regretfully ticked the white/black African box.

One of Margaret's friends is a French lady named Nathalie. She told

Margaret such tick boxes are unheard of in France. I am not suggesting we follow the French model on integration, as they seem to have more problems than us, but I think she has a point. By all means keep records for important issues such as promotions/grading, etc but.........a child's toy?

I find it so wrong that ethnic origin is something that appears so important in modern day England. We are all British, regardless of ethnicity. By continually going on about it, I feel we are merely making differences more apparent. It seems as if we are using ethnicity as a barrier between people, rather than celebrating or ignoring it. Take the issue of adoption. Our local authority care homes host a disproportionately large number of black kids. Despite many white families wishing to adopt/foster black children, our authorities are reluctant to do so, arguing that a child is better suited living in an environment that reflects his/her ethnic background. Whilst appearing sensible, this is actually a cruel way of ensuring more black kids stay in care than in a loving family. Now, it may well be better for them to grow up in a black home but surely a family background, irrespective of race, is the starting point for a placement to be made? Yet again, this type of approach is demonstrating that ethnicity is the number one issue when it should be irrelevant if all parties are of a British background. Our nationality, rather than our colour, is the main thing that binds us together as a society.

I see, on this point, even celebrities are getting in on the act – best shown by the ridiculous furore that erupted over singer Madonna's fostering of her Malawian baby. As usual, the do-gooders leapt out of the woodwork using the 'cultural awareness' line when criticising her. Stupidly, this criticism was aimed at someone who was offering a stable, financially sound, home for this child. Why was this deemed wrong?

Personally, I would have thought her entire back catalogue of music was more deserving of abuse but no-one picked up on this. Instead, we had lovey dovey, wishy washy, hippy style lines from *ersatz* Yoko Ono types lecturing people on how to lead their lives. What a load of bollocks. Ignore the child's colour and concentrate, instead, on why Mali has so many orphans deprived of a loving upbringing.

This ethnic profiling nonsense even applies to the union I belong to. For the 2007 elections we were asked to vote for our representatives from a brochure that listed all the candidates. Alongside their mug shots every one of them proudly stated their racial origin. Why? It is irrelevant to me what colour they are. I am far more concerned about their ability to represent me in times of strife than I am their race.

Another ethnicity incident cropped up in December 2005 and was briefly reported on Ceefax. It involved an FA Cup football match between

Oldham and Brentford at Oldham's Boundary Park ground. The report alleged that the Brentford manager at the time, Martin Allen, (who is white) complained about a flag the Oldham fans had produced. The flag proudly stated: 'Born in England, live in England, die in England'. The report went on to say that Martin Allen was approached by some of his black players who believed the flag to be racist.

Why was it thought to be racist? Presumably the black players would also have been 'born in England, live in England, die in England'. Unless the flag had a Nazi message on it as well, I fail to see how this flag could be offensive. As a result of Mr Allen's complaint the BNP probably acquired a few more votes.

The supreme irony here is that Brentford play in red and white striped jerseys and are sponsored by a London property company called 'St George.'

Amazing.

Another area where the races divide is entertainment. How many nightclubs are labelled as 'black'? How many clubs have 'Bhangra Nights'? How many black or Asian people do you see at Marilyn Manson gigs? Not many – they are inevitably Caucasian only occasions with colour only visible behind the bar or in the shape of a burly security guard. Even in something as relatively trivial as music we are segregating ourselves. But it has not always been this way.

If you look at punk rock shows from the Seventies, one of the things that stands out, are the amount of black faces in the crowds as compared to today. To emphasise this, the whole 'Rock against Racism' movement made a big statement of putting punk on the same bill as reggae bands. The idea of this was to shove two fingers up at the National Front (NF) by showing that punks and Rastas were united against two common enemies; fascism and the police (the boys in blue and not Sting's plastic punk by numbers band). On this point though, the whole reggae/punk togetherness thing is much overplayed. Whilst bands such as The Clash, The Ruts and The Slits were heavily influenced by the Don Letts/reggae connection, most other punk bands remained in blissful ignorance of its appeal. Individuals like Johnny Rotten and Jah Wobble also dabbled in dub and reggae, but the overall myth of Bob Marley's 'Punky Reggae Party' should be consigned to the dustbin of history. But at least it is a nice myth.

So, why has this noble sentiment been allowed to fade? Where are the Somali origin punk rockers to prove we are an integrated society?

Let's face it, apart from events such as Live 8 (where even German punk legends Die Toten Hosen played), such musical mixing no longer happens.

Instead we are seemingly content to live in isolation of each other, in this country at least. America, I am glad to report, is at least a bit ahead of us in this regard as they have the burgeoning Afro-Punk movement; literally what it suggests via the title. How refreshing it is to see black punks in the US with no hang ups over supporting a music scene that is now predominantly white. If only we could follow suit in England.

It is at times such as these, we look to the government to set the ethnicity agenda. I have been critical in this book about the role played by government but it is only fair to acknowledge that, whichever way they turn, they run the risk of ridicule. A clear example of this was when I read about a government initiative to get more black and Asian people to attend fishing. To encourage this, they started up an advertising campaign to sell fishing to more 'diverse' people. At first glance I laughed at this suggestion as leisure pursuits are a personal choice. Thinking about it a little longer, though, I feel they should be congratulated over this approach. It may still seem weird to read of this publicity campaign but at least they are trying to break down the segregation between races.

Another example of how we like to segregate ourselves with entertainment happened to Margaret just last Christmas. My sister asked Margaret what she would like as a present. She answered the DVD of *Downfall* would go down a treat. My sister was puzzled at Margaret requesting a film about the last days of Adolf Hitler. She said to me: 'Isn't this more for you?'

Whilst I would be lying to say I didn't want to view it, the DVD really was on Margaret's Christmas shopping list. Doubtless, if she had requested *Shaft in Africa* or *Songs of Praise* I would not have had the same question.

The very same logic applies to such a humble item as a theatre flyer. For our *ersatz* lower middle-class sins, Margaret and I have attended a few shows at Stratford East Theatre, in East London. Just because one of those shows was *Urban Afro Saxons*, a play about identity within both black and white communities, we are bombarded with publicity about forthcoming attractions at the same theatre.

Without exception, all the advertising relates to shows that highlight either 'black' or 'Asian' issues. Part of me just accepts this as sound business practice, as the targeting of an audience is nothing new. However, I would also like the opportunity to know about any other plays/shows that are on at the same theatre. I am not drawn to a play for the ethnic subject matter. No, I go to see something entertaining, informative and educational – whatever the colour of the writer or actor. By pigeonholing my presumed interest they are potentially losing future custom. It also means their shows are playing to a restricted clientele. Perhaps they should infiltrate the BNP and send 'Asian and black' flyers to their members instead? Heaven knows, they could probably do with mixing with a few 'ethnics'.

Even on a trip to the Imperial War Museum with my son, I was touched by the segregation on display. Not between races, but ages. In the museum's comments book I read numerous sentences from, presumably, young people, stating it was a good museum but that it was mainly for old white people.

To go off on a quick tangent, this is one area that always disturbs me (and links with the segregation theme). Why is it a lot of black people feel that WW2 was a white person's war that holds little historical interest for them? This attitude is so wrong as 421,000 troops alone were called up from Britain's African colonies to fight German/Japanese imperialism. Then there are the millions from Asia who were drawn to service for 'Queen and Country'. Indeed, a staggering 2.5 million Indians enrolled for the British Indian Army, despite the lure of the Japanese Co-Prosperity Sphere propaganda.

WW2 also discredited the whole issue of white supremacy that had been encouraged by many countries, not just Germany, up to that point. It was precisely because many white people were forced to see the logical results of these supremacist theories – the Concentration Camps – that they were questioned. In addition, the war also accelerated the civil rights and black-power movement in the United States, caused in part by the scandalous treatment meted out to black and Asian people after the cessation of hostilities on 15 August, 1945.

And yet, history instead tends to link the Vietnam War much more closely with the advancement of black people. This is incorrect as the seeds were sown in WW2. By effectively segregating an important part of black and white world history, we are doing a grave disservice to all, irrespective of colour, who fought for freedom.

But it doesn't have to be this way. Why do we restrict ourselves to things that only our age or racial group 'should' like? I am not suggesting old people start going to nightclubs or going on Club 18-30 holidays (although it would help to keep the levels of binge drinking under control). Oh no, I am just suggesting we should all open our minds to different things. Which is presumably why I just like English food and punk rock/skinhead music. Aw shucks, I must come over like a right old hypocrite but I really do feel enlightened over this issue. Or maybe I am just turning into a moany pompous old git?

Poor old Margaret feels this segregation mentality more than I do as her interests are constantly blamed on her being married to me. Whenever she is on her lunch break at work she tends to read *The Daily Telegraph*. Almost without fail, people pull her leg about her reading a 'white man's paper'. They then go on to point out she should be reading a paper more in tune with her ethnicity like *The Sun* or *The Mirror*.

How stupid.

Apart from the *Telegraph* being the most Christian of all the broadsheets, it contains lots of balanced features concerning Nigeria. It also credits its readers with having a brain and promotes the idea that people should empower their own lives – a very Nigerian character trait. Why, then, should Margaret read *The Sun* or even *The Voice*? It is precisely because Margaret sees herself as a person first that she can do this.

It should also be remembered, it was *The Sun* that published story after story in the early Eighties aimed at discrediting Red Ken's Greater London Council (GLC). It was they who were behind those spurious scare stories about Hackney Council banning banana shaped pens and 'baa baa black sheep' nursery rhymes. These stories may have appeared funny to the editor but they probably caused real hardship to ordinary black people on the street. So, if anything, black people should be boycotting *The Sun* rather than encouraging others to read it.

One of the areas where people are still segregated, to a certain extent, is that of mixed marriages/relationships. I know there are lots of problems that can hinder a successful mixed marriage (see previous chapters). But, hey, most marriages have these problems even if both participants are of the same colour. If you are in a mixed marriage, though, and it goes wrong, you can guarantee that someone will say, 'I told you it couldn't work – he/she should have stuck to his or her own race.'

People outside of a relationship can only ever get part of the picture. Yes, mixed marriages have their difficulties but they also have their pleasures, pleasures generally not emphasised enough by the world at large. The consequence of this leads to people developing a negative mindset as to the viability of mixed marriages. Once this mentality is in place, it is then hard to shift, and normally only by personal experience. One of Margaret's friends once said to her, 'I never used to believe in mixed marriages until I have seen how happy Bobby makes you.'

Granted not everyone has my good looks and sense of humour, but at least I had made a positive impression on her friend's attitude. Her own husband was against me to start with and said some strong words to Margaret at the time we started dating, even though he now talks to me on a level basis. Since then though, their two daughters have been given the green light to date whoever they deem appropriate. To my mind, this has to be progress. If Margaret and I have managed to change just one person's opinion then that is worthwhile.

So, how come mixed marriages are not more common? In some ways they are. According to the Office for National Statistics, via their census of April 2001, 219,000, of the 10.3 million married couples who completed the census, were classified as 'inter ethnic'. Patterns of 'inter ethnic' marriage were broadly similar with one exception; black women were less likely to marry outside their ethnic group. Whilst 48 per cent of black men born in England married a woman from outside their ethnic group only 33 per cent of black women did. The census in America showed a similar outcome. So why the discrepancy? Why do black women appear so reluctant to date outside of their race?

I have already covered some of the issues regarding this – slavery and the sexual myths. Other factors also come into play. A black female friend of mine said she would never date a white man because she wouldn't know what to do with him. She felt it would be a step into the unknown.

Another black lady – who was asked out by a white male friend of mine – replied that, although she liked the man in question she could not do it because of what her family might think.

My old friend, David Nunn, had problems of a similar nature. He was dating a Nigerian origin woman for six months. During their entire relationship, the lady in question had to keep their liaison a secret, as she was scared of what her parents might say.

Yet another lady, (Keisha, an ex-friend of Margaret's) could not do 'it', as her mother warned her at an early age she could never date a white man. She was told that, however bad a black man may treat her, she must accept it, as she is a black woman.

One of Margaret's black colleagues was also told by her mother when she was a teenager, to 'never date either a Rastafarian or a white man.'

Our near neighbour Sheena, whilst herself being open to dating outside of her race, was gently reminded by her uncle that she was best off not having a white boyfriend.

When news of Margaret dating me first broke at work, her friend, Sylvia, was working with a young black lady. Unfortunately for her, she did not realise Margaret was one of Sylvia's closest friends. She, therefore, put her foot in the proverbial 'it', when she told Sylvia that Margaret was wrong for going out with a white man.

I give all these examples to prove, albeit on a local level, that many black women do have an aversion to dating white men. So, is this resistance justified? No. Although I can understand some of the objections, as in the first two examples, they are still wrong. I would actually find it easier to accept if they just said, 'I don't find white men attractive.' By giving these excuses, the women are helping to keep barriers up in society.

As for the 'I must suffer because I am a black woman' bit, how is this taking forward issues that affect black women? Sorry, but why exactly should they have to suffer? Given that black men are dating outside of their race so much, why can't black women follow suit?

Margaret also informs me that a lot of black African women are put off dating white men because we are perceived as lacking in one important area: religion. To be fair this is true. For whatever reason, a lot of white men are not religious in the same sense that many black women are. I can at least understand why people object on these grounds, as religion can be too important to be compromised via the fragility of human emotions.

Another reason to object, is the notion that some white men seek black women as partners to prove their anti-racist credentials, that they are 'colour-blind' and contributing towards racial harmony – by dating someone who is non-white. Of course, if this was the case, who in their right mind would want to step out and be patronised by a liberal whitey type who was feeling guilty over the slave trade? You can imagine the conversation, 'oh my pretty ethnic girl I am so sorry for the crimes my ancestors committed against yours in the past, please forgive my poor white soul and let me worship your black beauty'. Sorry, but this is ridiculous, not to mention deeply offensive. Most black girls I know would prefer to dress up in a fancy number from Primark, rather than wear the sackcloth and ashes conferred on them by the white liberals.

Black peer pressure also applies its squeeze on black women who are tempted to stray to the 'white man'. Margaret had a classic case of this within the past year. She was talking to a black teenager named Simone and the subject of relationships reared its complicated head. Simone inquired of Margaret if it was true that Nigerian men looked after 'their' women better than Caribbean origin men. Margaret, as is her way with any young woman, told her to forget about men until she was at least twenty-five!

Poor Simone, unused to Margaret's feminist style rantings, persisted with her line of questioning. Margaret told her not to believe everything she had heard about Nigerian men. She went on to say that Simone should consider dating other men.

'You mean someone who isn't black?' asked a wide-eyed and incredulous Simone.

Margaret merely said, 'You should keep your eyes open to any colour.'

Simone considered for a second and said, 'No, I couldn't go out with a white man, I love my black 'brothers' too much.'

Margaret didn't answer and merely gave Simone one of her 'don't mess with Auntie Margaret' looks.

To deflect attention away from her, Simone changed tack and innocently asked Margaret who she was married to. Margaret smiled and showed my handsome picture to her. Surprisingly Simone smiled back.

Why all the smiles? Was it a picture of me in my birthday suit, proud and erect for all to see?

No.

The reason for the all round *bonhomie* was that Simone was actually dating a white French man at the time but was too scared to admit it! It was only when Margaret played her hand and revealed me as her husband that she confessed the truth.

This is so sad, how many other black women are hiding white men as partners around the country? Are we doomed to be forever lurking in the shadows, only coming out when the coast is clear?

Simone went on to tell Margaret that she had also experienced the stares and kissing of teeth from other black women when she is out with her boyfriend. This was the reason for her not coming clean about her 'Jean Paul'. It was only when Margaret admitted that she, too, had joined the 'Milky Bar' club that she felt confident enough to do so.

Peer pressure. Pah, as they say in France.

It seems that, everywhere one looks, black women are imbued with a fear of the 'white man' when it comes to finding a partner.

I see that even the humble email has its part to play in the racial dating game. My wife received an email this year entitled *Love the Black Woman, Respect the Black Woman and only date the Black Woman*. It included the following lines;

Only a Black Woman: Can make a black man and his non-black date feel nervous without saying a word.

Only a Black Woman: Can be admired and fantasized about by men of other races.

Only a Black Woman: Can make other women want to pay plastic surgeons and tanning salons hundreds and thousands of pounds for physical features she was already born with.

Only a Black Woman: Can be the mother of civilisation.

Propaganda bullshit! Although its main vitriol is aimed at black men who stray away from 'sisters', the email has only one message; segregation. I dare say that many readers of this book have probably also read such a mail. Quite clearly the words of *Love the Black Woman* are meant to act as a defensive mechanism to promote the notion of black female strength and beauty. I have absolutely no problem with this, and indeed I have tried to do the same with my writing in this book. But, the people who swallow this part of the email confuse black female strength as being anti to those of us who do cross race. How many more times do I have to read about the 'fantasy' myth? Why is this crap still believed by so many? If you extend this then, surely, I should be seen as a 'fantasy' for black women?

My brother-in-law shed further light on why black women are reluctant to date white men. He told me many Nigerian women talk to him, asking for help in finding a husband as there is a shortage of Nigerian men in England. He always suggests to them that if they cannot find a Nigerian they should consider dating a white man. Without exception, they don't entertain this as an option. White men are so far off the radar; we are just not thought of as potential boyfriends. Indeed, we are just not recognised as sexual beings at all. Instead, we are seen as a race of latent homosexuals with a penchant for clasping onto mother's apron.

He then went on to tell me that the women he speaks to can't even understand why white men would find them attractive. Well, all I can say by way of response is; wake up, 'sisters' of the world, 'we' do!

Eventually though, this reluctance to 'cross over' will change. If the statistics are correct and half of black men are marrying outside of their race, it stands to reason there must be a lot of single black women and white men knocking around in England. Through circumstances beyond their control they are being squeezed into the same lonely corner.

As a consequence, the next few years, I believe, will see an explosion in this type of coupling. You only have to check the personal ads in the local paper for confirmation of this. Certainly, where I live, many black women are now requesting white men as partners. Crucially, most of the women are over the age of thirty. It is almost as if these older women have given up waiting for 'black love' and so are looking further afield. This is progress but I still find it difficult to understand why so many young black women are averse to dating white men.

The funniest thing I heard over this issue was yet another colleague at the care home where Margaret works. The lady in question was criticising a contestant on the *X-Factor* – one of those naff reality singing competitions I believe. The singer was called Brenda and was black. Her life story was featured in the *News of the World* – written from her black ex-husband's point-of-view. Apparently, the fact she ditched her husband to live with a white guy was basically the story's main point of 'interest'. So Margaret's colleague asked, 'How could she bring such shame on her family by going out with a white guy after marrying a black man?' She went on to say, 'Doesn't matter what her ex-husband was doing she should stay with him.'

She then resolved not to vote for her anymore!

Maybe as a consequence of other people doing the same, poor Brenda was voted out in the next round after the newspaper article was printed. Sad but true.

Albeit indirectly, this was an example of how the media can play a large part in shaping black women's opinion on the subject of mixed marriages. For a more direct example, I suggest you search out the *Guardian* newspaper, dated July 31, 2004. The issue in question featured an article by the female Nigerian writer Helen Kolawole. In it she was allowed to explain why she would only date black Africans, as she felt others could not have the same African spiritual connection to her. Fair enough, I thought first of all. But why not white Africans? Are they not African as well?

Her article also carried the usual suspects as to why she couldn't date outside of her race. She didn't want to be someone's (yawn yawn) 'exotic fantasy' or 'rebellious experiment'. Again, I defend her right to have such rubbish printed but why no corresponding article in praise of such relation-ships? Why were her views aired in the public domain with no redress or right of reply? Would the *Guardian* have published it if it came from a white woman professing she can only love European white men? I suspect not. So why the double standards?

I did write to the *Guardian* at the time, but had no response. In my somewhat naïve mind, I imagined a Left-wing newspaper would seek to bring races together under one banner but obviously not in this scenario.

The BBC also showed a programme in 2005 called the *No1 Ladies Zambian Detective Agency*. It was a harmless enough thirty-minute programme until the final ten minutes. It then contained a scene with two black Zambian ladies discussing sex. The gist of their conversation was they both agreed not to go out with white men because of their unusual sexual demands. Apparently, they had gleaned this information from a friend who informed them of a white man she had dated, who just wanted her to masturbate whilst he looked. It is funny but this sort of informed opinion always seems to come from 'friends'. Just for once, I would like to be given concrete evidence of this white perversity.

I do not understand why black (especially African origin) women/white men relationships are subject to the level of scorn that they receive – especially from the black community. For sure, Africans have had their culture in the past exploited and demonised by Europeans but why take revenge on innocent couples whose only crime is to love one another?

Politics also play their part as to why some black women will not date white men. Due to the numbers of black men marrying out of their race, peer pressure is sometimes applied to black women to keep producing black, rather than mixed race, children. I believe it is this taboo subject that keeps many from 'crossing' over to other races. A sister of one of Margaret's black female friends declared she had to have children with a black man as her other sisters had ended up with white men. She felt it was her duty to continue the black bloodline in her family; to save it from dying out.

Cherlyne, the American lady I interviewed, also advised me that black American women who date outside of their race are made to feel guilty for not staying with their 'brothers'. The idea goes that, by sleeping with the 'enemy', black women are stabbing black men in the back and adding to the feeling of hate that society sometimes has for them.

I am sorry but I find these reasonings so spiteful. They are divisive and merely heap pressure onto people who are colour 'open' when it comes to relationships. Regretfully Cherlyne, a deep thinking lady who certainly does not hate her race or any other, has herself been labelled a 'white man's whore' and an 'Afro whitewash' just because she prefers to date white men.

On the same issue, I notice that even celebrities cannot escape the attention of the inter-racial black police. Part-time tennis player, and full-time sex bomb, Serena Williams, had to go on US national radio, no less, to deny that she only goes out with white men. Why did she feel compelled to do this? Because of a rumour going round the internet discussion sites alleging this of her. As a result, she had to defend her integrity by stating she does find black men attractive and that she has nothing against them.

I don't know what is sadder; the people that gossip like this or the fact she had to go on the radio to defend herself. It has nothing to do with anyone who she prefers to date. It is the political notion again of someone's ethnicity restricting their choice of partner. For me, this is the saddest aspect of the relationship debate, as politics should never be allowed to spill over into an individual's personal life.

But why do I appear so sensitive and maybe even paranoid over this subject? Why should it concern me that so many black women/white men relationships have the odds stacked against them from outsiders and mythmakers? As I am already married to my 'Nubian Queen', why should it matter to me who people date or have children with?

Because the underlying thread of 'sticking to one's own' is the mentality that leads to women treating Margaret as they do. The women who kiss their teeth at her are the type who read articles such as Helen Kolawole's or watch the Zambian programme. I know I can ignore it but I don't see why we should suffer in silence. This negativity will only stop if objections are raised against it and I for one certainly object.

I should stress that I don't want to give the impression that black women can solve all their problems at a stroke by dating white men. No, that is not my intention at all. I just want people to respond and respect other human beings in a humane way.

But why am I only blaming black women for not crossing the colour line? Why do I not blame white men as well? To put this to the test I asked my white male friends if they would date black women. Without exception they all said yes. Not because they want an 'experiment', or a 'fantasy', but because they are turned on by a woman's personality, bum or breasts, or, the more desperate ones, by her pulse. The colour of the female did not enter the equation.

I am not naïve enough to think all white men share this attitude, as many undoubtedly feel it beneath them to date black women. This was brought home to me when Cherlyne was perusing a draft copy of my manuscript, whilst working in America. Her white male boss asked her what she was reading. Truthfully she described it as a book that dealt with a white English man's marriage to a Nigerian. At this news, the guy was visibly shocked by its subject matter and took an involuntary step backwards. Apparently, he really couldn't understand how a white guy could lower himself by marrying a black woman. His reaction stinks I know but I put this down more to the backward attitude of the USA when it comes to race, rather than confirmation of white masculinity rejecting black womanhood.

Please don't misinterpret what I am saying here – it is the basic right of an individual to go out with whomever they see fit – I am just demonstrating that society deems it acceptable for a black woman to state she would not date a white man. Indeed, if anything, peer pressure *encourages* her to say this. It is this attitude we need to question. Otherwise segregation will persist.

I should apologise for the unremitting doom laden chapter this has become. I would, however, like to end on a positive note and advise the reader that I have a Sikh friend (Tars), who is a season ticket holder at the Wolves, a Muslim friend (Asif), who likes punk rock. In addition, my best mate (Nikki) is a confirmed lesbian and also a big Julian Cope/Crazyhead fan.

Oh dear, I sound like a racist using their last line of defence; 'some of my best friends are *coloured*'. This one always makes me laugh when it slips through innocent white lips. Do these people have no inkling as to how stupid they sound when they come up with this old chestnut? I used to work in the same building as a regional organiser for the NF. He was as nice as pie to black people at work – much to the surprise of the black folks themselves. Does this mean he wouldn't support 'voluntary' repatriation for his black colleagues if the NF ever came to power? Of course not. It doesn't matter how many colleagues or 'friends' people have of a different ethnicity, individuals still have the potential to hate another for skin colour alone.

In my case, however, I genuinely do have friends from a variety of ethnicities. I am not writing this to score any anti-racist/anti-homophobia credibility points, merely to show it is possible to live de-segregated lives.

I have, though, become aware that all of the above people have gravitated towards *my* interests. Maybe I should move more towards theirs to truly live my own de-segregated life? Maybe it is I that needs to be more flexible?

Margaret

My husband states that we are a segregated society. I would have to agree with him on this one, as my experiences have shown too many people just want to be with their 'own' kind. The fact that we are all members of the human race seems to be an irrelevance.

So why are we still so separate? For many (ethnic minorities) in England it is because they wish for their culture to remain untainted by Western excess, be it sexual or material, especially within African and Asian cultures. It is slightly snobbish I accept, but many Nigerians I know view our culture as being spiritually and religiously superior to that of white English or black Caribbean.

I would agree with this to an extent, as many white and black British people *have* forgotten their own rich culture and are thus more receptive to others, as shown by their desire to try other foodstuffs. It remains to be seen if this is a tolerance, a weakness, or a strength. Personally, I feel this is a strength.

I contend that the English have forgotten their culture, and on a spiritual level they have lost their religious verve. Britain is now, more than ever, a secular country. The popularity of Christianity has suffered – you only have to walk into a church on a Sunday to spot the dwindling attendances. Where is the will in this country to reclaim our Christian soul?

I would argue it can only come from African or Polish immigrants as we are still living our lives via the morality laid down by God. It is the absence of real Christian values that, therefore, leads us to the conclusion white England will never feel entirely our home.

This is certainly one of the problems we, as Africans, tend to have when it comes to the difficult subject of mixed relationships, as we feel that white people are too open when it comes to sex and prone to a lack of morals. At times, it seems to us that women are used in the West purely to sell sex to men. Evidence of this is found in abundance once winter mutates into spring. I am fed up with seeing young girls walking around with half their backsides exposed either side of skimpy thongs that barely manage to conceal brown skid marks! Why on earth do these women dress like this?

Because they have had it drummed into them that this is the look they must have if one is to be free and a real woman. They are wrong. This is not freedom, it is bondage. Sexual bondage, for men to get their kicks from spotting the female equivalent of builder's bum.

As a result of this sexual imagery, many black women have a tendency to feel that other races only want to use us for sex and a simple lingering look from a white or Asian man can put us on our guard – as our first instinct is to question the motives of the guy. Rather than acknowledge a complimentary gaze, we are sometimes hostile and oblivious to the idea that non-black men find us desirable as marital partners – as opposed to a quick shag. This attitude has to change, especially given the limited number of available black men in this country. Why should relationship 'fun' be restricted to the male of the species? Bobby has a lot of very nice white male friends. Friends that would make perfect husband material if black women gave them the chance.

Equally I have a lot of single black female friends, who would like nothing better than to nurture a home for a loving man. Instead of a man they come home to four empty walls. I may have a degree in economics but anyone with even half a CSE in Maths should be able to work out this equation.

For their own sake black women should open their eyes and seek happiness wherever it may lie. This can be hard, though, as black barriers to interracial dating are hard to break down.

I had a Nigerian colleague of mine (yes, at the care home from hell again) who asked me: 'Why did I marry a white man?' I refused to answer as I am fed up with this stupid question. Does my husband not have a character? Why is he continually seen as a faceless blob of pale skin rather than a human being? He is more than just a piece of 'uncooked chicken'.

Another Yoruba man came to my house, a friend of my cousin Joyce, and met Bobby and I for the first time. He was a sociable young man who was friendly to the both of us. Imagine my surprise then, when he confided to my cousin afterwards that I was 'lost' having married a white man.

I wish for a few seconds these people would sit down and think before coming out with such sweeping statements. I am certainly not lost because I married a white man; on the contrary, I feel that my mind has blossomed now that the burden of racism has left me.

This guy also suggested the reason I like antiques is because I am married to a 'white man'. I mentioned this to Bobby and he found this amusing because he always refers to my two favourite shows (*Antique Roadshow* and *Cash in the Attic*) as *Antique Rubbish* and *Crap in the Attic*. I truly find it baffling that this man, who had only known me for an hour, had made so many false assumptions about my character – all on the basis of whom I have married. He is not the only one.

I also knew a Mauritian lady whose son was going out with a white woman. He was told, in no uncertain terms, that, if he ever married her, the family would disown him as he had brought shame on them. What exactly was it they were scared of? They were worried she would look down on them if they ate food with their hands! She also did not want to have to make an appointment to see her son if he was married to one of 'them'.

This has echoes of what my mother once also feared; a fear that turned out to be groundless. The Mauritian lady was concerned about her culture being fragmented and so withdrew into herself – a natural human defensive mechanism but one that can be overcome.

The Africans I work with also often ask for my opinion when it comes to traditional English customs, such as the wearing of a remembrance poppy in November. I get asked these questions because: 'You are married to one of them.' Yes, that is correct but I also have a brain and knew before meeting Bobby what a poppy meant.

This question should actually be turned around as it is surely wrong that my African colleagues have remained in ignorance about English customs given the length of time they have lived here. Yet again, it is the box scenario. If a certain culture views itself as superior, it will always be separate and, therefore, segregated from the rest of society. Trevor Phillips was a lot more clued up on this subject than the majority of social commentators who queued up to ridicule his words. Both Bobby's and my own experiences show the validity of his timely comments.

I actually feel sorry for the English, as many Africans dismiss them as a nation of DIY experts, sexual perverts, loose women and David Beckham! You want more proof?

I was discussing the Zambian detective agency programme, that Bobby referred to, with a colleague who had also seen it. The lady, a Rwandan by the name of Vanessa, went on to say, 'Everyone knows that white men have problems getting it up so they have to pay someone to have sex with their wives.' She, as normal, acquired this information from one of her 'friends'.

Really, such nonsensical comments do nothing for race relations in this country. Is this what the BBC intended by showing this programme?

I have felt for a while that, to close the cultural gap existing in England, the English should be more up front with their nationality. Sure, the English have done many bad things throughout history in the name of colonialism but, whilst recognising this, we should not forget the good.

Religion is the obvious one but even some aspects of the Empire, for example the Civil Service, have long been admired internationally. Diverse figures such as the historian Niall Ferguson and the new Ugandan born Archbishop of York, John Sentamu, have pointed this out. By having more pride in their cultural achievements/traditions, I think the English would understand why other groups in England celebrate their own events. It is precisely because of this apathy that non-white Brits feel the English have 'no culture'. After all, if you yourself cannot be patriotic towards your own country, why expect others?

Look how this reasoning has even affected my husband – what with his comments regarding his lack of 'identity' at being English and reluctance to cheer on the England football team.

I suppose the argument here is why do black/white/Asian people now not have the same culture? After all, we have been rubbing shoulders together for many decades. How come we still have these segregated lives? Why do so many seek to divide us from one another, such as the Muslim extremists who want Sharia law in England? Then, again, why do we tolerate their behaviour? In this instance, there are plenty of countries that do have Sharia law. If these people feel so strongly about it why do they not simply move house? This is such an obvious question for the majority of people who live in England and, yet, I have never heard any religious 'cleric' come up with a satisfactory response. If you want to mix with people of different faiths, politics, races, then fine, stay here. If not, go, it is your choice.

Another Nigerian colleague admitted to me that, after eleven years in this country, he still had no English friends. Neither did his wife or his ten-year-old son who had spent his whole life in England. Rather than be ashamed or puzzled by this, he was actually rather proud he had managed to keep his culture free from Western corruption. I asked why he has no English friends. He answered, 'Because you cannot trust them.' He went on to say that you could work with them but that you cannot mix socially.

Persisting with the theme, I asked how he came to this conclusion. 'Because the English have no culture,' came back his somewhat predictable response. He embellished this with, 'I can't stand this country and all it stands for.'

I can sympathise with many who are probably thinking: 'Well piss off then, if it is so bad.' It is akin to a stranger going into someone's house, drinking their tea, eating their biscuits and at the same time ridiculing their wallpaper. I am not suggesting all people who live in this country parade around in St George underpants, merely that they show courtesy to those who do.

My colleague, and numerous others, needs to be aware of this and show more respect to a country that, by standards around the world, has welcomed us.

When I say respect I don't mean the tip your hat days of the Raj mentality, I just mean learning about England and its vibrant history. As it stands at the moment, many of my fellow Africans glean their entire cultural knowledge of the English via TV soap *EastEnders* or reality show *Big Brother* – hardly positive images! Without their experiencing other aspects of English culture, should we really be surprised if some Africans are of the opinion our civilisation is superior?

A lot of white people would be rightly horrified at many of the views I hear whilst at work in the nursing home. Without exception, all the comments are uttered by Africans. I have tried to understand why they express these views, and can only presume they feel personally demeaned at crossing continents, merely to wipe white people's bottoms. I believe Robert Mugabe made this very same point in one of his speeches. This attitude towards the English is so wrong, as I doubt that my co-Christian worker, for example, would have received such hospitality (in a religious sense) in Saudi Arabia.

My fellow Nigerian also made a derogatory comment about the English and their complete lack of fashion sense. I was going to defend the country's honour again on this point, but then remembered some of Bobby's clothes. I remained silent. Of course, his comments reminded me once more of how I used to feel about the English. Now, I actually find it embarrassing that people still have these negative thoughts about England and its culture.

It is also discourteous to constantly label the English as those 'white people,' another line I constantly hear by fellow Africans. We are forgetting that behind the skin colour of a person is a human being. The idea that skin colour denotes someone's type of character is so off the wall it is scary.

What is scarier, though, is the amount of Africans who tell me that this is true. Increasingly, we are suffering from a persecution complex and are unable to differentiate between normal white people and prejudiced white people.

To take it one step further, I even have the suspicion that black folk look on the majority of whites as racist; unless they can prove otherwise. By assuming this and writing off England's culture, we are slipping into the dangerous territory of the cultural supremacist.

It is because of this drive to ridicule England's past history, that many of the English are only allowed to look back affectionately at the Second World War and the Royal Family. Is that the sum total of English cultural achievement since the dawn of time? Absolutely not, and more should learn about England's past to forge ahead with its colourful future.

I ask a pertinent question: why are the English so embarrassed by their past? In my opinion it stems from the hangover caused by England's colonial legacy. Decades of well meaning, but wrong, lefty types have taught the English not to love their country, and to, instead, concentrate on others, whose cultural achievements are deemed more worthy.

It seems to me you've celebrated 'diversity' to such an extent that you have forgotten your *own* rich culture. You have become culturally unaware of English traditions and history, due to the misguided notion that expressing one's culture is racist.

Look at the celebrations which take place every year in London for St Patrick's Day on March 17. Numerous Irish themed events are held throughout London to help the party go with a swing. In contrast St George's Day, April 23, is allowed to pass with a brief show of Morris dancing, or maybe a reading of Shakespeare. Why the English act in this way is bemusing to those of us who celebrate our own culture. This is a very dangerous policy and I refer the reader here back to when I was constantly being told how black people had managed to achieve little. What was the outcome? I turned against white people.

If we are not careful, this policy of refusing to celebrate Englishness will rebound on the very part of society it was supposed to protect, and the far-right will exploit this to the detriment of all black and Asian people. Indeed, there are signs the backlash has already started. The clearest example came in the shape of the ITV Teletext poll, mentioned by Bobby in an earlier chapter, a poll that showed only 3 per cent of Britons deemed diversity to be good for Britain. 3 per cent! It is precisely because the English are not allowed to celebrate events, such as St George's Day, that this belief is spreading.

Zimbabwe's Robert Mugabe, that pillar of democracy, is equally at home denigrating the English, his African sense of superiority no doubt finely honed after years of fighting the 'white man'. He seems to have forgotten that Rhodesia was renamed in 1980. To the great sadness of any true African, it is his own people who now bear the brunt of his anger and disastrous policies.

Mr Osama bin Laden also demonstrates his hatred for the West, via the terrorist actions carried out in his name, actions that destabilise the entire Western hemisphere.

It may seem strange to link these two tyrannical figures as one, but each is speaking with a superior tone of voice. Each is effectively seeking segregation from the rest of the world. Each is wrong.

But how do I feel personally with all these different thoughts and cultures rampaging through my head? To be fair, I have sometimes felt in the middle of two different cultures. This is most noticeable whenever my family has a 'Nigerian' issue to discuss with me. In Yoruba culture, I would be equally at home discussing any subject matter with either set of parents. Although I love Bobby's parents dearly, I am aware certain issues are off bounds with them. I refer here to family problems 'back home'.

In English society, a lot of problems couples have are solved within the framework of the two people discussing them, or maybe with the assistance of a marriage guidance counsellor. In Yoruba land, we would have family conferences which would involve a lot more than the couple. Surely, I would argue, a family is better qualified to give a more accurate answer than a counsellor? I find it weird how such issues are dealt with over here. As a result, more than once, my parents have had to tell me, 'Tell Bobby's family this is the way we do things.'

Bobby says this is extremely arrogant, as his family have never told mine, 'Tell Margaret's family this is how we do things.' Maybe it is arrogant, but it's just the way it has always been, although I can see how this links to my colleague's attitude about the English having no culture. They do have a culture; it is just different to ours.

Another example is our attitude to our respective sisters. If I have a problem with Bobby, I am quick to phone my sister, Anne. She tends to side with Bobby anyway, whatever my complaint, but I always feel better after speaking to her. Bobby, though, would not discuss our issues with his sister, as he views any problems as private within a marriage – until this book anyway.

So, in some areas even Bobby and I are leading segregated lives. Both of us are constantly hopping around trying to appease both sets of parents. This is one of the main reasons why African men and women, a generalisation I stand by, do not marry out of their culture. They love their culture too much to risk it being diluted by intermarrying, viewing themselves as having a stronger spiritual belief.

An interesting historical parallel can be drawn here with the Japanese at the onset of WW2. The war planners in Tokyo believed victory would be theirs due to the 'spiritual strength' of the Japanese fighting man. This would, supposedly, make him more than a match for any number of effete and self-indulgent Caucasians. Whatever the material advantages the Western Allies had over them, the Japanese were confident their stronger culture would win through. Culture, luckily, cannot win wars. It can, however, restrict a person's ability to think clearly. By replicating the Japanese arrogance of WW2, Africans in England are setting themselves up for future conflict. The generation that have this attitude may think they are harmlessly protecting their culture but they are not. Instead, they are sowing the seeds of misery for their children, by keeping them at arm's length from other ethnic groups. However, much like the long heralded property crash, when the culture crash comes it will come big time.

This is so unnecessary. For, once you have committed yourself to marrying out, it's not really as hard as you may imagine. Sure, it can be frustrating explaining what seems obvious to us as Africans, but it's never too late to learn something new. Bobby is an exemplification of this. Since we have married, he has grown to love the way Yoruba culture is reflected in simple areas – such as Tupperware! For those not in the know, we like to celebrate and remember events by stencilling names of people onto plastic Tupperware. So, for instance, I enjoy a bucket bath with the name Madam Victoria Osunnuyi, a lady who sadly passed away in 1992, imprinted on the side of the bucket. It may appear tacky, but Bobby really likes the way people live on once they have died. And we don't just stop at Tupperware! Oh no, mugs, bottles, saucepans, basically anything that is useful in the house, we like to decorate with names from our past. It is our way of showing respect to the memory of the person. So when Bobby dies I am going to stencil his toilet – for reasons I will explain later.

Apart from the two of us, both sets of parents have also gained information via exposure to the other person's culture. Information they would not have discovered if Bobby had married Glynis Barber and I Denzel Washington! Indeed, Bobby's mother has become so aware of my culture that she now likes yam and plantain as much as I do. I remain hopeful that one day her son will share this 'diversity' towards my food.

So, if anyone is put off dating/mixing for this reason, I say give it a try – segregation is the safe option and ultimately just leads to disappointment. We all have to mingle in together eventually. Surely, it is better to do it on your own terms?

Another area of segregation is age. I have many elderly friends, mainly to do with my black doll *obsession*. I, personally, have no problem at all in talking to them about any issue under the sun. Some youngsters, however, find it odd that I seek the company of people forty or so years older than me. I find their attitude strange. Just because someone's skin may be criss-crossed with wrinkles and their hair is grey, it does not mean that their brain is not capable or their opinion worthless. Why segregate people because of this? This would never happen in Nigeria, where we value the wisdom of elderly citizens.

This is again the corrosive effect of Western culture, where youth is acclaimed and seen as a 'must have' even for people who have reached middle age. You only have to see the amount of anti-ageing, anti-greying products on the market, or the lack of TV presenters (especially women) in their fifties and sixties for confirmation. Fine, have the young guns for your eye candy, but don't cast aside a lifetime's knowledge once a few wrinkles appear.

We are also segregated where religion is concerned. Unfortunately, so many people today do not trust other people's faiths; as a consequence they withdraw into their own and become more fundamental in protecting its name. In Nigeria we have often been accused of this and, in all fairness, we have suffered religious riots in a few Northern cities like Kano. The problem, though, is not as bad as you may imagine in England, despite occasional flare ups such as those the Prophet Mohammed cartoons provoked in 2006.

Sure, as Nigerians we are passionate about religion, be it Muslim or Christian. However, the vast majority are content to live side by side in harmony. It is only when local issues erupt that violence can be seen to be along religious grounds.

Even in this country, we are divided on religious grounds. By this I don't even mean the obvious ones such as Muslim, Sikh, Hindu, Christian. No, take an average Pentecostal gathering. The congregation will be 98 per cent black. Most white people steer clear of such churches and stick to their 'own' somewhat staid services instead. On the flip side, black Africans actively seek 'black' churches that worship in a way more acceptable to those of us with roots in Africa. As Martin Luther King famously said in the Sixties; if we cannot even pray together what chance do we have in other areas?

Class is another aspect of segregation. In England, different classes tend to stay within their own tight confines and are quick to dismiss the others as either 'toffs' or 'chavs'. In Nigerian circles, we are more likely to segregate ourselves via our ethnic groupings, be it Yoruba, Hausa, Fulani etc. This is because we generally have only a small middle-class. Most are just rich or poor.

One part of segregation not immediately obvious is language. I do not mean someone unable to speak the English language, although that is another variation on it; I mean the usage of 'street' talk or 'Jafaican' as it is sometimes referred to. It used to be that only the black kids would adapt language to include words such as 'brethren' 'you get me,' etc. Nowadays, it is as likely to be white or Asian kids speaking like this. In some ways, I can see this as a positive – as it demonstrates on a practical level how we are becoming one people. Unfortunately, it is also restricting the type of employment opportunities available to people who insist on talking like this. Let's be frank here, what boss would want to give a job to someone who cannot speak a sentence using the Queen's English?

So, we are again segregating ourselves by a refusal to play the game when it comes to conversation. It may seem trivial but not being able to communicate properly has major ramifications.

Anyway, the white/Asian kids that are speaking 'black' are only picking up on a small negative aspect of black culture. Believe me, there is a whole lot more to being black than merely speaking like Ali G and wearing baggy jeans.

Bizarrely, segregation even applies to children's toys. It always makes me laugh when I see baby dolls being labelled as 'ethnic'. Why? You never see a white doll labelled as such. Is white not an ethnic group? Take the Argos department store. They sell a range of products for the Baby Annabell doll. 'Annabell' is totally white but she does come with a 'coloured' friend. Yes, you can get the Baby Annabell ethnic doll – exactly the same as the other one, only with slightly darker skin. In truth, she looks more mixed race than black, but I guess 'ethnic' suits all non-white dolls. Why have they done this? If you have to label the dolls just call them white or black dolls. 'Ethnic' is so all-embracing, it is actually offensive. By harping on about the different ethnicity, they are merely bringing it to children's attention.

The irony is that Argos probably think they are being 'socially inclusive' by selling these tacky dolls. Who knows, they may even boast at boardroom meetings how much they are in touch with ethnic 'culture' via their doll diversity.

I even noticed this ethnicity as brand name, when shopping at Makro. Within their aircraft hangar-like store room, they have an aisle labelled 'ethnic'. I wandered over, curious as to what 'ethnic' referred to. Basically, it seemed to describe anything under the sun. I could buy spices, herbs, rice and,..err...lots of tea. Tea! How quintessentially English is that? Yet it was labelled 'ethnic'. This may be technically correct in historical terms, but, surely, by now, it is recognised as a character trait of the English to sup tea all day? I guess tea is still 'ethnic' in the same way that I am. It is truly a strange world we live in.

Summary

We have no differences here. Both of us are of the opinion that Britain is segregating itself voluntarily along all sorts of fault lines – be it race, age, class, or even dolls. Whilst the herd instinct of humanity tells us this is correct, the brain should be able to work out it is wrong. By constantly emphasising the differences that people have, we are merely reinforcing already entrenched views.

The reality is no-one is emerging as a winner. We can all learn from the way another person may approach a problem. Just because one has done something one way for centuries, it does not mean it should remain that way indefinitely. Culture is there to educate us, not to keep us chained to its beliefs. Many things, in all types of cultures, are wrong. Society only progresses by challenging and changing those ideas that are morally and spiritually corrupt.

The whole rationale of segregation stems from the belief that one race/culture is better than another. Superficially, this may appear benign and unthreatening. The reality is somewhat different.

All around the world it seems as if people are rebelling and fighting against a perceived threat; a threat normally from within. It is time ordinary people, who don't mind who their neighbours are, started fighting back.

Rudyard Kipling produced his famous dictum that "East is East and West is West, and never the twain shall meet." Both of us, obviously, disagree with this suggestion and believe distrust of others can be overcome with just a little effort from everyone. Sadly, many now feel their own way of life is likely to be upset if they mix with people who do not physically/culturally resemble themselves.

In my opinion, this is the biggest area for confusion when people discuss the current hot potato of multiculturalism. As we have demonstrated, it is possible to overcome this feeling. Just because someone in your family, street, or place of work does something in a way you would not, it does not mean to say it is necessarily wrong.

Take me for instance. Do I feel threatened by Margaret liking Whitney Houston? Will it lead to me liking 4 Promille (German Oi! band) any less? Just because I do not necessarily believe in a higher authority, does that make Margaret less likely to believe the Holy Scriptures? Of course not. We both have our own beliefs and are confident in expressing them. The people who are more likely to segregate themselves are those who lack confidence in their own culture. By seeking to avoid its 'corruption', they are being defensive and showing that something is wrong with it to start with. By keeping it 'pure' and untainted, they are just subscribing to the ridiculous racial/cultural supremacy theories of the past. A past that eventually leads to death camps and the like.

The problem we have to face up to, in England, is that with ever more disparate groups of people living in our cities, the propensity is increasing for one 'community' or another to feel victimised. After all, as the saying goes; you can't please everybody all of the time.

Lastly I refer here to Margaret's favourite book: Jonathan Swift's *Gulliver's Travels*. In it Mr Swift makes the very valid point that, just because one day you are in a position of power, do not presume it will last forever. Roles are easily reversible. The moral of his book is; every individual should be fair to all. We share his hope.

CHAPTER 16

Fraud and Finance

Bobby

No real differences here but we do have some interesting opinions on the issue of finance and its uneasy bedfellow, fraud. Whilst Margaret and I had no 'clashes of culture', I did have some problems with her reluctance to accept my advice, as you will see..........

I will never forget the first week I moved in with Margaret. I could not believe how much money she was wasting. A simple look in her fridge/freezer betrayed her lack of financial acumen; it was full of out of date food. Food she was going to have to throw away and buy all over again. Plain stupid! I decided to introduce two simple words: 'stock taking,' into her vocabulary.

You may think I am being a touch arrogant here, but I was really bemused at how a lady, with an economics degree no less, could be so idiotic when it came to an elementary skill such as shopping. From now on, she (or I) was going to check the freezer before committing to buying any more delicacies like frozen fishfingers.

Feeling increasingly exasperated at Margaret's lack of planning, I moved on to her personal finances. My horrors were only just beginning! I discovered Margaret had a penchant for only paying the minimum on credit cards, whilst still having cash reserves. This to me seemed like the most heinous economic crime in the world. Oh no, I cried at her in despair, I cannot believe you are doing this. There is another way, as the admen would tell you.

Feeling not unlike a colonial of two centuries past, I rushed to Margaret's aid and lent her the money to pay off the debt. After putting her on the right track, we then began to save money for the more important things in life: German punk records, Marks and Sparks's chicken pies, etc. When I asked Margaret why she was a bit loose with her finances, she merely shrugged her shoulders and said: 'that is the way we do things.'

Well no, I admonished her in my ever so slightly condescending manner; it does not have to be like this. Just because you have been brought up in the 'Nigerian way', (whatever that actually means) with regards to finances, does not mean you cannot improve your own performance. Many Nigerians manage their money in perfect fashion. It is utter poppycock to suggest you cannot do so due to the stamp on your passport.

To be fair to Margaret, I did congratulate her on her intelligent decision to buy property when she did. She bought at the right time in the early 1990s and so was spared the financial heartache that claimed so many victims in the late 1980s property crash. Somewhat spookily, I also bought my first property in the same month and year.

I also had similar financial differences of opinion with Margaret's mother. To briefly explain, she needed a few thousand pounds to transport some goods (by ship) to Lagos. I was asked if I would be willing to lend some cash to help. Whilst I was keen to assist my new family, I was also aware of the, how can I put this politely, tendency amongst some Nigerians to be less than truthful with business transactions. I, therefore, felt it prudent to ask for some information regarding the company/individuals concerned with the shipping. At the time, this was a surprise to Margaret's mother, as she expected the cash to be handed over no questions asked. The information was not forthcoming so the money stayed in my account, whilst her mother obtained the credit elsewhere. Suffice to say, she was ripped off.

I mention this not with any feeling of superiority – they are my family as well – but to show that a little bit of common sense is often the best policy when it comes to economics. Due to the respect of elder's idea, it was thought unusual, and maybe even disrespectful of me, to ask such questions. The end result, though, may not have been the loss of hard earned cash. This is a clear case of where culture is allowed to get in the way of business and cloud practical financial thinking.

I could accept this somewhat loose attitude to money if lessons were learnt, but they are not. This was not the first time my other family has suffered at the hands of fraudsters. I really am at a loss to understand this continuing financial suicide. The 'this is the way it has always been done' line should be shown up for what it is; the wrong way of doing things.

I have found Nigerians also have another way of explaining away and accepting any financial wrongdoing; it is the 'the will of God.' Without wishing to appear blasphemous, I am always dumbfounded by this response.

And yet it is trotted out whenever a natural disaster occurs; such as plane crashes, or when an act of vandalism is committed, like tampering with fuel pipes. Fine, pray to the Almighty and adopt a Christian lifestyle, but do not absolve yourself of responsibility by using God as an excuse.

I also do not understand the Nigerian mentality for displaying wealth whenever it comes one's way via flash cars/silk shirts etc. This showing off temptation is really the number one reason why Nigeria has not fully exploited its natural resources. In my opinion, it is sheer lunacy to spend every penny one earns on fancy clothes whilst many around you are struggling to make ends meet. At the risk of sounding like a neo-colonialist, a dash of hard-nosed western business sense would help Nigeria rid itself of such 'virtues'. Only when the environment changes around them, can ordinary Nigerians grasp the mantle of opportunity that many take for granted in the West.

Of course, the irony is many of the 'ordinary' Nigerians have succumbed to this way of thinking and see nothing wrong with flaunting one's prosperity. They do not realise the rest of the world think they are stupid for doing so.

The one hope for Nigeria is that many of its citizens now live abroad and can see the long lasting damage this attitude has had. I have spoken to lots of Nigerians living in England, who deplore this show off mentality, and who are determined to see that wealth trickles down to benefit all. It is sad to note, however, that these people have had to leave Nigeria to do (often) poorly paid jobs due to the run down economic infrastructure in their home country. Their expertise and financial common sense are being wasted here, whilst their fellow citizens are fooled into believing a silk tie is the height of success. It is not.

Mind you, in this country we are perched precariously on our moral high horse. The last report I read suggested we Britons owe a combined total of 1.3 trillion pounds! Instead of servicing this debt, we are buying our flat screen plasma television sets and our top of the range motors. Credit card debt is spiralling and we are mortgaged to the hilt.

For some reason we, and the Americans, who adopt much the same mentality over financial concerns, feel we are immune to the global slow down as long as we continue spending our way out of trouble. As wise old Katarina said in *Heimat*, 'everyone is living on tick.' It may just be a line in a fictional TV show, but old Katarina was proved right about the Weimar Republic. I fear we are going the same way now. You can buy yourself happiness in a material sense, but eventually the price needs to be paid. Time will tell if we can afford it.

Still, I suppose that even if you can't, you could always do some fraudulent activity to cover the cost. Oh dear, I was going to leave fraud out of my book, as it is such a stereotypical subject to talk about for Nigerians, but I would rightly be accused of moral cowardice if I did.

First of all, fraud is often labelled a victimless crime. This is patently not the case. How many innocent Nigerians are lumbered with a reputation for being fraudsters purely because they were born in Nigeria? I would argue that this reputation, harsh though it may seem, is entirely understandable, given the level of fraud that does exist. It is just a pity that so many ordinary people are caught up in the fraudster's deals. Do these criminals not realise they are making life so hard for Nigerians all around the world? I suspect they couldn't care less. This is again symptomatic of the selfishness so endemic amongst those who commit fraud. So what if Mr and Mrs Average Nigeria cannot obtain a mortgage, or prove who they are, at least the fraudster has a nice car to drive and a smart suit to wear.

But maybe I am exaggerating the extent to which these activities affect the regular guy in the street? Where is the evidence?

I have a friend who is high up in the echelons of power for a well-known building society. He tells me they have a special policy for Nigerians, given the level of fraud they have previously encountered. It is subsequently a lot harder for a Nigerian to open up an account than it is for other citizens in England. The reason for this is that Nigerian documents are treated with scepticism and downright disbelief when they are produced as evidence of identity. This then makes it almost impossible for Nigerians to open accounts and enjoy even the rudimentary financial facilities the majority of us take for granted.

My brother-in-law also felt the effects of the Nigerian fraud legacy when he tried to book a simple flight ticket to Lagos via British Airways (BA). Despite being a loyal customer for a number of years, he was told it was BA policy not to accept credit cards over the phone for flight bookings to Lagos Airport. As a result, he had to go in person to Heathrow to pay cash for the said ticket – an inconvenience for him and for others using their planes.

At first glance, these examples may appear discriminatory but I cannot find it in my heart to blame the companies. They exist to make money not to provide a social service. If Nigerians were less fraudulent they would be treated like anybody else. As I stressed earlier, this is an unfortunate by-product of the fraudsters' activities. It is they and not the building society, or airline, who should be blamed.

Fraud is also sometimes a barrier to justice. The case of Zainab Kalokoh proves this perfectly. This poor woman was brutally murdered in Peckham in

2006 and three of the convicted murderers, all Nigerian boys of ages 14, 15 and 16, were sentenced to prison for a minimum term of sixteen years. Such a terrible crime would generally have attracted a longer sentence but the judge had to take into account their young age. However, their age is not known for certain as, according to the police, their birth certificates were crude Nigerian forgeries. Thus this 'innocent' act of fraud has enabled them to cheat the justice system, and cause more heartache to the Kalokoh family. Does the fraudster have this on his conscience as he goes to bed at night? I doubt it.

After speaking to many Nigerians, I have realised that fraud is just the accepted way of doing things. Of course people moan about it when they are the victims, but often they do the same thing to others.

To an extent, I can understand this mentality in Nigeria where corruption is more institutionalised. What I cannot tolerate though, is when Nigerians go to other countries and carry on in the same fraudulent manner. A classic case of this was Olawasegun Adekunle, an illegal immigrant Nigerian, who was sentenced on May 15, 2007, to five years imprisonment for stealing two million pounds from different bank accounts. It is precisely because of people like him that life is made more difficult for non-fraudulent Nigerians.

Take Margaret for instance. Every time we travel to Europe, she gets far more of a going over than I do at customs. She has a British passport like me but as soon as they spot her Yoruba middle names the interrogation starts: 'Why are you here?' 'What is your business?'

Whilst such questions are annoying to Margaret, I can appreciate the logic behind the clerk's inquisitiveness. We all have a job to do and Nigerians are, unfortunately, bearing the brunt of the fraudsters work. Fraud will continue to impact on rank-and-file Nigerians until more people change their own personal habits.

However, this will take time, for I have heard some horrendous stories about the ripping off committed by Nigerians against other Nigerians. One of Margaret's ex-boyfriends, to give but one example, was staying in a flat owned by a friend of hers, in exchange for a small rent. She was quite close to Margaret's boyfriend, so thought that nothing untoward would occur.

Imagine then her shock, when she received a gas/electric bill, after he had moved on, for a thousand pounds! It transpired the boyfriend had fiddled around with the gas/electric meter to get power for free. Fair enough, some of you may be thinking, the gas companies charge too much money for essential services, they deserve to be ripped off occasionally. I personally cannot agree with this (Mr Anarchy strikes again) but, what I found most strange, is the boyfriend then refused to pay the sum, arguing it was not his flat. I really cannot get my head around this one. The lady helped him out with somewhere to live and yet he burdens her with a debt caused by *his* fraudulent activity. Companies are anonymous, friendships and bloodlines are not.

My Ugandan friend, Daphne, has also told me countless stories about the Nigerian boyfriends she has had in the past. One of the guys she dated had a separate wallet stuffed full of credit cards – all with different names. In case you are thinking he was merely a rate tart, he was not. He was a criminal, simple as that.

I am aware, writing this, that I can be accused, after listing all these misdemeanours, of merely helping to perpetuate the stereotype about Nigerians and fraud. I know this to be the case, but you cannot change a culture by ignoring the bad and just praising the good.

Even Margaret's own father is very disillusioned about the fraud aspect of Nigeria. A totally honest man himself, he finds it distressing that so many of his fellow Nigerians cannot see this and lead more virtuous lives.

Instead, rather than being embarrassed by their worldwide image as a nation of fraudsters, some appear to be proud of this fact. This was brought home to me when I read about the widely reported case of the governor of Bayelsa state, Diepreye Alamieyeseigha. Crowds, according to the *Daily Telegraph* of November 22, 2005, cheered the returning governor when he sprung up out of the blue in his home village in the Niger Delta. They cheered him because he had skipped bail in England, whilst on charges of money laundering to the tune of 1.8 million (pounds not naira.) This puzzled me. I could not understand why an alleged criminal is so worshipped, when he has stolen *their* money. Surely a more natural response would have been anger at his actions?

To be fair to the Nigerian President, Obasanjo, the governor has since been arrested as part of his anti-corruption drive and faces criminal charges. The problem here though is not necessarily the alleged crime it is the response from others. If he was shamed and humiliated it might act as a deterrent for the next generation of fraudsters. However, given the applause he received, should we be surprised if any impressionable young man reached the conclusion that life as a fraudster was a good career opportunity?

I compare this non-judgemental atmosphere to the middle 1970s in Germany. Here the terrorist *Rote Armee Fraktion* (RAF) were tapping into Left-wing intelligentsia and creating an environment for terrorism to be allowed to breathe. Not realising the RAF were truly a violent terrorist movement many on the left sympathised with their main aim: the overthrow of capitalist society. Indeed, opinion polls at the time showed the level of support they had was extremely high (between 10-20 per cent) amongst ordinary Germans. Support that only vanished after Martin Schleyer, chief of Daimler Benz, was brutally murdered (by the RAF) following the suicide of terrorists Andreas Baader, Gudrun Ensslin and Jan-Carl Raspe in Stammheim Prison during the night of October 17, 1977. I suspect their arrests would have come considerably sooner, if such a large chunk of the population did not share at least a part of their ideology.

Even today, we are seeing similar sympathies develop with regards to the attacks on London in the summer of 2005. Yet again it is the Left-wingers creating an atmosphere for the apologists to thrive in. By that I mean most of the blame for the attacks was aimed at the government for invading Iraq and not the bombers themselves. A complete *volte-face* of moral responsibility.

Muslim groups that claimed to represent 'their' community, such as the Muslim Council of Britain (funnily enough I used to work with their spokesman Inayat Bunglawara), were also wheeled on to discuss the outrage. Almost without fail, the familiar words tripped out of innocent tongues; 'we condemn this terrorist atrocity, Islam clearly states the killing of civilians is wrong, *but.......*'. It is the 'but' that is the problem. The 'but', of course, then leads on to a discourse about British foreign policy. Why include the 'but'? By all means criticise British foreign policy, but please do not include a discussion of it whilst condemning terrorism in the same breath. All this serves to do is confuse a political notion (bringing the soldiers home) with a bombing campaign.

It is this tacit defending of the terrorist's political argument that the general public subconsciously inhale, leading to genuine Islamophobia and distrust of ordinary Muslims. By including British foreign policy, these spokespeople are inadvertently legitimising the terrorist's argument by blurring the lines between religion/democracy/terrorism. Consequently, non-Muslims have a ready-made excuse for treating all Muslims as potential suicide bombers and not the human beings they are. Organisations, like the Muslim Council of Britain, should focus their ire on the bombers, who purport to act in the name of Islam, and leave politics to the politicians.

The Populus Survey in the summer of 2006 also published a poll that indicated 13 per cent of British Muslims viewed the London bombers of 2005 as 'martyrs'. Crucially, this support has been declared *after* an act of wanton destruction – in contrast to the German RAF terrorists. This is important to note, as it illustrates how the student-tinged idealism of the '70s German movement has been replaced with the hard aggression of the Islamist supporters. This 13 per cent are helping to contribute to the largely negative image of British Muslims amongst the non-Muslim population. They do neither themselves nor Islam a favour with such views. I feel the continual linking of British foreign policy with terrorism is the main reason for this support, not the actual policy itself. It is the old Josef Goebbels line; if you talk about something long enough the population will eventually believe it.

The terrorists may be losing the war on the ground, but they are light years ahead when it comes to propaganda. They have managed to successfully merge religion with politics and blended it into a recipe for hate. We are all at risk of falling for their divisive spin.

That they are winning the propaganda 'sideshow' in this 'war' was brought home to me in a survey for YouGov/*Evening Standard* on September 5, 2006. In it, a startling 35 per cent of people admitted to feeling 'uncomfortable' whilst travelling near an Asian/North African person on public transport.

I write startling but I, too, have to admit to feeling this way in the immediate aftermath of the July 7 bomb attacks. I can vividly recall boarding a train to work and anxiously scanning every Asian person who got on as it sped towards London from Hertfordshire. One poor Asian guy attracted my particular attention as he sweated profusely under a heavy coat. I studied him closely to see if I could pick up any 'Arabic' chanting or other giveaway signs of terrorist intentions. In my head, I rationalised I was carrying out government instructions and being 'vigilant'. After about a minute, I realised I was behaving in a ridiculous fashion and switched off my imagination. To take my mind away from potential immolation, I started reading the book I had brought from home. Unfortunately, that day I had chosen Gunther Bloemertz's wartime autobiography; *Heaven Next Stop, a Luftwaffe Fighter Pilot at War*. In hindsight, this was not the most soothing title I could have picked!

I really had to grit my teeth and convince myself that the guy was looking nervous due to having eighty other passengers eyeballing him at the same time. This was no joke for any of us. No, this was life or death. He sat there; sweat dripping into and beyond thin eyebrows, as one hundred and sixty eyes frisked him for semtex or whatever explosives are fashionable in terrorist circles these days. In truth, this innocent man looked more like an Asian version of *Mr Bean* rather than a potential bin Laden, but I was emotionally drained and unable to separate fact from fiction. My actions, whilst understandable at that particular time, were blatantly wrong.

By categorizing him as a lazy stereotype, I was letting the terrorists win. I was allowing myself to be bullied into thinking along racial lines. This had to stop. After my tribulations at school, I was not going to let another group of bullies batter me into submission.

Fanciful comparisons (with Nigeria's fraud problem), you may well be thinking, but I cannot see how fraudsters can flourish without a network of sympathisers. Only when showing off and fraud are publicly frowned upon, will Nigeria manage to rid itself of its unsavoury image.

I have often asked Nigerians why so much fraud is committed? Especially given that their nation spends so much time praying to God. The best response I have had in reply is: 'We have to commit sin to be absolved by God.'

Weird.

In the West we have our own version of fraud. Be it benefit fraud, tax fraud, non-payment of rail fares, or running up huge debts and declaring ourselves bankrupt, the list is endless. I cannot sit here in my glasshouse and pretend everything is rosy in England for I would be, err, a fraudster if I did.

Despite the previous paragraph, I honestly do feel that most people in our institutions are fair and above board. It may be naïve in the extreme, but I do believe the majority of our police force, our politicians, even our humble civil servants, are free of corruption. Well, apart from the Immigration Service 'sex-for-asylum' scandal, the Stephen Lawrence case, or the cash-for-honours investigation. Ah well, maybe not then.

Margaret

Yet again, Bobby and I are in agreement as far as the fraud issue is concerned. I have to confess, though, that he did assist me in a few areas where my personal financial planning went askew.

Bobby accused me of a 'heinous crime', in his little moan about me, when it came to my paying the minimum amount towards credit cards. Why did I do this? Being a Nigerian, I never know when I could be called upon to send money home to relatives; as a result, I must have a cash reserve to raid. I can see the logic of Bobby's words; it's just my own personal circumstances negate against his 'western business sense'.

I am not alone in facing this financial quandary. I know of countless friends who have had to take out loans in England so they can pay relatives weddings/funerals/school fees, etc. They do this willingly knowing that our families at home have no access to funds such as these. It is hard, very hard, to continue doing this, especially when you are struggling to make ends meet for your own children, but we can see no other option.

I have also found Nigerians, who are married to non-Nigerians, are sometimes forced to lie to their partners and keep a secret exactly how much money they do send home. Even I have sometimes kept this knowledge from Bobby.

Bobby also castigated me for my lack of shopping nous, giving the example of the out of date food in my freezer. I find this sad. Indeed, it is so sad I am about to go off on a little rant. Has he, a grown man, nothing better to do than root around in a woman's freezer? Quite frankly, he should get a life and do something worthwhile with his time. I wonder just how many hours of his existence he has wasted peering into the freezer or comparing supermarket prices? I do not feel this is a masculine thing to do.

Bobby, though, is an animal who is certainly happiest when in his natural habitat – the supermarket. Oh how depressing I find it, when he proudly waves in my face an item that is 'buy one get one free'. He always looks at me as if he has just won the lottery, and is invariably disappointed at my stonewall face in response. I wish I could get him to see that shopping is a trivial matter, a necessary evil, and not the highlight of the week!

Bobby's attitude to shopping is especially ironic, given he frequently tells me the first lesson of military history is to 'always have a reserve'. Well, that is what I was trying to do with the food in my freezer. Is it my fault the expiry date advanced too quickly and encircled my fishfingers in a pincer movement?

To compound my irritation over this issue, our son has inherited his father's genes and also enjoys a good shop. Urgh!

Still, if I view shopping as the ultimate evil, many see fraud in the same way.

I know many of Bobby's friends have been waiting for this segment of the book as he is often teased about the fraudulent nature of some Nigerians. Indeed, when he first informed some of his friends about me, he was advised, on more than one occasion, to look at my passport to ensure I was born in England and not looking for a green card type marriage.

But it is true, I can't deny it and keep a straight face, Nigeria as a nation is susceptible to fraud. As Bobby mentioned, it is unfortunate that innocent Nigerians have lost their good name as a result of this. The problem is, fraud has been such a deep-rooted part of our culture, it will take decades to eradicate.

How do I know it is deep-rooted? Because I used to condone the activities of those who participated in it. Whilst I have always led a fraud free life myself, I found (in my anti-white Eighties phase) I was sympathising with those Nigerians who set up 419 scams – the invitation to westerners to send funds to Nigerian accounts so more cash would be deposited in them – to dupe white people out of their cash. The reason for my sympathy was because I saw black Nigerians taking money from white Europeans. In my head, at the time, I viewed them as getting reparations for the slave trade, so I had absolutely no compassion for gullible and greedy white men losing their savings to smarter more clued-up Africans. I had adopted very much a Pan-African attitude and took delight at seeing the devilish white man being ridiculed. I was so messed up in my head that if Robert Mugabe had given me a call, I would have willingly become his concubine!

So, why do we commit so much fraud? Why can't we eradicate this blight on our culture? The answer is to be found in our attitude towards business. Nigerian society is geared towards success and the idea of being at the top of one's profession is much admired. This is one of the reasons why some Nigerians take perverse delight at being labelled the world's number one fraudsters. A dubious accolade for sure, but one that rings true. After all, it takes brains to be able to commit fraud – any idiot can mug someone – but real cunning is required to financially exploit strangers, often from a different continent. This is where our high level of education comes into play.

So, I guess, the question must be asked, why did I change my mind and realise that fraud is wrong and immoral? Basically, I used to frequent many Nigerian parties in my twenties, I wasn't exactly a 'wild child' or a 'party animal' but I did like to shake my booty at social get-togethers. I got some attention from men, but began to notice that males with designer suits and fast cars ended up with the prettiest women. The reason being, these men were playing hard and loose with their cash. The cash, in more cases than not, came from fraud.

In my somewhat innocent mind, I imagined these fraudsters were ripping off the white man in order to benefit their local community. I saw them as modern day versions of Robin Hood. The reality, instead, was pure and utter selfishness. The community was left to struggle on alone, impover-ished and financially neglected, whilst they enjoyed materialistic pleasures from their ill-gotten gains.

Nigerians love to show off, as our culture celebrates and demands achievement. What better, more visible way is there than to dress up with Versace shirts, Dolce and Gabbana watches, etc. The loose women with these men were adhering to this culture by associating themselves with winners. Hard-working, honest Nigerians were left to wither on the vine whilst flash fraudsters cleaned up.

Seeing these men for what they are; parasites and criminals, was really an eye-opener for me. Having lived on both sides of the fence, I can honestly say it is better to love a genuine man than to be eye candy for a fraudster.

Even today, this showing off disease is to be found amongst Nigerians – including here in England. Whilst I was writing this book, a Nigerian acquaintance of mine, on a salary of £20,000, boasted of spending £8,000 on a birthday party for her three-year-old child. A three-year-old child! She would have been better off investing the money into a Child Trust Fund to help the little one into further education in the future. But oh no, we just love to impress people with our generosity, wealth and over the top celebrations. What nonsense. This kind of behaviour has to stop for us to progress as a nation. Nigeria will be forever cursed until we overcome this mentality.

I know the English have their 'keeping up with the Jones' attitude, but it is not in the same league as the Nigerian version. We are truly world-beaters in this field. The case of Olawasegun Adekunle that Bobby mentioned proves this. When arrested, Mr Adekunle had an £18,500 18carat gold Rolex watch, and an £87,000 Bentley Continental car, in his possession. Rather than do something useful with his fraudulent 'earnings' he squandered it on luxuries. This is because it is the 'African' way to flaunt our wealth. It is this attitude that leads to pressure being put upon innocent Nigerians to obtain money from dodgy dealings.

Another fraud incident, that has forever stayed with me, is when I went to the assistance of a Ghanaian man who was being violently accosted by a Nigerian policeman in Ibadan. At my intervention, the policeman stopped beating the man and instead arrested me. I was then taken to the Police Station. After a few hours, I asked to be set free as I was innocent of any crime, other than expressing Christian compassion. The man refused and made me stay in a cell for several hours. Whenever I complained to him, he just answered 'I am the law' and that I should pay him if I wanted to get out. Although the man did have a passing resemblance to Judge Dredd, I refused to comply with his blatant fraud.

As a result, I had to wait several more hours before a friend's dad came to the station to get me released. Abuse of such power undoubtedly still carries on in Nigeria, and the situation will only get better when such practises are banned, and the rule of genuine law enforced.

The fraud issue also affects family life. I had a Nigerian friend who was having marital problems. To 'cure' them, her husband re-mortgaged their property to the tune of £80,000. What did he do with the cash? He moved back to Nigeria and left his wife saddled with the debt. Subsequently, she had to sell the house and move into council accommodation, whilst he spent the money living the high life in Nigeria. This is fraud on a personal level. The poor lady was defrauded out of her home by the actions of her errant husband, and had only a lifetime of debt to remember him by. Fair?

Fraud in Nigeria will only be eradicated when our politicians finally face up to the issue. By that, I do not mean glitzy anti-corruption drives with all the attendant razzmatazz. No, I and millions like me, demand a sea-change of culture from the top. Anti-corruption ministers and speeches are fine, but amount to nothing substantial for the poor people on the street. We need proper policies and not excuses.

This was brought home to me when I was watching the BEN TV channel during the course of writing this book. A male member of the Nigerian government was being interviewed about domestic issues of electricity supply, and the criminal gangs that infest our cities. Rather than address the question directly, he went off on a tangent for some considerable length of time. Instead of questioning government or opposition policy, his words carried the usual excuses. Yet again, he blamed everything on the white man for stealing things from Nigeria's heritage. Whilst I do not dispute this happened in the past, Nigeria gained independence in 1960! How much longer can we blame white people for our own failings?

By doing so, this man was appealing to the lowest common denominator: race. By introducing race into the equation, he knew he was on solid ground, as a lot of Nigerians would be happy to hear this. He is then less likely to be asked probing questions. To build on his theory, he also mentioned how white people do not like our food as it is beneath them to eat it.

He then came out, with perhaps the oldest stereotype in the world; that we should be more like the Jewish people as they, 'control the world'. At this point, I wished the interviewer had been able to get him back to the question he had asked, as this had no relevance whatsoever to the price of electricity.

Frankly, I am beginning to wonder if Nigeria will ever have a government that can face up to the real problem of corruption *and* keep its hands out of the till. How many more years do we have to suffer these fools for?

On a broader point, I find anti-Jewish sentiment amongst some black people to be extremely distasteful and often unreported. It is largely based on economic jealousy but cannot be excused. It is as bad as the racism directed against Jewish people by the fascists. Even I have heard crassly disguised anti-Semitism in the workplace. A black colleague of mine was berating someone for supporting Tottenham Hotspurs Football Club. Why? 'Because they are the most racist football club in England,' came the reply. When I asked my colleague for evidence, that could at least pass as circumstantial, I was told; 'they are owned by Jews' (a reference to their Chairman Daniel Levy). How pathetic. Just because a club is owned by someone Jewish, how does this make them automatically racist?

For sure, racist Jews do exist but to label them all that way is stupid in the extreme. Are we no better than Himmler, Heydrich or the rest of the Third Reich dummies?

Black people need to study the Holocaust more and understand how it happened. Anti-Semitism did not end when Hitler blew out his brains in April '45 with a 7.65mm Walther pistol. No, it continues to this day amongst all sorts of communities. Indeed, anti-Jewish feeling is actually increasing; as witnessed by the startling rise in UK anti-Semitic incidents for the year 2006 (594 cases); an increase of 31 per cent from the previous year, according to the Community Security Trust, the Jewish security organisation.

Instead of understanding this racism, we tend to get jealous over the attention lavished on it, in comparison to the slave trade – our 'Holocaust' – and refuse to put it on a pedestal. Even my own sister, Anne, is unaware of some of the finer details of the death camps. Indeed, she once admitted to Bobby she had never even heard of Auschwitz. I know this is ignorance and not anti-Semitism, but historical knowledge is open to all – irrespective of race or religion.

Perhaps even more disconcertingly, I have heard many negative comments from black men and women, concerning the plight of asylum seekers in England. I am sick to death of hearing people with my skin colour describing them as 'parasites'. Have they short memories? How do they think their parents or grandparents felt when their own residence in England was questioned in the 1950s, or as long ago as the 15th Century? Why replicate hatred against the defenceless?

On this point, the people doing the slagging off normally include the line: 'yeah, but my parents didn't come here to sponge off the state'. Whilst this is true, it should be acknowledged that modern day asylum-seekers are not allowed to work, despite many possessing the skills we lack as a nation. But, quite honestly, this is irrelevant. An awful lot of white people in the 1950s did not want black people here full stop – work or no work. Discrimination doesn't begin and end with an Income Support claim form. The frustration I feel at these misguided comments is magnified one hundred per cent if the speaker is black. Blacks should be the one group in society that have no excuse for failing to recognise racial prejudice when it rears its ugly head. Have we forgotten the mentality that kept the slave trade going for so long?

Only when we face up to the issues and not allow ourselves to be distracted by rumour, stereotype, scapegoats or lies will black people progress. Take AIDS as a case in point. I honestly cannot believe how many black people around the world think it was invented by the Americans to deliberately kill off Africans.

To an extent, I can understand the suspicion that it is a man-made disease that somehow went wrong. What I cannot get my head around, is the amount of black people who are entirely convinced the disease was purposely intended to wipe us off the face of the map. I am also fed up with the looks of incredulity I receive when I dare to disagree with those who subscribe to this conspiracy theory.

If it was the case, why has a vaccine not been given to white people? If the rumour was true why has AIDS not been introduced to countries more hostile to America, such as Iran? No, I am afraid AIDS is more to do with the sexual attitudes of male Africans, than deliberate policy by western governments. If a woman's husband goes off to have unprotected sex with a HIV infected prostitute and then passes it on to her, who is to blame? George Bush or the man without control of his genitalia?

This conspiracy theory mentality has now infected many strains of thought in most of the world's countries. Apart from AIDS, the other most popular conspiracy is the one that suggests the Americans blew up the twin towers on September 11. Even Bobby's friend, Asif, believes this one to be 100 per cent true. 100 per cent? Absolutely barmy.

It is also sad to report that more than a third of Americans, (according to a poll conducted by Ohio University in July 2006), believe their own government assisted in the destruction of the twin towers or took no action to prevent their attack. Sorry, but it didn't happen that way. *The X-Files* was a television series not real life! By believing this nonsense, people are giving succour to terrorists and ensuring their propaganda has a platform of respectability to be aired upon. The individuals who spread this garbage around may as well be fully paid up members of al-Qa'eda.

Another one doing the rounds is, that the Americans deliberately blew up the levees in New Orleans when Hurricane Katrina struck, so as to kill off as many African-Americans as possible. I must confess that this one at least made me laugh. I am beginning to think most of the internet community, as these stories tend to start on the net, have been on one-too-many creative writing courses.

Taken as a whole though, these rumours are depressing and sum up the distrust that people of different races feel about each other. To progress, we have to ignore these rumours and concentrate on the matter at hand, without automatically looking to blame outside influences. Excuses, and yet more excuses, get us nowhere in the long term.

I feel that only when women obtain more power in Nigeria (and Africa as a whole) will issues like fraud be put to rest. At the present time, most of our politicians are men who have grown used to abusing their positions of authority. Only when we stop idolising displays of wealth will our continent take its proper place on the world stage. It is time the curtain opened.

Summary

With the exception of Margaret's mother and her shipping loan, we have had no real financial cultural clashes. I do appreciate Margaret's difficulties with regards to her own personal finances, and feel nothing but admiration for her, and others like her, who struggle on for the greater good of extended families.

I have, however, given up trying to pass on my shopping tips to Margaret, as she is too stubborn to listen to my better-qualified advice. I have even tried to convince her, by pointing out how many black dolls she could buy if she paid a little more attention when in the supermarket, but it all falls on deaf ears.

The fraud area, though, sees us in complete agreement. Both of us hate ostentatious displays of wealth and prefer to judge someone on their actions. Sadly, it seems we are in the minority over this issue.

Margaret is sick and tired of the usual raised-eyebrows looks she gets whenever she lets on she is Nigerian. She finds it humiliating to be 'known' as a fraudster because of her identity. I do not know how much longer she has to put up with this stereotyping, but I am pessimistic it will change in the foreseeable future. Fraud is not a victimless crime – Nigerians all over the world are the victims. It needs to stop.

CHAPTER 17

Mid-Marriage Report Strengths and Weaknesses

Bobby

This chapter is a bit different from the preceding sixteen. By now, the reader should have a pretty good idea as to our two characters. Some may feel I am a bit too pretentious, or Margaret a touch outspoken, or even the other way around. Others may have written us off as two self-opinionated individuals who deserve each other. Whatever, what is important is how we view each other after ten years of marriage?

I suppose this is going to read a bit like a bastardised version of the *Mr and Mrs* quiz show that was popular when I was growing up, but I think most couples should continually evaluate their relationship, as it helps keep it fresh. To my mind, those that blithely carry on regardless are the couples that drift apart.

So what exactly do I admire in Margaret?

The first thing I respect is her sense of injustice. By this, I mean she genuinely gets upset when she sees wrongdoing around the world. Crucially, it does not matter whereabouts it happens. If President Putin makes a mistake in Russia, Margaret is quick to condemn him. If Obasanjo errs in Nigeria, Margaret will point this out. She is quite ruthless in her condemnation as well and accepts no mitigating circumstances. For her, the world is very much black and white.

Her sense of injustice is a strength; but it is also a weakness.

Margaret brings this mentality into our marriage, and, as a result, everyday normal discussions frequently descend into my having to verbally defend myself against a perceived insult I may (or usually not) have said.

Whilst I am normally happy letting problems wash over me, to Margaret this is anathema. She views them as challenges in a marriage, only overcome by her inflicting her opinions on me, and anyone else who is within earshot. I think she reacts in this way as a result of her being bullied at school. Due to her having negative experiences at the hands of bullies, Margaret now stands up for herself at the slightest irritation and lashes out at any who offer her a difference of opinion. Her laudable aims, of standing up for the neglected, have become infused with her own sense of frustration that stems from childhood. As a result conflict is never far away.

I have put this to Margaret but she has none of it. Instead, she attributes her outspoken nature to the fact that she is short. Margaret feels, because she is only slightly taller than a cornetto ice cream, she has to air her opinions to stop people walking all over her. Nah, I don't buy that. She is too opinionated and treats talking as a hobby – it is nothing to do with her midget like tendencies.

What I do admire in Margaret is her genuine warmth towards people. Not for her the shuffle behind the newspaper if someone needs help. No, she really does believe in assisting complete and utter strangers whatever their nationality. I always remember a time when she rushed to the aid of a man who had fallen over on a tube platform. After picking him up she talked to him for a few minutes. She then told him that, 'You are Scottish aren't you?' He looked at her in horror, shook his head, and replied, 'No Sheila love, I'm Australian.'

Only my dear wife could mistake a Scottish accent for an Aussie one!

Although her linguistic skills are sometimes lacking, I commend my wife for being The Good Samaritan – a character trait absent in many.

Undoubtedly, her Christian faith is behind many of her attitudes and, whilst this is a good thing, it can make conversations a tad stereotypical. As an example, I know I should never make flippant comments concerning her religion. If I transgress, I am severely admonished by my dear wife. 'Ah ah Bobby, you cannot joke about God, some things are more important than your silly jokes.'

It is fair to say, I have heard this line more than once.

Margaret is also very much a social dream – with an ability to talk to any who will listen. Being the usual English stereotyped reserved type of guy, I can only look on with envious wonder as she feels, and sounds, totally at ease in most public situations. Not for her polite inanities about weather and the price of bread. Oh no, within a couple of minutes she will be lecturing complete strangers as to where they are going wrong in life!

Another of her strong points is her ability to spot propaganda whenever it is spouted. Seeing as how we live surrounded by the bullshit generation, this is a major plus point in her favour. Spin, be it political or social, is identified and shown up for what it is: rubbish.

It's funny but, reading this again, I've suddenly realised most of my compliments concerning Margaret are laced with sarcasm and contain as many negatives as they do positives. I should write that this is not my intention as she really is a lovely lady, albeit with some serious flaws.

So what are her main flaws?

Anyone who has rubbed shoulders with her, knows that her voice, whilst possessing sweet qualities, can be a struggle. For some reason, Margaret's volume control starts at eight and ends somewhere after ten. She is the human version of the amplifier in the *Spinal Tap* film. Please believe me, for this is not made up. Her voice should be recorded and used as a public address system to disperse gangs of lippy youths from outside shops. No sane teenager, with even half an eardrum, could tolerate her rantings for more than ten seconds. Ouch.

I am finding that even sitting down and typing these words is bringing me out in a cold sweat, for I know, any second from now, her piercing voice will be travelling up the stairs (I am in my loft) demanding I attend to our children or empty the bins. And, if I don't jump immediately, it manages (somehow) to go up an octave or two.

Apart from her height, I have no idea why she feels the need to speak so loudly. I truly wish she could moderate it, though, as I have suffered with headaches from the day we were married. Margaret, of course, denies she shouts. According to her, she is just being a passionate Nigerian. Utter balderdash. Some Nigerians are quiet and she should not stereotype herself, as it is possible to be assertive and softly spoken. It is the words one utters that are important, not the volume. I remain hopeful that one day she will realise this and reduce her shouting.

To compound this failing she, incredibly, manages to speak even louder when on the telephone. I really am not joking. I just pity our poor neighbours when she indulges herself in a late night call to her Auntie in Brighton. The walls of the house are often shaking at the outpouring of rage from her mouth.

This brings me neatly onto her biggest flaw – her temper. Call it what you will; being vexed, uptight, hormonal (my usual favourite, as I'm sure you've noticed by now) or simply husband rage – Margaret has them all.

Anyone, who knows Margaret and who is reading this, will now be nodding their head in agreement at these words. It is not a lie; she possesses an anger that has to be seen to be believed. I really have no idea why she gets so angry and can see no benefits for her in reacting like this. All she will get is high blood pressure and an early grave. I dare say that as I am the recipient of most of this anger, I will probably be keeping the ground warm in the grave next to her by this stage.

Her anger also ensures I am petrified of mentioning certain subjects, like her family or God, because I know what her reaction will be; ranting and raving, with facial expressions to match.

She wrote in the 'hobby' chapter about her love of '80s horror flicks. Well, I can only presume she spent so long watching these that they have left a permanent imprint on her brain! By that I mean, if you look at any picture cover of these films, they invariably show a person with a twisted look of terror on their face. Reader, this is no word of a lie, that is Margaret when she is angry. If only these video nasties were still being made, Margaret would have made pots of cash, as her facial expressions are certainly the scariest thing on planet earth.

No doubt, you may well be thinking, why on earth I stay married to someone who gives me headaches and scares the living daylights out of me. This would be a fair question to ask. I put it down to never having had a girlfriend before, therefore I can only imagine all women act like this in the home? So, because of my inexperience, I put up with my 'scary love,' as I like to call it, blissfully unaware that other men might not have the same problems I do.

Then again, maybe I am just an old-fashioned male chauvinist at heart who tries to camouflage his prejudices within criticism of others? Perhaps my actions are responsible for Margaret's temper tantrums? Whatever, scary love it may be but I still love her.

One of her other negatives is the way she puts other people's troubles before her own. On the surface, this may appear an admirable part of her character and in some ways it is. Other people, however, do not see the emotionally-drained wife I am married to.

Unfortunately, the majority of Margaret's friends tend to have absolutely horrific personal lives, normally revolving around the men-folk they have encountered. I appreciate it is a natural human reaction to seek solace in another in times of trouble and that is what they do by talking to Margaret. All well and good, but Margaret now spends so long getting involved with other people's emotional traumas, she neglects issues closer to home – such as: financial planning for our children's education, time spent with the kids, and emotional bonding with her husband.

This is probably coming over as unfair, but it is the way I genuinely feel about her. She really does need to discover the word 'no'. Sometimes, you have to look after number one.

I am a bit of a hypocrite here, as I was going through the same debilitating experience when I was working. I, too, was coming home with nothing left to give my wife; work having taken all of my emotional strength. This was unfair to Margaret and only brought home to me when we decided I stop. There can be no doubt about it: family life really is a struggle in England.

It is this struggle that is destroying marriages up and down the country. In Britain, couples are exhausted and without the time or inclination to discuss their personal matters. This is creating an unstable world as to flourish marriages have to be worked at. There is no overnight success in the world of relationships. And everyone knows that if you stop working for long enough you get the sack.

Another of my issues with Margaret is her stubbornness. In truth, she is so bad in this area I almost expect to see her name listed in the dictionary as a description of the word. Harsh maybe, but what other way can you describe someone who would rather wash (the infamous 'bucket bath') out of a plastic bowl in the middle of winter, when the other available option is a red-hot shower? It beggars belief that she sticks to 'cultural' tradition so much.

I referred earlier, in this character assassination chapter, to the fact that Margaret has a tendency to shout rather than talk to people. Unfortunately, she compounds this by having an addiction to talking. Yes, it is true, she just cannot stop herself. I have told her I find this a problem, but her argument is God gave her a mouth and she intends to use it.

Granted she does have a mouth, but I am yet to read the bit in the bible where it says humans must babble incoherently at all times of the day! Who does she think she is? A Nigerian Garth Crooks? (football pundit renowned for his erratic interviewing style.)

She should learn to restrict herself to comments that are relevant and cut out the crap. But no, she won't listen to my words of wisdom. Whatever she is doing (yes, even sex), she likes to give a running commentary on the way the world is being run. Doubtless her talking has its time and place, but it can be a bit intrusive – to put it mildly.

To add to my woes, our son has picked up this verbal diarrhoea habit of his mother's and also waffles incessantly. He, at least, can quote his age as a mitigating factor but can Margaret at the age of forty? I don't think so.

I know I am going to come over as extremely rude by saying this, but it really is mind-numbing hearing two people gibber jabbering away at each other with nothing sensible to say. I always prefer economy of effort when it comes to communication: i.e, only speak when you have something intelligent to say.

To make matters worse, she also has the incredibly irritating habit of repeating herself *ad nauseam*. I know I sometimes do the same, but only after seven pints of cider.

Lastly, my wife is given to panicking whenever something goes wrong. This was ably demonstrated when she tried to bleed our radiators. Being somewhat of a novice where plumbing is concerned, dear Margaret twisted the radiator knob rather vigorously. To no great surprise, she was then sprayed with a jet of dirty brown liquid. Rather than doing the sensible thing and turning the knob the other way, Margaret instead called out to Joshua and instructed him to 'put your thumb over the water'.

Joshua, being a game child, meekly did as requested and quickly became soaked to the skin. So, how much water was there? Well, if I tell you that our house hadn't seen this much liquid since Margaret's water broke when pregnant with our son, you may get the drift. It was so bad, I thought the BBC would have to give out a localised flood warning.

In the meantime, Margaret had run out into the street (it was around 8.15am) clad in nothing but a dressing gown, her ample breasts flip flapping from side to side. Desperate for masculine help, as I was at work, she cried out 'I need a man'. Luckily, a passing intellectual went to her aid and figured to turn the water off! Poor Joshua, by now resembling a drowned rat and not a little Dutch boy, merely said; 'I am sorry mummy, I couldn't stop it'. Ah, what a hero my son sometimes is.

It's funny but, re-reading this, I feel I am going to have to confront facts and accept it – I guess I am coming over as a pseudo intellectual snob. But when you are perfect it is easier to be judgemental of others. Can my wife prove otherwise?

Margaret

How can I respond to the man who is without fault? Truly Bobby is second only to Mother Theresa, given the words he has typed above.

As he has just demonstrated, his ego knows no bounds and is certainly one of his less-appealing traits. Indeed, he is so far up his own arse I'm just surprised he can manage a shit in the morning! But before I slag him off too much, I will concentrate on his more pleasant tendencies.

Anyone who knows Bobby will confess to his warmth and sincerity, not to mention his finely honed sense of sarcasm. He extends this to everybody he comes into contact with; white, black, Asian, Martian, in fact everybody apart from Tottenham fans. He really does treat all people exactly the same.

In fact, he is so Mr Right on that I sometimes feel humbled to be in his presence. In contrast to my past (the 'white hate' period), Bobby has a street cred I can never hope to match. He is so inclusive of society that his inner circle even contains a few white friends!

Joking aside though, his buddies would concur with me on this one, as he is always there if they need him for emotional support throughout their own lives. Being in touch with his 'feminine' side, Bobby is confident in talking one on one with his friends. An awful lot of men are not able to do this and would rather drown their sorrows in pint after pint of lukewarm beer. I find it disturbing that in England the 'tired and emotional' man only ever emerges after a heavy nights drinking. I will never understand why most men cannot talk about their feelings in the way women can.

Even with Bobby, it takes him a while before he unburdens himself to me. I have to probe for weeks on end to finally find out what is on his mind. The only clue he gives out, when he is upset about something, is a withdrawal into himself, a trot to the toilet, or a reluctance to engage in conversation. To Bobby it is bad form to be seen as too emotional, so he hides behind his stiff upper lip defence, his protection against 'hormonal' invasion. To me, this is wrong and I feel he'd benefit more if he let his emotions 'hang out' occasionally. By keeping his feelings locked inside, he is doing himself no favours at all and, by comparison, he makes me look too fiery by half. I concede he may have a point here but I like being volatile – it keeps Bobby on his toes.

Leading on from this, he is that very rare breed – an honest man. You will have to trust me on this one, for in my experience most men I have met are dishonest with: their money, their emotions, and their bodies. Mind you, it could be because: he has little money, cannot express his emotions and has a scrawny body. Perhaps he would be like all the others if he didn't have these weaknesses?

His financial honesty, though, is much appreciated by me. I have lost count of the times boyfriends have ripped me off with promises of money tomorrow in place of my jam for today. However, Bobby is in many ways too honest when it comes to money. He always lets me know exactly how much he has in his accounts and then wonders why I pick up a Butlin's brochure for an exotic summer holiday!

It is lucky for Bobby, I do not take advantage of his open generous nature and suggest Caribbean cruises or wildlife safari–type excursions. I often mention to him that if he ever had an affair a devious woman would find him rich pickings, for he is unable to recognise this mentality in women. Gullibility is certainly one of Bobby's weaknesses.

I can't, in all honesty though, see Bobby straying into the arms of another nubile black African woman, as he is loyal to a fault. Once he signs up to something, he tends to be in it until the bitter end. The best examples of this are his clothes and taste of music. Numerous changes and fashions have come about over the decades, but Bobby still insists on wearing his bondage pants and Doc Marten boots, whilst listening to music that hasn't progressed a single chord since 1976. He just cannot comprehend that other forms of music exist. For him, musical diversity means buying punk records from another country. It is in areas like this, that his loyalty most definitely has its drawbacks.

Bobby is also loyal to his family and friends and really believes a gentleman's word is his honour. I suppose old-fashioned is the word that best sums Bobby up and I mean this as a compliment. However, I do wish he could be more up-to-date with modern technology. For instance, he still does not possess a mobile phone and insists on playing music via his audio cassette Walkman. As mentioned earlier, I like my antiques but some of Bobby's stuff comes from the land that progress forgot!

These days, a lot of people view being slightly behind the times as a negative and not as something to be appreciated. As I told Bobby just last year, 'If every mother had a child like you, the world would be a better place.' This comment may at first glance appear vomit inducing but I refer here to his refusal to give in to peer pressure. I find this an agreeable part of his nature, as it shapes his character and sets him aside from the norm.

So what if he looks a bit different from the lager hordes out on a weekend pull, at least he is not doing things just to fit in. Unsurprisingly, a lot of people find this attitude threatening, and I've lost count of the number of insults directed at him by total strangers on the way home from a night out. Bobby refuses to change his ways or clothes though, arguing he gave into bullies for the last time when he was beaten into a pulp at school.

His friend Julian, same trousers and music but skinnier body, also gets this abuse. He is more vociferous than Bobby and normally responds with a similar rude reply. Still, he is a Northerner and, therefore, less likely to put up with rubbish. By way of a contrast, my Southern softie husband just tends to ignore them.

I cannot let this part of the book pass without mentioning Bobby's bad taste in jewellery. Not for him a Gaultier chain or a Versace ring. No, Bobby wears only the very best: Armitage Shanks. For those perplexed by this comment, I am referring here to his penchant for wearing a genuine bath chain around his neck – see picture in the book for proof. Yes, that's right, the very type of chain that is attached to the plug in a normal person's sink. The chain used to be a silver type of colour but has rusted over the years and now resembles a kind of grubby gold. One of these days he will be mugged for it and he runs the risk of being done for wasting police time when reporting its theft.

You may well be wondering as to why he wears this, ahem, decorative item. His explanation is that it is his 'anti-fashion' statement. By this, he is referring to the corporate mentality holding sway around the world – with its acolytes marching around clad in their Nike trainers. Again, I have to compliment Bobby on his attitude towards big businesses and the way it influences people's everyday lives. He really cannot believe that so many people buy into the 'feel good' factor of wearing designer clothes.

Of course, his own 'uniform' of bondage pants and studded leather jacket is a form of corporate dress sense, but he says – with some justification – that punk companies such as Knock-Out and Ruptured Ambitions are just serving their communities in the same way that antique shops do.

On a more personal basis, Bobby has been very supportive of my culture and this is important, as it was very much a step into the unknown for him. I at least had a limited understanding of the English when I met Bobby, whereas he hadn't a clue about the Yoruba way of life.

Despite being supportive, he is also critical, if needed, of some elements in Yoruba culture – but he expresses this in a positive and not a superior way. One of his more frequent complaints about Yoruba people is when he refers to them as being snobs. Pot calling kettle black is an old English expression and one that could easily be applied here.

Lastly, I just like the fact he is still here in the life of my children and I. A bit arse licky, I accept, but nowadays it is hard to find a man willing to play an active role in parenthood. That, to me, is his greatest attribute.

I may have painted a pleasant picture of my husband but he does have his faults. His first one is physical.

I will never understand why he is so reluctant to see the doctor whenever he is suffering from an ailment. Ever since I have known him he has suffered from irritable bowel syndrome (IBS), with severe stomach cramps affecting him whenever he eats. This is always worse when he is distracted from his food. As a result he tends to eat alone – away from the family.

He did go to the doctor once regarding his IBS and had the 'pleasure' of taking a finger up his anus to check if he had bowel cancer. An unpleasant experience for anyone to go through. The strange thing about the 'finger' was that the doctor first asked him if he was married. What on earth had that got to do with it? Bobby answered yes, the mind boggles as to what might have been inserted if he had answered in the negative.

I cannot understand Bobby here. If a man wanted to put his finger up my bottom, I would have had a whole host of questions for him to answer before allowing him access to my cheeks. Bobby, though, parted his without a moment's hesitation. I guess it's just as well that one of my husband's favourite songs is the Peter & The Test Tubes ditty, 'Up Yer Bum'.

His IBS was also the source of much merriment for his work colleagues who constantly teased Bobby about his trips to the throne. Certainly, he could shit for England if 'dumping it large' was ever brought into the arena of international sport. And boy, when my Bobby goes, he goes for a loooooong time! Yeuch!

Apart from his being full of shit, my other main objection with Bobby is his desire to be left alone – in peace and quiet. Seeing as how I grew up in a large family, with privacy at a premium, I have always been used to sharing my life with others. Because Bobby only had one sister, he grew up accustomed to life alone, with solitude his best friend. The residue of his upbringing is now best demonstrated by him occasionally eating his dinner in the toilet – so he can be left in peace to eat. Then again, after what I've just typed about his IBS, perhaps he was just ensuring he was in the right place at the right time!

I must say that his attitude concerning being on his own is certainly not conducive to a happy marriage and family life. How on earth can he expect to lead a solitary existence with a 'gibbering' wife and children to accompany him? He should have thought all of this through before agreeing to marry me. In the years prior to our marriage, Bobby lived by himself and I guess he got used to keeping his own company. Now that he is in constant close proximity with others, he struggles to keep sane.

This may come over as melodramatic, but Bobby really is a person who needs to be by himself. When there are too many people in the room, Bobby finds it hard to relax and his nerves play him up leading to mad dashes for the toilet. I believe all of this stems from his childhood, when he couldn't tell his parents about the bullying. His IBS started around this time and it's fair to say has accelerated since. I guess his desire to be alone is just his way of showing that he is feeling under pressure. When at school, it was his self-defence mechanism against the bullies and he used to spend hours in his bedroom – effectively in 'solitary confinement'. Even now, in adult life, this is the first place he sub-consciously retreats to when he is feeling the pinch. The toilet (obviously) is the second place.

This desire to be alone clashes with my, how has he put it, 'verbal diarrhoea'. So, with one person a self confessed 'talkoholic,' and the other not, you have, yet again, the potential flashpoint for conflict.

Bobby may not say much but when he does his words are somewhat acidic and hard-hitting. I still remember from a few years back when he referred to me as a vegetable. He never specified which vegetable, but I can only imagine it was a potato. Another occasion he invited me to 'get my fat arse off the sofa' and help him in the kitchen. True, my bottom is a little larger than average, but Bobby wrote how he is attracted to women with more rotund bottoms. He can't have it both ways. Bobby only needs one or two words to have an impact. Economy of effort he calls it. I just call it lighting the powder trail and standing back whilst Margaret explodes.

And by golly, do I explode. I will never understand why he resorts to these personal insults as he knows I will be mad at him for days afterwards. He should just bite his tongue and do what I tell him.

The ultimate irony here is that Bobby complains about our house being full of chaos and the chattering of noisy mouths. I respectfully remind readers that this is the same man who bombards his eardrums with the delicate sounds of bands such as The Neurotic Arseholes! I rest my case.

Another of his irritating habits is his adherence to routine and neatness. Whatever the situation, he does things in exactly the same order. This is best shown when he returns home inebriated from football. He always insists on unpacking his football bag – despite the state he's normally in. During the course of his tidying up, he manages to wake the entire household as he stumbles from one room to the next. I do not mind him getting drunk, it's his noises in the house (not to mention his constant high velocity cider farting) that irritate me the most.

Bobby's neatness is best shown by his attitude to his records, CDs and DVDs as he files all of them alphabetically. He says it is so he can find things quickly. I just feel it's him demonstrating his anally retentive side. What is perhaps worse is that I have even noticed he has the strange habit of putting his paper kitchen towels in the correct order in his cupboard – in case their expiry date, err, expires. I'll write that again in case you didn't get it; his *kitchen towels*!

Bobby is also a practical man and whilst this may seem a plus it does have its drawbacks. As confirmation of this I need only refer to our daughter's hair. If you are not black you may be wondering what I am on about here. Well, it is a sad fact that black/mixed race hair needs more work on it than white hair. This can be problematical, especially when combined with a child's low pain threshold. Oh how our daughter Olivia cries when we touch her hair. I have lost count of the times she tells me she is 'not my friend' anymore, just because I have pulled her hair into bunches or combed it through. Tired of her whining, I asked Bobby for help. His suggestion?

'I'll get my clippers and give her a skinhead'.

It is at times like these, I wish I had married an African!

Sitting side by side with his routine fixation, is his obsessional nature towards hobbies. I have so many examples here, I could not list them all. They include: he likes music so he has to play the guitar and make records himself. He liked Wolverhampton FC so he buys a season ticket. He liked reading so he wrote a book.

I mentioned earlier that one of his good points is his idea of loyalty. However, he does take this a step too far. He liked Doc Marten shoes when he was thirteen so has worn them every day since. Why can't he change?

Bobby explains it away by saying you can always judge a man by his shoes. In the land of Bob, this means; a man who changes his shoes frequently is the man who will jump just as easily into someone else's bed. I used to mock him for this suggestion but it does have a grain of truth. A man who can be satisfied with doing the same things for a long time is more likely to stay with someone for the length of a marriage. The person who chops and changes his shoes may go elsewhere when they wear out.

One of the most striking characteristics of Bobby's is his sense of humour. I'm really not sure whether to put this down as a good or bad point of his. I guess his humour is best taken in small doses and it is an acquired taste that many have not acquired. For some reason though, he feels that he's the funniest man around. What he doesn't realise is; people are not laughing at his jokes, they are laughing at the idea of a grown man possessing the wit of a seven-year-old.

To be honest here, his humour was one of the things that first attracted me to him as he always had a smile on his face. I sometimes complain to him that his jokes have dried up. By way of response, he just answers: 'My name is Bobby Smith not Bob Hope,' or 'What do you expect after ten years of being married to you?'

What a right bastard my husband can be.

My final complaint against Bobby is a practical one: he cannot drive – apart from driving me crazy. He says he doesn't have to as I can, and that he has a bicycle for emergencies. This is true but more than a little selfish. To give the reader the full picture, I should inform you that Bobby did attempt to learn a few years ago, to stop me from nagging. Indeed he took it so seriously, he paid for forty driving lessons in the process, even getting as far as having a practical driving test. At last, I thought, as he got in the car for his examination, no more trips to the supermarket acting as his chauffeur.

Sadly my optimism was misplaced. His test was cancelled after fifteen minutes as he had failed it twice over in that short space of time.

I did feel sorry for my husband, though, as he had to call in on the lavatory during his test when his nerves played him up. Surely his examiner should have made allowances for Bobby's bowel condition? Nope. All Bobby got was a shake of the head and a lecture about road safety. What was he to do? Carry a colostomy bag around in the car in case he got caught short?

His confidence shattered by this disheartening experience, Bobby has not got behind the wheel of a car since.

Oops, I nearly let the chapter go without mentioning one of his biggest faults – he has an absolutely pathological fear of wasps. Fair enough, you might be thinking, no one likes wasps that much. Yes, this is true, but how many grown men do you know who flap their arms around like a windmill on acid whenever a wasp is spotted at a distance of fifty metres? Truly, I am not exaggerating. You would think the humble wasp was masquerading as an al-Qa'eda suicide bomber the fuss Bobby makes. It's quite pathetic the way he quivers at the mouth and goes all bendy knees just at the sight of the little gold and black insects. You would have thought, given the fact that his football team play in gold and black jerseys, that he would have some kind of an empathy with wasps. Oh no, nothing of the sort. My dear old Bobby has a phobia that turns him into a lily-livered pansy.

I am sure I'm not the only one of his family who finds this totally pathetic and an un-manly way of behaving. Bobby really needs to come to terms with this, otherwise he runs the risk of passing the phobia onto our son.

So that is my Bobby after all these years. For sure, he has his faults, but I guess he is still the sausage for my mash.

Summary

Slightly different to the previous chapters here. I (Bobby) will comment on Margaret's comments and she will do likewise to mine.

Bobby

Well, what can I say about her observations on me? Not a lot – as they are all true. I really am the kind of guy who is loyal, honest and maybe a little mad (about my hobbies).

I am the classic case of the 'boring man syndrome' – best proved by my interests remaining the same after all these years. I try to be exotic by the wearing of crazy clothes and weird music but, let's face facts here; I could not be more boring if I tried. I am a civil servant, married with two kids, living in an end of terrace three-bedroom house. I am the epitome of conformity and of everything average. Instead of the Sex Pistols, I should be listening to Barry Manilow!

Saying that though, I think it is my boring trait that makes me a better family man and husband. Without blowing my own trumpet too much, I feel the ability to be 'boring' is one frequently neglected when women go shopping for a partner. It is fine to go out with the hip young gun-slingers when you are of similar age, but another altogether if you go chasing the same man or woman when you reach the age of thirty.

Would a Julie Burchill of today's world find Tony Parsons as attractive as she once did in the late Seventies? Unlikely, especially since their divorce and her flirtation with lesbianism.

In my experience, the women who do not change their type of partners are the ones that end up unhappy. The nerdy spotty youth of yesteryear may now be the smart kid on the block with his own company and income to match. As an aside to this, when I was growing up the nerdiest thing a boy could do was play computer games. It is fair to say, I lived up to the nerdy image in this respect. Nowadays though it has gone into reverse and it's seen as untrendy not to play Playstation 2 or PC games. Trust me to have been born too early. I would have cleaned up in the girl department if I were a teenager today.

So yes, I may appear boring but to me that is a compliment. I am too old to keep up to date with fashion or stick gel in my hair to look cool. I am certainly not interested in checking out the latest club – well, unless it has raisins in the middle and a chocolate coating on the outside. Nah, I just want to read a nice book of an evening and relax in a comfy armchair.

In some ways, I feel I am the human version of the Russian T-34 World War Two tank. For those without the faintest idea of what I am referring to, the T-34 was the workhorse of the Soviet army. A tank with no frills and yet a tank that was utterly reliable on the frozen steppes of Russia. A tank that won the war, but a tank with no aesthetic values whatsoever.

To ram home this point, I have left instructions for my headstone. It will read: "Here lies Bobby Smith – a man of substance, but of no style whatso-ever."

As for the rest of Margaret's comments: yes, I agree I am a man of routine and habit. I really find it hard not to do the same things all the time. Because of this, I appreciate I must be hell to live with at times and give thanks to the Lord Almighty (it will keep the wife happy if I say this) that Margaret puts up with my strange little ways.

The most important lesson we have learnt from this chapter is that it shows how our past experience of bullying is even now affecting our lives –

as demonstrated by Margaret's shouting and my withdrawing into myself.

I cannot stress enough, how damaging the act of being bullied is, to parents. It does not stop after Sixth form; the memory lingers on well into adulthood. It may be affecting me even now – what with the self-disparaging comments I have littered the book with.

I must confess, though, Margaret's observations about me are spot on. Over to my wife, now, to refute my allegation of her as a shouting talkoholic who spouts nothing but complete and utter garbage.

Margaret

Although Bobby came up with some redeeming points for me, the majority of his comments were in the negative. Really, if I was as bad as he makes out, he should see the doctor – for putting up with my mood swings and anger. He is either exaggerating or hinting at a degree of sado-masochism. Yeah, I like talking, it is one of my hobbies, but is this such a crime?

I only end up talking and repeating myself because Bobby has a tendency to 'switch off' when I am talking or telling him where he has gone wrong. Talking is a natural way of expressing one's emotions. To Bobby it comes over as shouting, to me it is merely passion. Bobby is a more reserved dispassionate creature, who would rather sit back to reflect on any action before he takes it. I am a knee-jerk reaction type of woman: passionate and proud. No doubt Bobby would say I am ruled by my emotions and lacking in common sense. I would answer that I'd rather be a hot temptress than a soggy wet fish.

He should also not refer to me as stubborn. He only calls me this because I am right more often than he is.

Crucially, my being Nigerian and him being English does not cause the differences between us. It is the age-old dispute between male and female, testosterone and oestrogen, Jack and Vera Duckworth. Men and women are just physically and mentally designed to have arguments and to find the opposite sex: attractive or ugly, pleasant or vengeful, kind-hearted or tight – normally all at the same time. It is getting the balance right and finding someone who is at least 51 per cent attractive, pleasant and kind-hearted – this is the key to happiness. Both of us feel we have met that person – despite our words within the cover of this book.

Our son, inadvertently, perfectly summed up our marriage. Bobby took him to Wolverhampton last season for a match and Joshua played up quite badly. Feeling a bit pissed off (and not just pissed for a change), Bobby asked him why he was so naughty.

Joshua merely answered, 'It's called tough love Daddy.'

Bobby and I both agree that married life is certainly that.

CHAPTER 18

The Future, Personal and Political

Bobby

"No future, for England's dreaming" – Johnny Rotten, 1977.

So where is the future for Margaret and I?

Whilst she has been living in England for the bulk of her life, I sense a yearning in her to return to Nigeria. This is primarily because she feels a deep frustration over our children growing up in an environment where the absence of manners, sorry, 'respect' is becoming all too prevalent. Both of us long for a time when pleasantries were exchanged between strangers on the streets and 'happy slapping' was something that only occurred when goals were scored at football matches. I too share her frustration at the lack of discipline throughout society and the gradual dismantling of the institution of marriage – mainly through changes to the tax system and the promotion of the idealistic single-parent lifestyle.

That the idea of marriage is dying out was brought home to me the Christmas just passed. In the local card shop I searched endlessly for a card that bore the message; 'Happy Christmas Mum and Dad'. I did eventually find one that was suitable, but what disappointed me was that it was hidden away behind other, I guess more fashionable cards. By this I mean a whole legion of cards that said; 'Happy Christmas, to Mum and her fella' or 'Seasons greetings to Mum and my Step-Dad' or, even, 'Xmas snogs to Mum and her bit of rough'. I exaggerate with the last one, and I know I sound like a typical *Daily Telegraph* reader here, but is this progress?

To combat this disintegration of once-sacred ideals, Margaret has fallen back on the one constant in her life – her faith. Her faith, though, will not protect our children from peer pressure at school when they reach puberty. Her faith will not protect them when they suffer the inevitable racism that society spews out. Her faith will not be of help when our son is travelling home late at night on the beer bus with all its accompanying dangers, for despite what the powers that be tell us, our streets are still full of danger and violence.

I write here with personal experience as I was once beaten up at a bus stop by a complete stranger on the way home from a punk gig, whilst standing with Julian and his wife Tracey. Julian, contrary to his image of an abrasive Northerner, left his wife and I to face the ire of our attacker alone – whilst he ran to get help. What a mate.

Is it, therefore, any wonder, that Margaret wants to save our children from being exposed to this gradual decline in English behaviour?

If I was interested in point scoring, I could retaliate by comparing our problems with the ethnic or religious violence that erupts every now and again in Nigeria, or highlight the armed bandits that roam its Delta swamplands. This is without mentioning the corruption or the lack of discipline on its dusty roads.

It seems to me the problems we are experiencing in England are being followed right around the world. Discipline and self-respect are no longer words that people use with pride. Instead, the ability to know ones 'rights' is the modern mantra of the day. Here is a concept that may unsettle some of these people: responsibility for one's own actions.

So, I see no point in running away from the problems we are having in England and jumping ship to live in Nigeria. It is far better to confront problems here head on. Margaret's problem is; she still views Nigeria as the Nigeria when she was growing up – with total respect for elders and adherence to parents' instructions. In her head, Nigeria is forever crystallised. It will never change.

Unfortunately for her it has. Exposure to mass media, via satellite and the internet, is slowly suggesting to its population that they can challenge once-accepted forms of behaviour. An example of this is the creation of groups promoting homosexual rights – unimaginable in times past. In my opinion this is a pleasing development, as it shows tolerance is on the increase. To Margaret, this is just plain wrong.

Another example came from the lips of Margaret's cousin, Joyce, when she informed us that her brother in Nigeria is an atheist. At this news my wife's jaw literally dropped open in amazement – as in Nigeria atheists are as rare a sighting as Lord Lucan. However, these developments prove that like everywhere else, Nigeria is changing. This does not have to be a bad thing. The advancement of women, as we have argued, is long overdue and may finally see them achieve parity with men.

The price to pay, though, is the dilution of Nigeria's rich culture and traditions by the globalised world economy. How long before the Naira goes the same way as the Deutschmark? Whilst the Euro is still far off for Nigeria, there will come a time – maybe fifty years from now – when it will happen. Progress (or regression – take your pick) grinds relentlessly on.

So, if Margaret does decide to live in Nigeria, I think she will be shocked by its changing values. Of course, she does return every now and again for holidays and always returns saying it is pretty much the way it was when she was growing up. I think she is in denial.

Holidays are unreliable litmus tests of a countries smells, tastes or desires. If she spent, say six months there, I'll wager a fiver she would be surprised at its changing face. I appreciate it may be unfair of me to say this – as I have never been to Nigeria – but it defies reason that any country with media access will not rapidly evolve.

Margaret's dad is a more accurate barometer of Nigeria as he spends as much time in Nigeria as he does here. He frequently complains that the younger generation have lost touch with their culture and how they nowadays tend not to offer automatic respect to elders. Most of his barbed comments are directed at Nigerians living in England but if some of these retire to Nigeria it will surely accelerate the dismantling of its culture there.

Because of the social/physical intercourse between Nigeria and England, Nigeria and the USA, Nigeria and the world, this is a fact that cannot be denied. Its citizens have grasped social mobility and boldly gone where no Nigerian has gone before. But this is no fancy star trek – most Nigerians are happy with a simple pay cheque.

So, assuming Margaret at some stage does decide to live in Nigeria what would become of me? I would be forced to either live alone or swallow my Englishness and depart the white cliffs of Dover for sunnier climes. At this moment, I cannot believe I can do this. Living in Nigeria would have its advantages but the disadvantages would outweigh the positives by around five to one. At the moment I commute to Wolverhampton from Hertfordshire to watch Wolverhampton Wanderers FC. This is currently a tiresome journey but it pales in comparison with the thought of having to get the plane from Lagos. So, by moving to Nigeria, I would have to give up football. It is also fair to say, I cannot think of any punk bands that play in Nigeria on a regular basis. The Clash may have 'Rocked the Casbah' but they never got as far as West Africa.

But, if Margaret does go and I stay, what kind of a conundrum will that create for our children? The absence from Margaret's life of her mother has had – in my opinion – a damaging effect on her mental well-being. In her sub-consciousness, Margaret felt rejected by her mother for not always being by her side. So, after going through those feelings herself, I find it hard to believe she would put her own children through this.

Personally, I would want to be as near as possible to my children as they progress through the difficult teenage years and on into adulthood. I want to be by their side offering them the love and support that I took for granted from my own parents. Just because a child is old enough to vote, does not mean it is able to think clearly. The wisdom and experience of parents should be a constant mine of information that offspring can tap into at any stage of their lives. For sure, you can offer financial support from afar, but it is sometimes hard to gauge a person's feelings just by email or the phone. Human, physical contact is paramount in maintaining the bond that exists between parent and child – whatever the age.

That is why I could have problems if Margaret decides to send our children to Nigeria to be educated. On one side, I can see the logic of sending the children to a poor third world country – as their schools are still imbued with the disciplinarian approach to education that our rich country jettisoned in the Sixties – but it would be hard not to see them every day.

On this topic, I honestly cannot understand why we have allowed our school behavioural standards to slip, to the extent that we have to seriously consider sending children to Nigeria to be educated. How on earth has it come to this? We have so much more cash to spend on education, yet it appears to have all been in vain – if the feral youths on our streets are anything to go by. I know I run the risk of sounding like a grumpy old man but this free and easy approach to education and up-bringing is now having an effect on me. My children will possibly end up in the same school as these youths, being exposed to corrupting influences such as: drugs, gang warfare and under age sex.

And even if they avoid this – by being shipped off to Nigeria – I will suffer, as they will grow up away from their father. That is why I raise my head above the parapet and criticise disastrous policies that create an environment for single-parenting and crime to flourish. Eventually, we all become victims of this weak-willed approach.

Of course, many may think it's unfair of me to link single-parent families and crime in the same sentence and to a degree they would be right. Whilst I do not automatically assume that one follows the other, the evidence suggests it is a contributory factor. I hate to come over as a pre-David

Cameron Tory party member here, but some of the statistics are damning. According to the Family Policy Group, around 27 per cent of children in this country are brought up in single-parent families and yet 70 per cent of young offenders are from these households. Whilst it would be remiss of me not to mention the sterling work that many single-parents do, the conclusion is quite obvious: children need their fathers.

It should be included here that the young offenders' statistic is also undoubtedly heavily influenced by the poverty that a lot of single-parent families have to endure. Poverty normally involves poor housing, sub-standard education and petty crime – so is it any wonder that people in this environment are starting off at a disadvantage?

Politics will not help women forced into the hard life of the lone-parent. The idealists on the Left will argue for more financial aid to remove single-parents from poverty, whilst the Right will curtail financial incentives to deter others from following on in their footsteps. The truth is neither of these approaches will change attitudes of a population disillusioned with the circus that now passes for politics in England. I write here in my capacity as one of the disillusioned who will never vote for any party again. I have been let down too many times by those elected to govern us.

So, assuming that at some stage Margaret does hitch up her skirt and hot foots it out of here, what will become of our children?

If they are of the age when education has been completed, I suspect they will decide to remain within this island, as they have very little in common with Nigeria. This, and not some faraway country on another continent, is their home.

Opportunity in Nigeria is also lacking, as proved by all of Margaret's brothers and sisters being desperate to leave its restricting economics. They can see no way to improve their situation in Nigeria – with its limited employment and backhanders as a way of life. The irony is they are trying to leave just when Margaret wants to return.

In all honesty, I cannot say I am too worried about Margaret coming over all romantic with her idea of returning to Nigeria. It is way too reminis-cent of those who dream about doing something exotic when they retire – only to discover that the dream they had in their youth has dimmed with age. In my heart of hearts I really believe she will not decide to live full-time in Nigeria. She may go for longer holidays in the future but I think she is heading for a disappointment if she continues to believe she will be returning 'home'. Margaret would find it hard to readjust to everyday life in Nigeria and she will just have to accept that England now has first claim on her body – if not her mind.

So, what will the future hold for the two of us as a couple? I guess the fact that we have lasted this long is in our favour. We have witnessed so many of our friends/colleagues marriages collapse around us that we sometimes feel like an endangered species. An awful lot of people tend to marry with the mentality that finding a mating partner is the hard part. It's not. Keeping a marriage, or any relationship, healthy is far more difficult. Over a period of time both individuals change. Priorities become blurred, hips become fat, clothes become fashionable, bodies become as one. Lighting the flame is easy, putting it out is easy, ensuring it stays alive is more problematical.

I honestly cannot say if we have found the magic formula but we persevere until the light dies out. It is still burning as I write these words.

Margaret

Our future, hopefully, will be as one. Whatever the problems that await us, we have to show a united front to combat them. This may appear somewhat obvious, but in the past I have run away when confronted with difficult situations. In my childhood, I was the cause of much anguish to my parents as I ran away from home on more than one occasion. Whenever I felt pressurised, I saw flight as the best available option. Maybe, deep in my head, I see Nigeria as a bolt hole to run away to – to escape the rigours of parenthood and domestic 'bliss'.

The sad fact is that once there I would probably need somewhere else to run to when times got hard. I am beginning to think my family must have gypsy blood in their genes as I rarely find comfort in being trapped within the confines of a job, a house, or a country. I think I am just too sensitive and emotional for modern day life. I should have: 'Please be gentle – fragile goods' stamped across my forehead. I try to cover this up by being brash and outspoken but inside a little girl is still hiding.

It is only with Bobby's help I can overcome this feeling of wanting to flee to pastures new. And we will only get past this urge by communicating our feelings to one another. It is crucial that we do not worry about how the rest of the world sees us and instead concentrate purely on how we see each other. I have to learn to ignore any stares in the street and just be content that I've married a man who has a central core of decency about him.

This is hard for me because I often feel like a piggy in the middle – torn between what Bobby wants and what my parents and Yoruba culture have deemed appropriate. I know now that I've got to ignore some of my parents' wishes and put my own family first, although this is difficult for me to do as

I've been brought up to always adhere to my elders' instructions.

Sometimes, rather than merely displaying his English 'reserve', I wish Bobby would put his foot down and tell them that we cannot have distant relatives staying with us for months at a time, or that he objects to money being sent to relatives. Bobby is too tolerant and polite to do this but I know he is not entirely happy with the way my family control certain aspects of our marriage. As our marriage lengthens I must lean more towards him.

That does not mean, though, I will sacrifice my children's education, by sending them to a sink secondary school, and, if it comes to the crunch, I really am quite prepared to send them to Nigeria. I feel that their being exposed to a difficult educational environment will make them appreciate those things we take for granted in England – electricity, books, etc. To view abject poverty will help shape their characters and make them realise that a pair of trainers are not the most desired objects in the world. Is this fair on Bobby?

Not really, but sometimes you have to sacrifice yourself for your children.

Following on from this, I purchased a plot of land in Nigeria in the early Nineties before I met Bobby, as I intended to retire to Nigeria and live a life of luxury in my purpose built house – with maids seeing to my every need. Marrying Bobby has given me a dilemma, as I cannot see him living happily ever after in such a hot country. It would resemble a scene from the *It Ain't Half Hot Mum* TV sitcom, with Bobby mincing around in a pith helmet swatting away the wasps.

So, at this point in time, my plot of land is still barren – protected by a few swirls of rusty barbed wire and my fading dreams.

Then again, is it fair of Bobby to expect me to remain here with only my government 'Winter Fuel Payment' to warm me up in old age?

Perhaps a compromise will be for me to spend six months of every year in Nigeria – only returning to England when I need my cataracts done or my hip replaced?

Somehow, I guess I am destined to roam this planet until I meet my maker, forever scratching away at its boundaries. The world may be my oyster, but it seems I can never have a permanent home.

Aside from us though, where are race relations in this country heading?

As we have already mentioned confusion abounds over this subject. England is now a seething mass of different cultures, races, religions, and foods. Each are fighting for their fifteen minutes of fame. Each is isolated.

Instead of being open to fresh ideas, we are seeing more negative entrenchment of attitudes towards asylum seekers or disputes over religion. At difficult times such as these, it is imperative that we all leave our brains unlocked for data to flood in. Instead a hardening of already developed stereotypes is threatening to overcome us. Stereotypes that go both ways – as we have demonstrated in this book.

What should happen is that our similarities are emphasised as much as our differences. Nigerians are great entrepreneurs, much like your very own Sir Richard Branson.

True, most Nigerians do not go on madcap balloon rides or grow hippy style moustaches and beards, but they do share his sense of business adventure. I know that most readers are now probably thinking back to the 'fraud and finance' chapter but I really do mean legitimate business-minded people here. Nigerians are ambitious and like to succeed, much like the lower middle classes in England. We are hard-working people who want to get on in life. Strangely, we are never described as such in the media. In contrast, the recent influx of white Eastern Europeans tend to have the prefix 'strong work ethic' before any mention of their nationality. The poor African is relegated, once again, to the bottom of the pile with this type of racial favouritism.

Bobby made me aware of this when he noticed how the employment agencies, near to where we live, tended to recruit their labour from African sources. By this, he was referring to the huddle of Africans who used to cluster around the agency doors before they opened each day. Almost immediately, the Africans disappeared once Britain was opened up to the other European accession countries in 2004. Queuing up outside are now the omnipresent Poles and 'sexy' blonde Lithuanians/Latvians/Estonians. Everywhere one looks, their presence is seen; Polish plumbers, Polish brickies, Polish bakers. I even once walked past a seedy club that was advertising for Pole dancers! Talk about multi-tasking.

Where have the Africans gone? Have they moved up the social scale or are they now out of a job? Maybe they are flocking to Poland to do the jobs the Poles no longer wish to do over there? Or maybe the Africans are now becoming like birds, migrating to whatever country wants them to clean their toilets or wash their offices?

Whatever, I for one know that our care homes and supermarkets would collapse without the 'hard working ethic' that African staff bring with them from home. Fraud is not the only thing us Africans are good at.

It is also striking how many Nigerians are also now going to live in America – my sister amongst them. The Americans, even more than the English, like to celebrate success so I can see many positives from this mixing of cultures.

And this is the key really of the whole book – that cultures have to mix. It is never too late to learn from another. Do not be put off by what you imagine a person to be like, find out instead what really makes them tick by talking to them.

You may be pleasantly surprised.

Summary

We are both determined that whatever is round the corner for us has to be met head on by two strong individuals.

In some ways, marriages can resemble the Thames Water Barrier – always erect and ready to call on at a moments notice. Dependable. Paradoxically it is that very strength that can lead to their downfall as, without even knowing it, the ability to take a partner for granted is never far from the surface. Couples should constantly be on their guard against it. My advice is; if your partner does the ironing or cooks a meal, compliment him or her about it. Do not presume your dinner will always be on the table for you. If you do, one day you may just find an Iceland ready meal is your sole comfort.

Still, I'd rather have that than pounded yam.

The future (for us) is obviously going to bring with it certain problems. Not least is the longing of Margaret to go to Nigeria. The funny thing is many Nigerians over here would do almost anything not to go back there. Really, I have lost count of the number of people who have told me this.

When I ask Margaret why she has this desire to return, she always states she wants to help her siblings, to be there physically as they struggle through life. Whilst this a laudable aim, I cannot see how it will help them if she gives up her job here and wanders the streets unemployed in Nigeria. If the worst comes to the worst and a civil war breaks out again in Nigeria (Muslim north versus Christian south) her family would need somewhere to flee. Margaret's being in Nigeria would only serve as a drain on her parents' already-stretched resources. She would just be another mouth to feed.

However, if she remains in England, she would be of far more use to them – as we see even now, with us accommodating relatives when they visit England.

As I said before, I cannot see her going, whatever she may say. Margaret would miss things about England she holds most dear: Joshua, Olivia, cod steaks, apple pie, antique shops, my parents, her church, her sister Anne, the telephone, David Dickinson, *Cash in the Attic, Antiques Roadshow....*

One day, she may even learn to miss me.

The future for England is not quite so straightforward. I often hear from others as to how successfully we mix as a society. Whilst I wish this were true for many this remains a myopic issue. I note that the American academic, Cornel West, said, after a recent visit to our shores, that although our streets appear cosmopolitan he wondered about the friendships across the colour line. He followed this up by criticising the amount of 'ethnic' friends that white people have. I feel he should equally have asked; how many white friends do black/Asian people have? The blame for this should be apportioned equally between all races.

Perhaps more credible evidence of this lack of friendship was provided by a MORI poll released in November 2006. The results showed that 70 per cent of people polled admitted to hardly ever choosing to meet someone of a different ethnicity within the bricks and mortar of their own homes. Although somewhat alarming, what surprised me the most about this was the inactivity of the government. You would have thought, given the racially sensitive world we live in, that a target figure ought to have been agreed by now for councils to meet ethnic 'friendship' quotas.

And, if it did come to pass, I presume it would operate along much the same lines as the congestion charge – where people who currently drive 4x4 vehicles are charged a higher daily rate. White people with black and Asian friends might see their council tax fall, whilst people who remain in ignorance of their neighbours would see an increase. Let's see how many people wish to remain segregated once they are hit in the pocket.

I may write in jest but the reality of this survey is a sobering wake up call to all who work in the race relations field. Troubles undoubtedly lie ahead if we do not mix more.

As a result of our living apart, different communities are having their own sets of values, cultures, clothes, foods, and drugs. This is fine until they rub shoulders with another. Whereas racist violence used to be the preserve of white against black, now we are seeing differing factions emerge, normally based around drug turf wars and the ownership of certain streets by the omnipresent gangs that plague our cities.

Youth gang warfare, of course, is not new to England; since youth cults first emerged in the 1950s, young people have found a reason to hate other groups. It could be Mods v Rockers in the Sixties or Punks against Skins and Teddy Boys in the Seventies. Whatever, testosterone has its violent side and the English are nothing if not good at fighting. These days though, we are witnessing youth fighting other youth along ethnic lines, not for the music they like or the clothes they wear. This is a crucial difference as skin colour cannot be changed.

It could be Somali youth against Caribbean origin kids in Woolwich or Romanian youth against Albanians in Palmers Green. Slowly, without many realising it, our streets are beginning to echo with police sirens as a backdrop to the racial/cultural intolerance that is spreading.

I hate to come over all Enoch Powell in the last paragraph, but it is always advisable to spot social trends before they become more common-place. We still have time to combat them, but that time will be wasted if more are not made aware of the issues involved. It is obvious to us that we urgently need a 'Rivers of Love' message to be spread to all communities for this to happen. As our own lives have shown, it can be done with the right motivation.

The media are very much in the front line here and they need to be seen as a voice of reason and not merely sensation-seeking if reason is to emerge victorious. It is of critical importance that they remain politically neutral – otherwise extreme political parties will use this as a vindication for their existence.

However, I have found a lot of this violence is reported in a subdued manner by the media. Those from the Left seem to be especially troubled by inter-ethnic violence, such as the Asian v Black riots in the Lozells area of Birmingham in 2005. They are much happier in commenting only on the odious activities of the white supremacist types. This is wrong. All violence directed at anyone for whatever reason is unlawful and should be commented on the same. A classic example here is the BBC Ceefax information service. Whilst researching this book, I noticed that they rarely use the words 'asylum seeker' if a person has been found guilty of a crime and fits that category. The ITV text service, however, has no such qualms and happily informs the reader that the person who has been sentenced was an asylum seeker from whichever country they came from.

To continue this theme, BBC Ceefax also fails to report a suspect's race or ethnicity when the police issue an appeal for a particular person. ITV, by contrast, nearly always mention their race.

Now, a case can be argued that it's irrelevant listing someone as an asylum seeker or referring to their colour. Surely though, if a man has committed a crime and is wanted by the police, the first thing the guy in the street needs to know is his race. Not for any ingrained stereotypical reason but because it's the quickest way to eliminate someone from their enquiries.

A good demonstration of this occurred on January 29, 2006. An incident happened the night before where an eighteen-year-old youth was stabbed (in

Camden, London). Twenty-five men were arrested at the scene of the crime and taken to varying Police stations around London. Both the victim and all the alleged murderers were Somali. I read this on the ITV text pages and also the *Telegraph*. Of course, BBC Ceefax just listed them as 'twenty-five men'. Their ethnicity had been removed.

So why do I make a fuss about this – especially given that a large chunk of this book complains about ethnicity tick boxes? Well, what would have happened if a witness had seen a large group of Somali men abusing an individual on the night in question? If the witness read about the death the next day in the paper and the actions of 'twenty-five Somalians', he may realise he has important information for the police. However, if the potential witness was not aware of their ethnicity – via reading Ceefax – he may be more inclined not to link what he saw with the murder. Justice is therefore being hampered by some misguided kind of PC approach to crime.

It is a sad fact that the vast majority of black people who are murdered are murdered by other black people. By ignoring ethnicity or by reporting such murders via a cursory couple of lines at the bottom of a page – normally with a reference to Operation Trident – the media are giving the impression that a black life is somehow less important than the life of, say, a white lawyer. The Metropolitan Police commissioner, Sir Ian Blair, commented on this in January 2006, accusing the media of 'institutional racism'. His comments were roundly condemned at the time, but I think he was correct with his allegation. The underlying thread seems to be, 'ah well, yet another black kid murdered by another,' yawn yawn; move on to the business pages.

This is unfair, as each life is as valuable as the next. *The Daily Telegraph*, I have noticed, takes this even further and seems to give so much more publicity to anyone murdered who was a solicitor, an accountant or someone who once sneezed at Eton. It could be said that they are being: 'economically racist'.

This whole attitude towards crime and ethnicity is perverse and insults the reader's or listener's intelligence. Does the BBC not think the population of this country are adult enough to differentiate between a criminal, who happens to be an asylum seeker, and one fleeing persecution who has never committed a crime?

Personally, I feel insulted by this inference and think it is actually playing into the hands of extremists by giving them a ready made chip on the shoulder to exploit. Since the Tories are moving further towards the centre ground of English politics, the potential is there for the BNP to acquire more votes – not a pleasant thought for the majority.

Right now I feel their increasing electoral success (nearly one million

Britons voted for them in the 2006 local elections) is reminiscent of the growth in popularity the NF enjoyed in the middle/late Seventies. Popularity that was only destroyed by the emergence of the much denigrated Margaret Thatcher – in many ways her lasting legacy for British politics.

The irony is that it is partly her 1980 policies – such as selling off of council homes, destroying manufacturing industry – which the far-right are capitalising on to feed and exaggerate white working-class fears of immigration/housing. It is clear, with the benefit of hindsight, that the superficially liberating policies of Margaret Thatcher destroyed the self-esteem of the working-class, or, at least, those in it who lacked the drive to get through the glass ceiling to middle-class 'utopia'. With the collapse of the family unit, white working communities are now feeling just as disenfranchised from society as some Muslim elements are. However, whilst you can switch on the telly and view numerous Muslim 'community' leaders talking about how they are victimised, you never see a leader speaking for ordinary white working-class folk. Nick Griffin, whatever I or anyone else may think of his simplistic and divisive policies, has spotted this gap in the market and has ruthlessly exploited it. I get pissed off by this, as he doesn't represent me or any of my white friends. But then again, which politician does?

The only way to combat this new approach is to meet the BNP on their own terms. At the moment, the Left are fighting a 1970s race war with regards to the BNP. It may make one feel better shouting 'Smash smash the BNP' or 'Nazi Party never again' but what does this achieve? In my opinion it is gesture politics, much like those who wear 'Make Poverty History' wrist bands. The sloganeering approach is also self-defeating. Why? Because Mr and Mrs Joe Public see only a middle-aged guy (BNP leader Nick Griffin) in a suit talking in a calm moderate manner. On the other side, they see a chanting abusive mob. Is it any wonder, then, that many white working-class people are falling for their benign version of disguised fascism? All they have to do is promise to get the trains running on time and they will be in number ten Downing Street before you can shout *Mein Kampf*.

No, the Left really have to think again about combating the BNP. What they should do is engage in dialogue and defeat them with logical clear argument. Talk about their policies and what they actually entail. At the moment, all the BNP seems to stand for is withdrawal from the EU, de-politicisation of the BBC, an extra Bank Holiday to commemorate Trafalgar and 'voluntary' repatriation. They seem to think that cleansing Britain of brown skins will lead to automatic prosperity for the rest of us. Err; I think Idi Amin said something similar when he threw the Asians out of Uganda in the 1970s. Is Uganda now an economic superpower?

The Left should also discuss the BNP and their zero tolerance attitudes to crime. I would love to know just how many members they have who possess criminal records, I'll wager it is more than the national average. This is the way to reduce their impact on the white population – by showing them to be liars and hypocrites. I know this policy is fraught with danger, not least because of the publicity they would enjoy, but by refusing to engage in debate, we are laying ourselves open to the charge of moral cowardice and appeasement. Appeasement, because we are tolerating them as a political force, instead of slaying their hijacked St George's dragon, and cowardice, because by not talking we are sending the message we are scared of them. This is wrong. Their arguments are weak and therefore easily defeated by counter political thought.

Another way is to use humour. They are certainly ripe for parody with their anti-gay, anti-Islam, and anti-nowhere league comments. Laugh at them; pity them even for their faintly ludicrous ideas. Beating them up on the street is lazy, old-fashioned and way too easy. A new modern way is needed to reduce their appeal, for if we just stand still they will continue to gain popularity.

And yet all the government does is talk about how they despise the BNP, that their views on Islam being a "wicked, vicious faith" are not representative of the voting mainstream. Well, I don't know where the government go to canvas opinion on such ideas. I hear, on a regular basis, views expressed like Nick Griffin's by white, working-class people. Why is the government in denial of what is on their own doorstep? In contrast, minister after minister queue up to accuse Muslim leaders of being in denial about Islamic terrorism and sympathisers in their midst. I actually agree with this line of thought regarding terrorism, but why, then, do we replicate the head in the sand approach? As it is, at the moment, the government consistently underestimates the ability of the BNP to infect the white working-class with racial hatred. Shouting them down is no longer enough.

We should also point out that their version of up-market fascism does nothing historically to help genuine white, working-class people. Take their hero; Adolf Hitler. How did he benefit the German working-class of Hamburg, Berlin etc in 1930s Germany? He got five million of them slaughtered in WW2. How is this standing up for their own self-interest? Who is stabbing who in the back now?

There will always be 2-5 per cent of the population who are a serious danger to others with regards to terrorism and/or right-wing extremism. These people cannot be defeated through rational argument. The real problem is the 10-15 per cent of the respective communities, the sympathisers, these are the men and women we need to reach out to with a 'hearts and minds' campaign. The type of person who might say, 'I don't agree with bombing but I wouldn't tell the police if I knew of someone up to no good'. Or the person who ignores the man who shovels excrement into someone's house, because 'it's not a nice thing to do but the Asians don't integrate'. I firmly believe that, with the right tactics, we can influence this group of 'swinging voters/fascists'. Do we have the moral willpower, though, to admit our society is not as inclusive as we like to believe?

Another area ripe for the BNP to exploit concerns the reporting of racist murders in the UK. I have noticed that whenever a white person is the victim of racist violence the story disappears in a flash from the media and especially from BBC news bulletins. This is disturbing as over the period 1995-2004, according to official Home Office figures, twenty-four of the fifty-eight people killed for reasons related to their colour were white. People like Kriss Donald, a white Scottish teenager who, in March 2004, was bundled into a car, beaten, stabbed and finally set on fire. His murderers, five Asian men, were found guilty of racially aggravated murder. Unless you were the type to study the news religiously, this murder probably escaped your attention, seeing as how it didn't receive the same prominence accorded to cases such as Anthony Walker. Now, considering that white people make up around 92 per cent of the population, it stands to reason they would make up a sizeable percentage of the victims, as well as the perpetrators but, why does the BBC act in such a nervous way by ignoring these murders? Why are they so scared to confront the violent reality of our streets?

Because they are worried about stirring up the passions of the white working-class in England, ironically the one group of people the middle-class 'inclusive' luvvies at the Beeb haven't a clue of how to reach. This is the wrong approach. Racist murders are just that; racist murders. All mothers shed the same tears; no matter the ethnicity of the victim. All are crimes that should be condemned in the same manner. The BBC has to be above this kind of social engineering. They are paid to provide a public service for all citizens of this country, irrespective of political views or colour. Everything should be reported on an equal basis. If they don't do this they risk giving the far-right an excuse for their hate filled propaganda.

I should stress, though, that percentage wise you are still far more likely to be on the end of racist violence/murder if you are black or Asian – a fact we should not forget.

Another thing that irritates me is 'Red' Ken Livingstone and his continual trumpeting of the multicultural nature of our capital. If you have ever had the misfortune of reading his *Londoner* free newspaper, you would know what I am on about here. Story after story, within its pages, show how multicultural London is a success story for the whole country to be proud of – what with all its different languages and cultures. According to the paper, we all rub along fantastically with no problems whatsoever.

Good old Ken then compounds this glossing over of problems by barely being able to complete a sentence without including the word 'diversity'. Really, I'm not joking. Check out one of his speeches for proof – you won't have long to wait before he slips it in. It is so bad, I used to think he was sponsored by the Commission for Racial Equality (CRE) to mention the magic 'd' word, well, until his much publicised spat with ex-CRE head, Trevor Phillips, that is.

He really seems to view it as a personal crusade to convince everyone that we are all one big happy family. I genuinely wish we were but, as we have shown with the examples littered throughout this book, it is not always that way.

As if he wasn't lefty enough, I notice Mr Livingstone went on a 2006 trip to Cuba to get lessons from an ageing dictator (Fidel Castro) on how to run the world's economic hub (London.) During the course of the visit, it was alleged that he spent nearly £36,000 of taxpayers' money. Why is such nonsense allowed? Then again, his political opposite, Nick Griffin, bases his party's strategy on the last will and testament of a mass murderer (Adolf Hitler.) Has the world gone mad?

It is obvious to any, who are politically aware, that Nick Griffin and his acolytes are using the white working-class as *Sonderkommandos* (special commando) in their lust for power. Equally, George Galloway is using Muslims as his foot soldiers in a *jihad* against western style democracy. Neither of these men are happy giving their opinions in the margins of politics – they both live off the oxygen of self-publicity. Galloway has had his ninety minutes of fame on *Celebrity Big Brother (CBB)*, how long before Griffin receives an invitation?

I say again, though, that Mr Griffin should be given the chance to make a fool of himself. A political debate with him may increase his notoriety but only at the expense of showing the population his true beliefs. As a depressing sign of the times, I contend that we really are more likely to see him on *CBB* than on BBC's *Question Time*. Remember where you read it first!

Incidentally, I have noticed that whenever Nick Griffin is mentioned in the papers, a reference is always made to the fact he was educated at Cambridge. Why is this? Because the perception exists that only illiterate, working-class people can be racist. As most of our journalists are that way inclined (middle-class not racist), should we really be surprised at their apparent shock over Griffin's educational background?

Neither of these two individuals has the answer to the problems on our streets, whatever they may think. Oh, how I wish we could just shove the two of them into a bear pit and say 'may the best man win'. Sadly, we can't.

Instead of a bear bit, we have denial and a refusal to acknowledge the problems caused by race. Our elected politicians – in their rich houses cut off from the naked streets – can downplay the race issue, but it will increasingly affect people going about their day to day lives. They will only realise when they leave their flash Jaguar cars at home in the garage and start to travel around the capital on a daily bus pass.

So, why does Mr Livingstone ignore the problems between different races? Why does BBC Ceefax remove race from the equation? Because we, as a nation, are too put-off by the word 'race' and all the myriad subjects that come under its multi-coloured umbrella. As stated in the introduction to this book; it is a topic the same as any other. Demystify race and divorce it from its elder brother, racism. One does not automatically lead to the other.

Rather than being scared of talking about race, we should concentrate instead on defeating racism. It is up to all of us to grasp this opportunity to stop this disease in its tracks, and reach out the hand of friendship to any who cross our path.

And, once you have done this, you will soon find out that most of us in this country share the same hopes, fears, and worries. We really have to concentrate more on what we have in common as a nation, rather than what we are perceived to have as a difference. We really are all in it together.

CHAPTER 19

Friends

Bobby

As you may expect, both of us have friends from a wide social and ethnic background. I should add though, for whatever reason, a high number of my friends have something a bit 'odd' about them. Very few are the usual 2.4 kids, semi-detached house, and safe job types. To me, this is a compliment to them.

Take our friend David Nunn, for example. He loves travelling and has visited a high proportion of the world's low spots. Not for him a week in Spain, sunning himself to a frazzle, or nicking the German punk rockers bath towels round the swimming pools. No, for him, holiday bliss is mixing with the downtrodden locals, be it in Cuba, Cambodia, or any other economically destitute part of the world. A man of culture, of sophistication, of.... curiosity.

Then, there is my friend, Nikki Upperton. Can you think of any sane person who would dedicate twenty-five years of their life following a failed pop star around to all ends of the earth? Well, she does. The irony is that the subject of her affection, Marc Almond, has told her to her face he is fed up of her being in the front row of his shows and has requested she sit further back! I am sorry but, if one of my favourite bands said that to me, I would have made a funeral pyre of their records.

Then we come to Julian and Tracey Smith. Dear, oh dear. Whilst the rest of the country has woken up to the 21st century, poor old Jules and Tracey think the world is still turning Day-Glo, and surround themselves with all manner of punk rock clothes and artefacts. Indeed, it is so bad that, unless an item is stamped 'punk rock authenticated 1977', they don't want to know, as ably demonstrated by their proud flaunting of a Sex Pistols clock (that I bought them) in their kitchen.

Walking into the rest of their house is like falling backwards in time, as punk rock screams at you from every direction. Oh dear, but it gets worse. The majority of their clothes comprise fishnet tights, purple bondage pants, wacky shirts (including their own home-made stencil designs) and tacky bum flaps. They also ride a tandem.

What!

Yep, I guess it ruins their punk rock credibility, but they enjoy cycling the country with nothing more than a thin tube of metal keeping them together. My goodness, the last person I saw riding astride one of those contraptions was Bill Oddie and the rest of the *Goodies*. And yet, they declare themselves 'Mr and Mrs Punk Rock.'

I ask you!

Mind you, they are nothing compared to well-known comedy duo 'Nik and Alex' from Blackpool. Not content with being famous for its breasts, sticks of rock and debauchery, Blackpool is also renowned (in the punk world at least) for spawning one of the punk 'faces' of all time: Nik. This man is fifty years old and still sports a pink mohican. To compound this, he insists on wearing a leather jacket that must be thirty years old to the day, his face is adorned with more tin than Metal Mickey and he has a cartoon 'carry on' squeaky voice.

Bizarrely, he once met the then leader of the Tory Party, Iain Duncan Smith, when he was awarded a prize for employee of the week at the plastics factory where he works. He was seen on camera shaking his hand. How punk rock is that? He should have gobbed in his face and shouted "Anarchy in Blackpool, take that you dirty Tory ★★★★★."

Another old friend of mine is Scott Allin. Canadian by birth, but very much an assimilated English geezer after living in England for many years. He hasn't forgotten his roots, though, and is proud of his Canadian ancestry. Indeed, so proud is he that he has a stuffed moose mounted on the wall of his front room!

Other aspects of his character are English through and through. As an example, the English are often criticised for not having a winner-takes-all mentality and, instead, being gallant losers. Eddie the Eagle springs to mind as confirmation of this cultural trend. As a nation, we clutch to our bosom these brave but foolhardy sporting icons, even though the rest of the world is laughing their socks off at our English ineptitude. I am glad to report that Scott has taken this idea fully on board and supports a football team renowned for being losers – Tottenham Hotspurs!

Of course, to be fair to the above, they could probably retaliate with their own views on me, especially after reading my somewhat caustic comments on them. I stress again, though, that I mean all the above as a compliment.

But, just in case any are offended, I have given them the option for revenge. This chapter will close with a questionnaire, completed by joint friends/family members enabling them to give feedback regarding Margaret and I as a couple. Some of their views are spot on, some are, quite frankly, ridiculous.

Where necessary, I have added comments in italics to indicate if I agree with the opinions aired.

The reason we decided to include this questionnaire was to enable readers to see for themselves confirmation of the views we have exposed throughout the book. Their answers also verify many of the points that Margaret and I made about each other.

Whatever their views, we are both just glad that we have met some interesting people over the years, with stories and passions that dovetail with some of ours. Neither Margaret nor I will ever understand why society views it as being normal for men to only talk about: cars, beer, clothes, women, football and gambling. Or for women to munch over weighty issues such as: washing powder, penis size, TV shows or dieting.

What is so good about being 'normal'?

Nothing.

Margaret

My best friend is not actually a friend at all, she is my sister, Anne.

I guess, because we have gone through so much together, I view her as my confidante and number one person to run to, if I have a problem. For her part, she never turns me away and always lets me ramble on without complaint. In many ways, she is a typical African woman living in England. She works hard, as a care home manager, and pours all her spare cash into enabling her daughter to attend private school, sacrificing holidays, expensive cars and designer goods, so that Whitney can attain a decent level of education. I admire her tremendously for this.

As I mentioned earlier, she is not entirely comfortable with Yoruba culture, and feels that Yoruba women living in England need to modernise certain beliefs held within the culture. Certainly, she does not accept the blind worship to men that some Nigerian women feel is natural. If her husband comes home tired from work and wants to bounce up and down on her to relieve himself, she will say no – unless she is in the mood herself.

She really is a woman that needs to be replicated and not shunted away as someone who has 'lost' her culture.

One of my closest friends is a Jamaican origin Essex girl (without the blond hair), named Natasha. Very much a sociable person, Natasha is without prejudice and always judges people as she finds them. Like me, she likes to talk, and our conversations are often a competition to see who can get the words out first! Certainly, the two of us would make a perfect advert for Duracell batteries, as we jabber away to one another.

Apart from Natasha, I have many other friends of a Jamaican background, such as: Norma, Judy and Carol. Over the years, I have learnt so much from them and I know they have picked up many nuggets of information from me – such as how to talk for two hours non-stop.

No, seriously, I am truly blessed to have got to know so many pleasant people over the years. It makes my heart go all gooey when I realise the big bad world can still throw up decent human beings.

What, though, do our friends really think of Bobby and I?

Questionnaire on Bobby and Margaret

Many people contributed to our questionnaire – we extend our heartfelt thanks to all who did.

Even though we are against the ethnic labelling of people, we figured it may be useful to readers to know the origin of those who replied. So, in no particular order: David Nunn, (white English) Glen Baldwin, (white English) Sheena, (black Ghanaian) Scott Allin, (white Canadian/English) Daphne Biribonwoha, (black Ugandan) Anne Dennison, (black Nigerian) Julian and Tracey Smith, (white, Northern and English) Andrew Gwinnett, (white, Black Country English) Asif Dar, (British Pakistani) Natasha Hylton, (black, Essex and English)

For ease of reading, we have condensed all the replies into one amalgamated response – with the author of the comment noted beforehand.

So, onto the questions:

Are Margaret and Bobby well suited?
Scott: Surprisingly yes. At the core, there is probably more in them that is similar than there are things that make them different.
Julian & Tracey: Although they have dissimilar interests, they are well suited to each other.
How would you describe their characters?
Sheena: Very different, yet very similar.

Scott: Bobby; a strange mix of the contrary and the conformist. On one hand he is a punk who stands out from the norm, and on the other he is Mr Suburbia with his 2.4 kids, *Daily Telegraph* and sensible savings plan. In short, a nice, honest bloke who is more thoughtful than most and has a keen intellect. He oscillates between being surprisingly immature and very mature, depending on what context he finds himself in.

Margaret: Where do I begin? The first word that springs to mind is ebullient, the second is definitely loud. Margaret is a person that doesn't put a lot of stock in concealing her emotions and you are always acutely aware of where you stand with her. She enjoys debate and discussions (*arguing!!*) on issues that range from the trivial to the very deep. She is very naïve at times and can often get hold of the wrong end of the stick and shake it vigorously. She is very caring and kind, but does have a temper that is best to avoid.

Julian & Tracey: Bobby; His appearance can suggest both confidence and perhaps aggression. The truth could not be further from this, as he is often shy and definitely a chicken! (*this from the man who ran off and left me at the bus stop with his missus when we were attacked in Tottenham!!*)

Margaret; She likes heated discussions. However, she can be very deep and enjoys a long conversation.

Daphne: Bobby is both weird and funny. Margaret is strict and yet understanding.

Natasha: Bobby: Opinionated, not willing to listen to others. He is also a bit of a piss taker.

Margaret: She can go off on a tangent quite frequently. Definitely the queen of waffle. Known to misunderstand a conversation.

Who got the best deal out of the marriage?

Glen: the two people who were saved by them marrying each other!

Scott: Neither. I believe that they are one of the rare examples of a truly even partnership which benefits both equally. I'd say that their two children probably get the best deal, as they get to grow up in a loving family unit.

Natasha: Both benefited; Margaret wanted kids and saw Bobby as a desirable father, whilst Bobby wanted to prove his sexuality!

David: I wasn't aware that the marriage was a business transaction.

Good/bad points of each of them?

Scott: Good points for Bobby; Intelligence, decency, reliability, bravery (by persisting in wearing his punk clobber in the face of hostility.) He is also friendly and can be very funny (although not as often as he thinks).

Bad points; His knee-jerk reaction that makes him go against popular opinion, just so he can retain what he thinks is a punk ethos. He can also be very dismissive of certain things or opinions. In addition, he has an obsessive fascination with WW2, punk and Wolves.

Good points for Margaret; Intelligent, good at listening to people, caring and compassionate, a lack of cynicism. Good conversationalist.

Bad points; Overly emotive, sometimes naïve and gullible. Too religious by half. A fairly childish and repetitive sense of humour. Can be too easily offended and has been known to be a little attention seeking!

Julian & Tracey: Bobby; His good points are his music (Oi! Oi! Oi!) and his clothes. His bad points are lack of different clothing and too much German Oi! He also shows his Southern softy origins by only drinking cider.

Margaret: Her cooking is fantastic. (*Julian and Tracey like Nigerian cooking and love nothing better than coming round our house for a slap up Nigerian meal.*) Her bad point is that she doesn't cook enough!

Natasha: Bobby; His intelligence and shopping skills are high up on any list. His problem areas are most definitely his sense of 'humour', that is often too dry for the majority to get. As is probably obvious by reading the book, he is also a bit of a snob.

Margaret: Her bad points are that she stresses out too much over relatively trivial things. This, though, is balanced out by her sympathetic and caring nature. She is willing to go the extra mile for her friends.

Was his/her race ever an issue for you?

Julian & Tracey: I remember that, the first time we met Margaret, we were just happy Bobby had a girlfriend and was not gay! (*Can you believe this?*) It never occurred to us she could be black (*with a name like Oshindele??????????*) It had no bearing on our relationship with them whatsoever.

Natasha: Yes, Margaret was Nigerian – I was dubious of her because of this. I have since grown to realise that she is not as bad as the stereotype of most Nigerians.

Do the English have a culture and what is your response to those who suggest otherwise?

Scott: Of course they have a culture. Anyone who suggests otherwise is being ludicrous and insulting. The English have great traditions in all the areas that one might associate with having a culture; food, music, literature, arts, customs, dress, sport etc. My reaction to those who make such claims is; improve your education and don't listen to the fashionable opinions of self-hating English journalists, or bigoted foreigners, that dislike the English and wish to belittle them by making such outrageous claims. Alternatively, a simple f**k off will suffice with a two fingered salute an optional extra.

Daphne: They don't have a culture – well, not one that I've seen anyway. (*that's because your box isn't open to others Daphne.*)

Andrew: Yes, of course they have a culture. People who suggest otherwise must be West Brom fans.

Julian & Tracey: Obviously they do. Be it the so-called British disease of football hooliganism or the stiff upper lip of Noel Coward. Our country is steeped in tradition, such as the may-pole, touch woods, standing stones etc. Folk traditions, both musically and artistically, are alive and well. People, who say the English have no culture, do not deserve to participate or contribute to such riches.

Asif: I think that the English do have a culture and people who suggest otherwise are misguided.

Natasha: Of course they have a culture – such as going down the pub and beating people up!

Would you personally cross the 'colour line'?

Scott: Yes. The only impediment that I have encountered so far is a distinct resistance from some women I have liked to cross over the line towards me!

David: I crossed it many years before Bobby jumped on the bandwagon. I have also crisscrossed this line repeatedly since.

Asif: Yes, I would. Because I am Muslim, I do not view any race/culture/religion as superior/inferior to another. I believe that our treatment of others is how we are assessed, and that is the real criteria of who is "better", or "worse" as a person.

Daphne: No.

Who would play the both of them if the book were made into a film?

Glen: Charles Hawtrey and Barbara Windsor.

David: The guy who plays Harry Potter in the films (for Bobby) and, for Margaret, the guy who played the cute black kid in the *Different Strokes* TV show (*Gary Arnold*.) Otherwise, the Krankies for Margaret.

Sheena: Whoopi Goldberg and Robbie Williams.

Daphne: Tom Hanks for Bobby and Angela Bassett (*yes please*) for Margaret.

Asif: Whoopi Goldberg for Margaret and Tim Roth for Bobby.

Andrew: The Krankies or Laurel and Hardy. (*It is only fair to point out that Andrew was a tad tipsy when he completed this questionnaire!*)

Natasha: Mr Bean for Bobby and Barbara Windsor for Margaret. (*told you her tits were large!*)

Did either of them change when they came into contact with each other?

Glen: Yes, Bobby lost something.

Scott: Bobby's diet has changed for the better. This was the man who lived on a diet of bread & butter and fishfingers for years.

Julian & Tracey: Bobby became happier and interested in other things apart from German Oi! punk and Wolverhampton.

Asif: I think that Margaret had already realised by then that not all white men were perverts! Bobby saw that, for some people, faith and their religious belief(s) are still very relevant subjects in England today.

Has their marriage been an inspiration to you?

Scott: I like the fact that they truly accept each other for whom and what they are. It shows the rest of us that you might find happiness from an unexpected source, so long as you are prepared to keep an open mind.

Asif: It is nice that two people of different backgrounds have overcome ignorance and prejudice to remain together and start a family (ah, cue the violin music.)

Natasha: It proves that opposites attract.

Daphne: Yes, it shows that even weird people can make a successful marriage.

Andrew: Oh, my God, no!

What do you think about punk music?

Scott: I must confess to actually liking quite a lot of it (*I introduced Scott to bands such as Terrorgruppe, Die Toten Hosen and Government Issue.*)
Unfortunately, Bobby has such an obsession with German punk that he is unable to sort the wheat from the chaff – he just buys anything that is punk and German. I also think he should ditch his blinkered refusal to listen to anything that is popular or trendy – i.e, anything outside of the punk/Oi!/skinhead world that he has immersed himself into.

Andrew: I'd rather not.

Natasha: I have learnt a lot about punk since knowing Bobby – I now appreciate why some people like it – even though I don't.

David: Repetitive and coma inducing. Every time I go to Bobby's house, I am forced to endure yet another version of some three-chord thrash by some obscure Kraut band that I've no interest in.

Asif: I heartily approve of Bobby's eclectic music, although I sometimes don't understand the lyrics of German Oi!

Julian & Tracey: Rubbish! No, really, we feel it is sometimes a little one dimensional. At times, it appears that every song he plays us includes the chorus: *Poebel und Gesocks*, Oi! Oi! Oi! We are surprised he does not study

256

the roots of punk more. (*not true as my record collection contains a huge volume of Sixties garage music – the precursor of punk rock.*)

Sheena: Interesting. (*Ah, so polite – West Africans just cannot slag off elders.*)

And Margaret's black doll/Golliwog interest?

Scott: It is good to have some kind of hobby – even if it is a bit strange. However, we should not lose sight of the fact that we are talking about a forty-year-old woman, who is still playing with dolls.

Sheena: Very interesting (*even more polite.*)

Natasha: Dolls are good investments – like houses. (*Barmy.*)

The best and worst elements in Nigerian/English culture?

Scott: The English have a good dash of scepticism, tolerance and humour. Their bad points are a tendency towards jingoism and the suppression of emotion – the stiff-upper-lip stereotype.

I like the Nigerian respect of elders and the wider family in general. The negative factor is their over-reliance on faith and a fairly pronounced slant towards xenophobia.

David: You are the one writing the book not me.

Julian & Tracey: For the best English attributes, see our answer for culture. The worst would include binge drinking. Other bad points are the lack of knowledge, and capitalism. (*punk rockers of the world unite.*)

For Nigeria, the worst is their punctuality. They also have reverse racism towards the English.

Their best qualities include their cooking and basic friendliness.

Asif: Best thing about English culture? The truly diverse nature of modern Britain. Also, old-fashioned values about sex, parents, elders, discipline and community.

The worst has to be the hysteria about illegal immigration and asylum-seekers, football hooligans, rise of the Nazi BNP, debates about "integration", the apparent "clash of civilisations," end of the world, etc.

For Nigeria, the best is their genuine respect for elders and traditional family values. The worst has to be their insecurity and instability leading to corruption on a massive scale. Also the fractured nature of ethnic and religious groups and their on-off feuding.

Anne: The best thing about Nigeria is the way respect of elders is still adhered to. The worst is the hypocrisy of some of the men.

Natasha: Nigerian; The men are largely bastards! By that, I mean that they tend to look down on women as second class citizens. As a race, they are also cold and not welcoming of non-Nigerians. (*I think Natasha is confusing the 'coldness' for the snobbery that many Nigerians display towards people of a Caribbean origin – due to the Nigerian obsession with education.*)

Many Nigerians feel superior to Caribbean people, as they feel they are un-educated compared to them. In return, Caribbean origin men and women feel they don't get the respect they deserve from Africans, for their challenging of racist attitudes from the Fifties onwards. The slavery legacy is also a major factor for the animosity between the two groups.) Another irritating habit is their desire to dress up at the drop of a hat – even for trivialities such as shopping. This, combined with a serious addiction to designer wear, just looks tacky. (*Oh dear, and Margaret said Natasha treats everyone the same!*)

Aside from Margaret, I am struggling with the good side. Maybe, being so good at fraud?

English; We are more humane, tolerant (see above!) and open-minded. The bad side is that black people are still not competing on a level playing field.

Do the English have the best sense of humour in the world?

Scott: No. The thing with English humour is not that it's better than any other; it's just that it is much more widely used than in other cultures. This prevalence of humour in every facet of English culture is unique and baffling. So, we probably have the most acutely sensitive senses of humour but that doesn't equate to being the best, in my humble opinion.

Julian & Tracey: No, just the quirkiest.

Asif: Perhaps, see Tony Blair's reasoning for war in Iraq!

What do you think of the Nigerian stereotype (fraud) and the English one of being reserved?

Scott: To be frank, I was not aware of the Nigerian stereotype (*I am sorry I just cannot believe this*) and having worked alongside several Nigerians, this seems ludicrous to me.

The English stereotype is more accurate – especially in the South. Outside of London, people tend to be more open and friendly from my personal experience (correct, especially those from the West Midlands.)

Sheena: The English are reserved.

Anne: The English are reserved, but I think this is a good thing as it makes them respect other peoples.

Asif: Both of these are just stereotypes and nothing else. It's like saying all black people are muggers and that all white people are paedophiles.

Julian & Tracey: It is funny how the English are often seen as reserved in our own country, yet when we go abroad we are seen as rude and arrogant drunkards. When the two of us go on foreign holidays, we are mistaken as non-English. We once spent a week with people who thought we were Dutch!

Andrew: But Margaret is reserved and Bobby's just a cider drinker (*sorry, but* *he was even more drunk at this stage).*

Could you imagine either of them with another?

Andrew: Bobby could be with Looba Loo. Margaret could shack up with Russell Crowe.

Anne: No, I can't. They wouldn't last without the other person.

Natasha: If Bobby died, I could imagine Margaret going back to her roots with a black guy. He wouldn't, though, be Nigerian.

I could not imagine Bobby with another woman as no one else would have him!

David: I could imagine Bobby entwined with Julian in some tartan decorated love nest.

Julian: No thanks!

CONCLUSION

One Love Two Colours

We started writing this book with the intention of promoting a rounded image of mixed marriages, encompassing the pain, pleasures and pitfalls that are wrapped up within our 'two colours'. We have tried to show the reader that our relationship is not about Margaret being a black woman or I being a white man. No, it's about two human beings truly believing in the notion of loving thy neighbour.

We have been totally honest with all the issues raised, and have not found it necessary to exaggerate any of the vignettes we have described.

So, what have we found to be the pain of our relationship?

Apart from our disputes over food, we have been remarkably pain free. For certain, we argue quite a bit but it is very rarely over 'cultural clashes'. We are just two strong-minded people who happen to disagree over household chores. But, we would argue, this goes on up and down the country in just about every house. Most of our problems do not come down to me being white/English and Margaret being black/Nigerian.

It is important I stress this, as people from outside can assume that skin colour/culture is the root cause of a couple's arguing. I have felt for sometime that people not in relationships such as ours really believe that men and women wake up in the morning and gaze at their partner thinking: 'What a nice white man/black woman I have married'. I am sorry to appear boring but a couple being a different colour is completely irrelevant to the everyday trivialities of life. Even cultural matters are not that severe. This is best shown by our worst flash points being the potato or 'bucket bath'. I guess we must be doing something right for this to be the biggest problem after ten years of marriage!

What I would say, is that I did have a lot of cultural clashes with Margaret's cousin, Joyce, who stayed with us for a few months. Seeing as how she had not spent anytime in England before, she found it hard to adapt to a new country and way of life. This may come over with more than a whiff of hypocrisy, but I found her to be too respectful towards me in my role as her elder. By this I mean that every time I vacuumed her room or removed her dinner plate, she snatched it back, as she had been brought up not to let someone older than her do menial tasks. Whilst I respect her upbringing, I got fed up that I had no control over the way I did my housework. I am sorry if I come over like a control freak, it is just that, if I want to do the washing-up, I want to feel I have the freedom to do it anytime I wish.

I am sure many parents, reading my words, would think me a right Bus Station Loonie for thinking this and wonder what my problem is. Even my friends from football advised me just to sit back and let her wait on me hand and foot. Truth is though, I have always been independent and like to arrange my work the way I want it.

Her cousin also found it hard going to the church with Margaret. Coming from Nigeria, she was used to a more vocal style of worship with singing, clapping, chanting, etc. Much to Margaret's embarrassment, she actually started laughing at the way the congregation worshipped. She quite clearly had little time for the way people behaved in English churches, and soon found an 'African' church where she felt more at home. The two points to make here are: one; she is able to find in England a church where she was at ease, and two; that she didn't realise she was causing offence by her actions at the 'English' church. It remains to be seen whether this welcoming attitude we have towards others is a plus or a minus.

What is obvious is that she should have shown more respect towards those who worshipped in a way different to what she had become accustomed to.

I do feel sorry for her, though, as she is journeying very much into the unknown – by coming to live in England. I'm not sure I could do the same thing in her shoes.

It is also fair to say, she has much to learn about England and its peculiarities. For instance, she had no idea about the gamut of choice regarding apples on sale in the supermarket and begged Margaret for assistance. As ever, Margaret was pleased to help and informed her about the qualities of each variety. Cousin Joyce digested what Margaret told her and asked a final question, 'Auntie, what apples do you like?'

Margaret innocently replied, 'I like English Cox.'

Indeed!

It is important to add here that it was only after Joyce arrived that Margaret was forced to look again at herself. She, then, realised she was no longer '100 per cent Nigerian'.

Margaret had glaring differences with Joyce, a woman who had lived all her life in Nigeria and could rightly claim to be 100 per cent. Most of these differences revolved around timekeeping and organisation of one's finances/domestic chores. This had quite a sobering effect on Margaret, as it made her question her earlier comments about sometimes being culturally different to white English people, and her having zero confusion regarding identity. To my mind, this is a positive development as it shows that even without realising it, Margaret has assimilated into English culture. My Nigerian/German brother-in-law, Lawrence Dennison, also went through the same transformation, via his living in Germany for a number of years. He strenuously denies it but he too has picked up the habits and thinking of a true *Deutscher Mann*.

By the way, cousin Joyce also insists on using a 'bucket bath' and spends hours shouting on the phone – some stereotypes are closer to reality than others!

The only other obvious pain – if it can be called that – is in the religious field. I have accepted I will never be able to fully understand Margaret's religious motivation, and I wonder if I will be able to relate to my children in later life, when they start asking me questions about the good book? Without my sharing their faith, I can see possible troubles ahead.

Our children may also find it hard to connect with me in later years, when peer pressure may encourage them to label themselves as 'black'. The ridiculous idea that mixed race children are 'black' is actually quite offensive to those of us who have them. They are not 'black' in the same way as they are not 'white'. This reminds me of the bad old days of the South African apartheid regime, whereby mixed race children had a comb inserted in their hair. If the comb stood up they were declared black. If it slipped out they were 'coloured'.

The whole 'one drop of black' heritage notion, that means a child is black, is an outdated American concept that should have no place in current society. The idea, that a dash of non-white 'blood' makes someone black, belongs to a different era, from when races were kept apart and inter-racial marriages banned. In 1924, for instance, the American state of Virginia defined a white person as someone who had 'no trace whatsoever of any blood other than Caucasian'. This basically meant that even having a 'Negro' great-grandparent would make someone black. Have we not advanced at all since 1924? Mixed race means just that. One is not superior to the other, both are equal. Both are part of the same person.

I should add that even my dear lady wife thinks of our children as 'black'. She justifies this by arguing that, as most of society will label them that way, it is best not to confuse them at an early age. Our friend, Norma, who herself has three mixed race children, similarly sees her offspring as black. Colin, her white partner of fifteen years, has come to the same conclusion. In my opinion, this is wrong, and I feel that the groundswell of opinion is changing. Even the last government census of 2001 included the option of mixed race to define someone's ethnicity. I really do see this as the way forward, and assert that children are not confused by being called mixed race. It is surely better to give kids the honest facts and let them be comfortable choosing who they wish to be. No-one else has the right.

But will they be given the right? Personally, I am not sure. Way too many people, involved in the media, for instance, call those of mixed race 'black'. After collecting her well deserved 2002 Oscar for her part in the *Monster's Ball* film, Halle Berry was immediately labelled the first 'African-American' winner of the leading actress gong. Seeing as how she has a white mother, I fail to see how she is just 'African-American'. Why not the first mixed race woman? I am glad to report that she herself was more clued up over this, as, during her emotional acceptance speech, she dedicated her award to 'women of colour' – a far more accurate reflection of her heritage. Why, then, do the media continue to call those of mixed race 'black'? Because they are lazy, ignorant, and just misinformed of the history behind a label.

One of the practical problems of being married to Margaret, and most Nigerians I would wager, is her reluctance to embrace the English weather with all its ups and downs. Really, unless the thermometer is showing 35 degrees centigrade, she has a tendency to shiver un-controllably. Truly, she must be the only woman who can't wait for the menopause and the consequential 'hot flushes' to keep her warm on a cold winter's night! By way of contrast, I have a problem only with heat. As a consequence, our house has a room we keep as an icebox, during summer, and then excessively hot, in winter. The downside of this means that we normally only see each other in spring or autumn – as summer and winter sees us hibernating in our respective room!

The pleasures of our marriage, though, far exceed any of the negatives. We have both learnt so much from the other and seen our own lives enriched by knowledge.

For instance, Margaret did not know much about German history or WW2 before she met me. She is now interested in these subjects almost as much as I am. It's fair to say that she hasn't yet developed a love of German punk music, but I remain optimistic.

I have also gleaned much from Margaret that I appreciate. Before knowing her, I couldn't pick Nigeria out from a global map of the world. Nowadays, I am at ease prostrating myself in front of elders and can happily discuss the price of yam or sweet potato. I understand the state of mind of most Nigerians I have met in this country, and share their sorrow at how their country's wealth is being eaten up by dodgy-dealing politicians. I even find myself buying Wolves shirts, with Olofinjana (a Nigerian international who plays for Wolves – an average player, but damn expensive at £3 per letter) stamped on the back, to send home to relatives in Ibadan.

In my own quiet way, I guess I resemble a bastard son of Bob Geldof – with my attachment to the Nigerian way of doing things. True, I will never like the food or adhere to 'Nigerian time', but I do feel that I have a second country to run to, if England continues to go down the pan.

I can now also spot the difference between a Norah Wellings black doll and a Heubach. Truly I am blessed to swallow Margaret's dolly knowledge.

Both of us also feel enlightened by having our minds and souls enriched by our union. It is only as time has gone on that we have begun to realise a lot of people we have bumped into over the years are not as tolerant as we are. Too many are quick to dismiss others as 'white trash,' 'fanta,' (a derogatory Yoruba word used against Nigerian women who date white men) 'Jamaican yardies,' 'Muslim terrorist,' or 'Nigerian fraudsters'. This is lazy and will only change if people mix more. That is why the segregation chapter, to us, was the most important in the book.

The saddest thing is that the people who stay in their own homogeneous boxes are the ones losing out. You, dear reader, will have to trust our judgement over this issue, as we are writing with plenty of hands-on experience.

Being married to Margaret has other useful spin offs as well, such as an evening's entertainment at karaoke. We are certainly never stuck for something to croon – with 'Ebony and Ivory' a near cert to be on any song list.

Tacky?

Maybe, but it always gets a laugh.

Lastly then, we come to the pitfalls of marrying someone from a different culture.

Although I would be lying to suggest we've had no problems, our experiences show they are easily vaulted. For sure, Margaret's parents/friends had initial reservations about me, but eventually most of these cleared up. Anyway, how many mothers and fathers are always happy with their offspring's choice of partner?

It may have been my colour that was in the way to start with, but another parent may have found my occupation, clothes or music an obstacle. Whatever, time and patience tend to overcome prejudice, leaving only a naked human being for people to love or hate.

We do appreciate here that family acceptance of a partner is the hardest area to get over. We were relatively lucky. Others may not be so. We would argue, though, it is worth persevering if you really believe you have found Mr or Mrs Right. Life is too short to waste time missing opportunities for happiness because of skin colour, cultural differences or even the food that goes in your belly.

Crucially, neither of us had any desire to see our marriage as a cultural battleground from which one side would emerge victorious. This might appear strange, but I have often read of how one has to 'go over' to the other side due to marrying out. Maybe it is just our nature, but this has never been a problem in our marriage.

The start of our book asked the question as to how we have made our marriage work (if longevity is a sign of success). So what 'good practice' can we share with readers?

For us, the crucial point is that, once you strip away all the labels, be they punk, Christian, black dolls, white, black, potato, rice, two human hearts remain, beating away softly to each other. It is the ability to see beyond these flimsy labels that is the key to our success. Sadly, we live in a country obsessed with pigeonholing people by putting them into boxes based on race, gender or religion. This policy is doomed to fail, as humans are not robots. Yes, we have weaknesses, yes, we have desires, yes, we make mistakes. That is the beauty/despair of humanity.

I guess, maybe, it is because both Margaret and I have been labelled so often that we are more sensitive than most over this issue.

Rather than make an issue of differences between us – cultural or otherwise – we feel it is really important to stress the similarities that have enabled us to enjoy our marriage. Whilst we visibly look different, our values and morals are entwined together around a core of humanity. That is why we find it strange when people can't understand how we are a couple. To our minds, we are very similar people indeed. The mystery is how others cannot see this.

In all honesty, even we have sometimes over-played the superficial differences between us. The very title of our book alludes to this; *The **unlikely** marriage of a Punk Rocker and his African Queen'*. Why is it unlikely?

It is not, of course. The title was chosen merely to lure the reader into picking it up from the book shelf. 'Ha ha, ever get the feeling you've been cheated?'

Seriously, we have not set out to cheat anybody. We just want people to know the truth about mixed marriages. Contrary to popular belief, they are not always based on sex and physical infatuation. No, they are about love finding a way through the obstacles mere mortals put in their path.

Margaret and I are very much alike in so many areas. Both of us try to see the best in people and are patient with those whose views we deem objectionable. We both respect the older generations and the suffering they endured for us to lead more comfortable lives. Neither of us is happy that the elderly are the most neglected of all groups in society. We resent the way they are shunted off into care homes and made to feel worthless if they can no longer work. Many seem to view the elderly as 'coffin dodgers', who are merely taking away oxygen from those that can breathe easily. This is so wrong and unfair.

We also share a belief that we all have a duty to ensure children are brought up the correct way – within marriage and with discipline a priority.

Lastly, we both have passions for hobbies and are not content to waste our lives glued to *I'm a Celebrity…Get Me Out of Here* and the like. This sounds incredibly pretentious and condescending, but neither of us can understand why so many people waste their lives watching this tripe. Have they no imagination?

Doubtless many would observe the same about me, with my German punk interest, or Margaret's dolls – but at least we made the effort to like something away from the norm. Anyway, what is the 'norm'?

Is it 'normal' to do everything exactly the same as everyone else?

To us that is boredom and suppresses the human spirit – like those who sit in the pub every night supping themselves into an early grave. Alcohol, *Big Brother*, drugs – all are used to stop the population thinking for themselves.

Perhaps that is the plan?

So that is our story. Hopefully you, the reader, would have got to know us by now, and feel sorry for one or both of us.

Some may be intrigued by the idea of a 'mixed marriage'; others may be viewing it as a step too far. What is important – and please forgive our somewhat lecturing stance here – is that people fall in love with people whom they respect as human beings first. As we have shown, everything else is superfluous.

To sum up, I guess both of us come over as hopelessly idealistic, naive people, blinded by love. This may be correct, but we really believe it is better to be a disappointed idealist rather than a satisfied cynic.

So, what can we say to anyone reading this book who is seeking the answer to the wider modern day conundrum; of getting along with one's neighbour?

We only have a single, simple, one-dimensional plea for readers: give each person you meet an identity and call them by their first name with yours swapped in return.

Segregation, assimilation, integration, all these 'tions' are dominating the news. It is time we disposed of all such notions and concentrated instead on the basics, like friendships and human compassion. All these other barriers are put up by extremists or by people who are prejudiced, ignorant or just plain scared.

Sad. As our experiences show, there really is nothing to be scared about.

The introduction of this book posed something of a trick question: 'How a white man can love a black woman and have his love reciprocated?'

Why a trick question?

Because, as should be blatantly obvious to any who have absorbed our message, the answer is; you love them the same way that you would someone who is your own colour.

There can only ever be 'One Love', no matter how many colours are involved.

It really is as simple as that.

Ghana Braid Girl

I see you walking down the street,
type of girl I'd like to meet.
Rotund body it's calling me,
you can take me, take me for free.
I love those hips that shake around,
your cellulite it bounces off the ground.

CHORUS
Ghana Braid Girls are so hard to beat (Oi! Oi! Oi!),
their plaits they are so false and neat.
Long black hair down your back,
it even goes right up your crack.

I must confess your voice isn't nice.
It's as hot as your pepper spice.
Heart of gold it lurks beneath.
Hidden by all those pearly white teeth.
And those teeth are shining bright.
Drawing me into your light.

Beautiful skin so clear and dark.
It's certainly better than your bark.
You hate my music and my punky clothes.
But I just love your sweet flat nose.
So purse those lips that I love so much.
And feel again my tender touch.

A song I wrote for my wife this year. Who said romance is dead?